T0322574

HOUSE OF SILENT LIGHT

*The Dawning of Zen
in Gilded Age America*

BRIAN RIGGS *&* HIDEMI RIGGS

THE BUDDHIST SOCIETY TRUST

The Buddhist Society Trust is a distinguished press in the United Kingdom which enriches lives around the world by advancing the study and practice of Buddhism. Its activities are supported by charitable contributions from individuals and institutions.
For more information visit: www.thebuddhistsociety.org

House of Silent Light: The Dawning of Zen in Gilded Age America.
By Brian Riggs & Hidemi Riggs.
First published by The Buddhist Society Trust, 2023
© Brian Riggs and Hidemi Riggs and The Buddhist Society Trust

The publisher gratefully acknowledges the support for this book provided by Dr. Desmond Biddulph CBE and Darcy Flynn for their generous support and encouragement.

All rights reserved. No part of this publication may be reproduced, stored in a retrieval system or transmitted in any form or by any means, electronic, mechanical, photocopying or otherwise, without the written permission of the publisher:

The Buddhist Society Trust
E: middlewayandpublishing@gmail.com

ISBN 978-0901032-67-6 (The Buddhist Society Trust)

A catalogue record for this book is available from the British Library.

Frontispiece: From a Tōkeiji group photo, 1903. Courtesy of Tōkeiji, Kamakura, Japan, through arrangements made by Oikawa Kenji, editorial section, *Mita Hyōron* Online, Keiō University Publications Department, Tokyo.

Designed and edited by Wayne S. Yokoyama.

Jacket designed by Toby Matthews.

Printed in Cornwall, TJ Books Limited.

Frontispiece: Ida E. Russell (in white), Shaku Sōen, Elise Drexler (in black), Louis Howe. Engakuji, 1903. Courtesy of Tōkeiji, Kamakura.

CONTENTS

HOUSE OF SILENT LIGHT

HOUSE OF SILENT LIGHT

PROLOGUE

L ITTLE about the Sunset District was unfamiliar to Dominick "Shorty" Roberts. The proprietor of the Sea Breeze Resort at the far end of Ocean Boulevard, he had grown up in the lonely district, miles past San Francisco's westernmost suburbs. Over the years that ushered in the dawning of the twentieth century the innkeeper watched the scattered shanties increase in number and concentration to form small, ramshackle communities. A few modestly sized dairies had also sprung up, though miles of windswept sand dunes still filled most of the coastal district south of Golden Gate Park. Without the rumble of motorcars, which put-putted down the boulevard mainly on Sunday afternoons, the crashing of waves and the howling wind remained the dominant sounds of the neighbourhood.

Roberts was also a witness of sorts to the doings of his curious neighbours, the Russells. Unlike most of the humble structures of the Sunset, the Russell mansion—massive, squat, russet—sat like an alcazar on its low coastal promontory. Its inhabitants tended to keep to themselves, their privacy protected by a towering fence that encircled two city blocks. The estate was well maintained and obviously inhabited. From the Sea Breeze, just three blocks away, Shorty could hear a few of the cows behind the rampart bellow before their evening milking. In the spring, the scent of fruit ripening in the Russells' small orchard wafted past his saloon. As a child he might have crept up to the compound and sneaked a glimpse between fence planks of the elaborate garden—curiously similar, with its stone lanterns and exotic pagodas, to the Japanese garden in Golden Gate Park. From time to time, Roberts watched as a chauffeured roadster rolled down the driveway, transporting grandly dressed society matrons or—more gripping—a depilated Asian gentleman sometimes festooned in flowing silk robes, sometimes in a dark suit and bowler hat.

The mansion's remote location combined with its imposing barricade and foreign visitors to excite the imaginations of a generation of San Franciscans. Though he never knew his neighbours well, Shorty was a local repository for the rumors that swirled about them. Some said the lonely residence housed a foreign cult. A colony of religious fanatics. Hindu recluses who shunned society. Fire worshippers abiding by some unnamed and heathen creed. They were presided over by a "Mother Rafael," as Roberts called the reputed priestess and leader of the community. Her husband was said to be her student and at the same time superintendent of the mysterious assembly. What wild rites they conducted was as much the subject of schoolboy banter as bar room gossip at the Sea Breeze. Before long, all San Francisco knew the place as the House of Mystery.

Yet there were some in the city to whom the mansion was not so mysterious. To the mayor, it was the home of a political ally with whom he regularly visited. Certain circles of high society considered the Russell manor a local mecca of art, culture, and practical philanthropy. Some of the city's immigrant Japanese knew it as home to a group of broadminded Americans who appreciated their art, their history, and—most of all—their religion. They correctly knew the Russells' home as the place where Zen Buddhism—borne by the famous Zen prelate Shaku Sōen, along with his friend and disciple D. T. Suzuki—first washed upon American shores.

Those to whom the mansion was least mysterious were, of course, the Russells themselves and their many guests, some of whom resided with their host and hostess for years on end. A number of these houseguests filled domestic roles, such as governess or private secretary. Others had no domestic responsibilities whatsoever. All participated in a religious life whose orderly, monastic qualities were unmistakable. They gathered for communal prayer and sat in private meditation. They sang hymns in the mansion's richly appointed chapel, sat together in quiet contemplation, convened to attend Mrs. Russell's orations. They were vegetarians and teetotalers. Domestics abstained from meat and alcohol; horses in the stable refrained from work on national holidays and the Sabbath. To this community, the Russell mansion was a place of silence and serenity, far removed from the secular distractions of San Francisco's bustling business district and crowded suburbs. No less, it was a place of enlightenment, where residents devoted themselves to spiritual "unfoldment" through quiet meditation. To them, it was the House of Silent Light.

INTRODUCTION

PART 1

Z EN is the most conspicuous form of Buddhism in the United States today. It has inspired the verse of Beat-generation poets, the musings of existential literati, and the working methodology of psychoanalysts. It became an adopted religion of counterculturalists who founded Zen centers and monasteries that have endured throughout the country to this day. Most recently it entered pop culture through a paperback press that associated it first with motorbike repair and then with a myriad of unrelated yet easily commercialized themes. Yet exactly how Zen Buddhism first began to capture the American imagination remains a half-remembered, poorly-understood chapter in the history of religion.

This is by no means due to lack of interest in the topic. For more than a quarter of a century, researchers have time and time again returned to the subject of Zen Buddhism's history in America. These include Rick Fields (*How the Swans Came to the Lake*), Richard Seager (*Buddhism in America*), Charles Prebish (*Faces of Buddhism in America*), and Thomas Tweed (*American Encounter with Buddhism*). In greater or lesser detail, each draws attention to the international conclave that sparked a comparatively widespread American interest in Asian religions in the early 1890s, to the mendicant teacher who vigorously propagated Buddhism throughout the United States in the dawning years of the twentieth century, and to the San Francisco socialites who were the first Americans to formally learn Zen meditation from a qualified master. However, the best researched studies to date have treated Buddhism only in its myriad cultural and sectarian manifestations. Such a broad focus prevented their authors from dwelling at length on Zen in particular. This is unfortunate because taking such a broad view has caused scholars to overlook a plethora of largely untapped primary source material that provides a startling amount of previously unpresented detail on how Zen started off in America. This lack of access to the necessary sources has prevented researchers from answering the most fundamental question surrounding Zen Buddhism's early American history: If Zen was actively propagated in America in the early 1900s, why was it not until mid-century that it finally began to attract a sizable American following and become as ingrained into the popular mind as it is today? This book not only answers this question; it provides a much more detailed account of Zen Buddhism's early days in America than ever before available.

Previous chroniclers of Zen's introduction to the West rarely fail to invoke the name of Mrs. Alexander Russell. She was the first Westerner to practice Zen meditation under the direct guidance of a Japanese Zen master, the first Westerner to live for an extended period at a traditional Zen monastery. It was in her mansion, on a secluded stretch of beach along the Pacific coast, that Shaku Sōen, the first Zen teacher to actively engage in missionary activity in the West, first spoke on Zen in America. Her monastic experience, her sustained interest in meditation, and Sōen's lectures at her home are the starting point from which Zen began making its indelible mark on the American psyche.

Yet Zen's American progenitor remains misunderstood, downplayed, or completely overlooked. She is sometimes presented as no more than Sōen's hostess, the proprietor of a kind of caravansary for religious mendicants. At other times her husband is given credit as the one with an interest in Buddhism so great that it led him to Asia to experience the religion himself. Occasionally Mrs. Russell's role as the first Westerner to formally practice Zen is bestowed on some nameless others. This is unfortunate because Mrs. Russell was absolutely instrumental to the religion's establishment in America. This book will demonstrate that her enthusiasm for Zen ignited in Shaku Sōen an almost extinguished flame to see his sect understood and appreciated internationally. Without her interest and support Zen could not have taken root in America the way that it did. In fact it can, and will, be argued that without Mrs. Russell Zen may never have captured the American imagination at all. This book will show how Mrs. Alexander Russell's unconventional religious pursuits led to her friendship with one of Japan's most prominent Zen abbots at the turn of the last century and directly inspired his work to establish Zen's first foothold in the United States.

Though all the incidents recounted in this narrative take place in Gilded Age America and Meiji-era Japan, the roots of the story actually dig deeper into history. The spread of Buddhism to America is only the most recent leg of its journey from west to east, a phenomenon known in Japan as *bukkyō tōzen*, "Buddhism's movement east." Originating in India 2,500 years ago, the religion is said to have made its first eastward migration when the monk Bodhidharma brought the teaching to China. Being twenty-eighth in a line of spiritual leaders, he could trace his religious lineage back to Śākyamuni, the historical Buddha himself. Rather than searching for religious truth in the pages of books or pious chanting, he turned his attention inward, seeking truth, enlightenment, in the silence and stillness of his own mind. After an unsuccessful attempt to interest the Liang Dynasty emperor in his particular brand of mysticism, Bodhidharma retired to a cave in Henan Province where for nine years he is said to have sat facing a wall, enrapt in contemplation. For his stress on seated meditation as a spiritual practice, Bodhidharma is credited with founding the Dhyāna sect of Buddhism, which in a series of phonetic abbreviations was in China called Chan and in Japan Zen.

Over the century following Bodhidharma's death in 532 CE his teachings on meditation and the inward search for enlightenment passed from master to student. They had not strayed very far from his Henan cave when they were imparted to Hóngrĕn, the fifth Zen patriarch, that is, Bodhidharma's fourth spiritual successor. He led a monastic community in the neighbouring province of Anhui. Here the Zen teachings remained until there arrived at Hóngrĕn's monastery an illiterate layman. Though from China's southern provinces, he was considered a foreigner, a barbarian in the more cultured north. This was Huineng.

During her life Mrs. Russell was directly compared to Huineng. Similarities between certain aspects of her life and the legends that have long surrounded this semi-mythical Buddhist figure are in fact striking. Huineng was first introduced to Zen by a mendicant, one of Hóngrĕn's disciples, who was visiting his land in the distant south. Inspired by the teaching, intrigued that the old master taught laymen as well as monks, and funded by a wealthy patron who encouraged his religious pursuits, Huineng embarked on the long journey to Hóngrĕn's monastery. A chance meeting with a foreign proponent of Zen, a teacher who welcomed devout laity, a wealthy patron, and a pilgrimage to foreign lands would all figure into Mrs. Russell's own introduction to Zen Buddhism. An illiterate foreign peasant also played a fundamental role in her spiritual development.

Huineng lived at the monastery for eight months, chopping wood, working in the kitchen, and eventually receiving the esoteric teachings of his master. Mrs. Russell had a monastic experience of similar length, during which she labored at menial tasks and pursued what she considered the esoteric teachings of the Zen sect. Recognizing that the foreign layman in his kitchen grasped the essence of Zen better than any of his monastic students, the old master appointed Huineng his successor. Knowing this would anger the others, he sent Huineng back south to spread the teaching to a new land. The newly enlightened master was hotly pursued by his fellow students. When they caught up to him Huineng instructed them in meditation, recommending that they "refrain from thinking of anything and keep your mind blank."

Similarities between Huineng and Mrs. Russell begin to break down at this point. She was never appointed Shaku Sōen's successor or recognized for having come to a greater understanding of Zen than the monks in his charge. However, both before and after she met the Zen master, she practiced seated meditation and advocated it to others. Her advice was reported in contemporary newspapers in words remarkably similar to Huineng's recommendation that students keep their minds blank [1]. Shaku Sōen first noted the parallels between Mrs. Russell and the man who would become the Sixth Zen Patriarch in a poem he dedicated to her. In it he noted that against common expectations—both in Huineng's time and his own—foreigners came to an unexpected appreciation of Zen and contributed to its proliferation to new lands. Mrs. Russell's enthusiasm for Zen seemed to place her at a similar point in its the eastward spread, in this case to the foreign lands of the New World.

Huineng's successors continued the spread of Zen throughout Asia. His teachings were codified into what became known as the "Southern School," which stressed a sudden experience of enlightenment in which the mind abruptly arrives at a state of awakening. This was accomplished by transcending dualistic thought, recognizing the underlying sameness of all phenomena. Besides seated meditation, religious practices of the Southern School included the contemplation of anecdotes meant to shock the mind into sudden awakening, as well as personal, sometimes intimidating confrontations with accomplished Zen masters. Mrs. Russell would be the first Westerner to experience both hallmarks that still characterize this branch of Zen Buddhism.

Though it was first introduced to Japan at about the time of Huineng, Zen did not immediately prosper. It was not until six centuries later that Eisai Zenji arrived from China, bringing with him the teachings of the Southern School. It was called the Rinzai sect, after the Japanese reading of Linji, the eminent master in Huineng's lineage who was the sect's founder. At about the same time, another branch of the Southern School, which emphasized a gradual attainment of enlightenment, also arrived in Japan and established itself as the Sōtō sect. Unless noted otherwise, references in this book to Zen as a sect of Buddhism refer specifically to the Rinzai sect. The reason for this is simply that the Rinzai sect, in the person of Shaku Sōen, was first to begin propagating Zen in the United States. No disrespect is intended toward other Zen sects, which began their work in America at a later period that is not to be covered in this book.

When it reached the Japanese islands, Buddhism to the medieval mind had reached its easternmost frontier. Of course, Shaku Sōen and other Japanese of late nineteenth century, with their accurate knowledge of world geography and increasing understanding of Western nations, knew better. They found that scholars in both the United States and Europe had already fostered an interest in Buddhism. Philologists and historians had long busied themselves over the Sanskrit and Pāli texts of India and Southeast Asia. This form of Buddhism was Theravāda, the "Way of the Elders." Japanese Buddhists tended to refer to it derogatorily as *Shōjō*, the "Lesser Vehicle," a form and interpretation of Buddhism that was somehow less complete than the *Daijō*, the "Greater Vehicle," transmitted to them via China.

PART 2

Since the formation of the Theosophical Society and the convening of the World's Parliament of Religions (the latter of which is the starting point for this book) Western interest in the Buddhism of China and Japan increased steadily. This interest was no longer restricted to academics. The teachings of the *Daijō* were being introduced and appreciated at a popular level. Shaku Sōen, in America for the first time at the Parliament, witnessed this firsthand. The experience left him eager to participate in Buddhism's eastward migration to the Western world. And not just Buddhism in general, but the Zen essence he perceived at its heart.

Shaku Sōen's two visits to America have been documented by chroniclers of Buddhism's introduction to America, but in a very cursory way. Previous approaches to this subject have also tended to repeat the same bits of information about Sōen and his associates. In some cases, details contradict one another to produce a considerable amount of confusion. In other cases, the reverence in which these religious forbears of American Buddhism are held has resulted in anecdotes that are apocryphal, biographical sketches that approach hagiography. This is very unfortunate since there exists a considerable amount of written material in Japanese about Sōen and his students that clearly present them as the flesh-and-blood individuals that they were. This includes three biographies of Shaku Sōen, two biographies of D. T. Suzuki, a series of biographical sketches on Senzaki Nyogen, several volumes of correspondence, diaries, and the reminiscences of a number of friends and colleagues. This book will be the first in the English language to draw from them extensively.

Readers familiar with the work of Rick Fields and other chroniclers of Buddhism's American instauration will encounter faces both familiar and strange. Uemura Sōkō, Sōen's devoted, eminently capable disciple, is introduced for the first time. Hopes for establishing Sōen's line of Buddhism in America were pinned squarely on young Sōkō, who has been largely forgotten by previous researchers. Also, the figure of Nomura Yōzō darts in and out of the text, which details his vital but previously unrecognized role in Zen's spread to America. Shaku Sōen, Shaku Sōkatsu, D. T. Suzuki, Sasaki Shigetsu, and Senzaki Nyogen, all figuring prominently in previous writings, also show up in this work. However, rather than simply repeat the same information already known about them, this book draws when possible on Japanese sources to introduce readers to previously unknown or underappreciated aspects of their lives, personalities, and contributions to America's introduction to Zen. For example, we will explore how daily life at the Russell mansion alternately inspired, challenged, and bored Shaku Sōen. We will monitor and account for Mrs. Russell's changing attitude toward her Zen education during Sōen's visit. We will catch a unique glimpse of D. T. Suzuki, a world-renowned interpreter of Zen in the 1950s, but at the time chronicled in this book, a young Suzuki in an early and clearly aggravating stage of his career. And we will clear up, to a certain degree, some of the prickly questions surrounding Senzaki's biography.

Unfortunately the same detailed examination cannot always be given to Mrs. Russell. Though she was clearly intelligent, educated, and articulate, little in the way of primary source material has survived. That which has survived will be examined closely. Fortunately she was also a highly charismatic woman. Months, years, sometimes decades later, people would recall in detail their impressions of and interactions with her. Many of these recollections were from her Japanese friends and acquaintances, again putting them off limits to researchers not familiar with the language. Supplemented by the recollections of two branches of her family and more than one series of newspaper articles, this first detailed look at her life, personality, spiritual pursuits, and place in the history of American religion is possible. And in the process we shall uncover the previously unknown role that the New Thought religious movement played in the establishment of Zen in America.

Most importantly, this book will for the first time account for the long length of time Zen Buddhism required to establish itself in the United States. Propagandists were in America as early as 1893 and active in at least a handful of urban areas since 1905. The interest in Zen fostered by the Russells and a number of their friends was far from casual. Other sects of Japanese Buddhism successfully established themselves in America under similar circumstances at this time, as did the Vedanta Society. Yet generations would pass, following the events to be described in this book, before there were more than a handful of Americans committed to Zen. This book will explain why Sōen's dream of transplanting Zen in America would remain unfulfilled in his lifetime and yet how, through the hard work of his disciples and the friendship of the Russells, he was able to participate in *bukkyō tōzen*, the eastward advance of Buddhism, by carrying Zen across the Pacific.

1

HERE IS A GLEAM OF LIGHT

1893

PART 1

S HAKU Sōen took a seat on the broad stage erected in the still unfinished Memorial Art Palace on Madison Avenue. His robes, silk of richly blended tints, were stifling in the humid Chicago summer. They identified him as a high-ranking head priest, not only the abbot of an ancient monastery but overseer of a complex network of temples throughout Japan. Others nearby on the rostrum were dressed just as colourfully— the Hindu swami in his orange turban, the Catholic cardinal in red, the Greek patriarch in a purple surplice, the pigeon-toed Singhalese ascetic in robes of pure white, the moonfaced Chinese diplomat with his delicate satin slippers.

It was 10:30 in the morning, the second Sunday of September 1893. The occasion: the opening ceremony of the World's Parliament of Religions. Officially, Sōen had been invited to represent the Zen sect of Buddhism, just as the other delegates on the stage represented their respective religions, denominations, sects, and creeds. At the moment, however, it seemed the Asian delegates were there mainly to make the proceedings a bit more picturesque. Throughout the event they would be seated conspicuously at the fore, where the audience could always get a good look. Surrounding and outnumbering them were the frock-coated professors and mutton-chopped ministers who organized the event and made up the majority of its participants. The opening ceremony proceeded on lines very familiar to those in the majority.

An organist pounded out the strains of traditional Sunday hymns—*Jerusalem the Golden* and *The Old Hundred*—as the delegates entered in a grand procession reminiscent of high mass. Once all two hundred of the delegates and dignitaries assembled upon the stage, a women's choir let loose with another hymn. The Lord's Prayer was then recited next. All remained respectfully standing for the hymn and prayer. All except the delegation of Buddhists [2]. It was an unlikely environment for the spread of Buddhism to America. Yet this is precisely what Sōen hoped to commence at the Parliament of Religions.

Just a few miles away to the east at Jackson Park, the World's Columbian Exposition was in full swing. Like world's fairs before, it was a place for people of different nations to meet together and display the fruits of their industries, the advancements of their science, the wares of their manufacturers. It was a place of discovery, where knowledge was shared, preconceptions torn down, new ideas adopted. A place of commerce where businessmen could survey the products of each nation and select what they thought best.

The World's Parliament of Religions was conceived along similar lines. Instead of exhibiting material, industrial, and mechanical achievements, however, the Parliament would showcase the distinctive truths prized and professed by the religions of the world. Christians, Jews, Muslims, Buddhists, Hindus, and Jains would stand shoulder to shoulder with Theosophists, Christian Scientists, Ethical Culturalists, Psychical Researchers. All were welcome to send delegates. (Everyone except the Mormons, still reviled for their polygamy, and the "primitive" tribal cultures, that is.) All were promised a receptive audience, an equal standing, a fair hearing free from argument, ridicule, or controversy.

Charles C. Bonney—Chicago lawyer, Swedenborg layman, and originator of the idea for the interreligious conclave—was first to address the assembly that not only included the 58 delegates on stage but also a keyed-up audience of 4,000. Welcoming the emissaries from around the world as "worshippers of God and lovers of Man," he introduced the solemn and majestic event as a stepping stone toward a "new epoch of brotherhood and peace."

> The religious faiths of the world have most seriously misunderstood and misjudged each other from the use of words in meanings radically different from those which they were intended to bear, and from a disregard of the distinctions between appearances and facts; between signs and symbols and the things signified and represented. Such errors it is hoped that this congress will do much to correct and to render hereafter impossible.
>
> He who believes that God has revealed himself more fully in his religion than in any other, can not do otherwise than desire to bring that religion to the knowledge of all men, with an abiding conviction that the God who gave it will preserve, protect, and advance it in every expedient way. And hence he will welcome every just opportunity to come into fraternal relations with men of other creeds, that they may see in his upright life the evidence of the truth and beauty of his faith, and be thereby led to learn it, and be helped heavenward by it. [3]

It was the draping of such sentiments in overtly Christian terms, as well as the Christian overtones that would characterize the supposedly interreligious event from beginning to end, that caused Sōen and his fellow Buddhists to remain seated at portions of the ceremony when they were expected to stand respectfully. Nonetheless, Bonney's words appealed greatly to Sōen. They were similar to those he had read a year earlier when a letter from John

Henry Barrows, Chairman of the General Committee on Religious Congresses of the World's Congress Auxiliary, arrived at his monastery in Kamakura. Barrows sought "the most eminent of men of different Faiths, strong in their personal convictions, which will strive to see and show what are the supreme truths, and what light Religion has to throw on the great problems of our age" [4]. Among the objects of the conference, the letter continued, was "to inquire what light each Religion has afforded, or may afford, to the other Religions of the world" [5]. Sōen was intrigued. He was determined that the opportunity would not pass him by.

PART 2

Shaku Sōen was by no means singled out as a recipient of the invitation from the chairman with the wonderfully elongated title. Enlisting the help of the United States Department of State, Barrows' General Committee sent generally the same letter to more than 10,000 people around the world. Received by the ecclesiastical leaders of all seven of Japan's Buddhist sects, they had caused quite a stir [6]. The overtly Christian language, recognized immediately, tended to solicit suspicion. Christian ministers, recipients reasoned, were organizing a Christian event in a Christian country to display the superiority of Christianity [7].

The deduction was, of course, absolutely correct. Chairman Barrows, himself an ordained Presbyterian minister, prayed that at the event "the Holy Ghost [would] be the divine apostle preaching Jesus to an assembled world." The Parliament would show that all religions of the world shared in "certain common truths." But by gathering together the religions of the world in one place, it would be obvious that any truth found in Buddhism, Hinduism, or Islam were mere reflections of the light of the Gospel. To Barrows, "Christianity claims to be the true religion, fitted to all and demanding the submission of all. The Church of Christ has a unique message, which she will proclaim to all the world, giving the reasons why her faith should supplant all others, showing, among other truths, that transmigration is not regeneration, that ethical knowledge is not redemption, and that Nirvana is not heaven" [8].

Such sentiments, published in a Christian magazine and read in Japan, contributed to the refusal of the country's most prominent Buddhists to attend. The Buddhist Transectarian Organization withdrew its initial tacit support for the conference [9]. The Japanese government declined to fund anyone who might want to make the long, expensive journey. The decision was mirrored by at least two of the sectarian bodies, which added that those choosing to attend could not proclaim themselves official representatives of their sect [10].

Shaku Sōen was by no means one of "the most eminent men" of Japanese Buddhism when he read Barrows' letter. He had just been elected abbot of his monastery, Engakuji, the "Temple of Perfect Enlightenment," at the remarkably young age of 34. It was an ancient abbey, tracing its origin back 600 years when it was founded by order of the shōgun. Now it was in financial straits. Though its many subsidiary temples dotted the map and owed regular tribute, Engakuji commanded an annual income that amounted to a mere ¥70. When the price of rice rose suddenly in the early 1890s there was not enough food to go around. Sōen and the ten monks under his direction walked the streets, begging food in traditional Buddhist fashion to sustain themselves. At the same time Sōen had been selected by the Conference of Chief Abbots to help edit a collection of Buddhist doctrine, *The Essentials of Buddhist Teachings—All Sects*. It was one of his few publications at the time, but it was enough to bring the otherwise obscure monk to the attention of the Barrows committee [11].

Sōen was the first Japanese Buddhist to accept the invitation to attend the Parliament of Religions [12]. Shimaji Mokurai, whom Sōen knew as one of his coeditors of *The Essentials of Buddhist*

Teachings, was probably expressing Sōen's own sentiments when he wrote:

> Already the *Shōjō* [that is, the Buddhism of Southeast Asia] has found many adherents in Europe and America. It has been taken there, not by priests of the faith, but by the foreigners themselves. The Western[er]s, proud of their own civilization, are thus becoming enlightened. Religion is the only force in which the Western people know that they are inferior to the nations of the East. Buddhism in all its forms is deep in doctrine and life. … If then the *Shōjō* is meeting with such wide acceptance abroad, what will be the effect if the *Daijō* [the Buddhism of Japan, Tibet, and China] is proclaimed there? … Let us wed the *Daijō* to Western Thought. Heaven has now given us the opportunity to do this. At Chicago next year the fitting time will come. Here is a gleam of light for our truth. Let us not ignore it. [13]

Responding to such sentiments, the General Council of Shimaji's Shin (Pure Land) sect agreed to set aside the sum of $30,000 to fund the propagation of Buddhism in France [14].

Sōen would receive no such support. Not only were Engakuji's coffers bare, his fellow monastics where opposed to him traveling abroad. They said it was beneath the dignity of such a high-ranking priest to travel in such a barbarous country as America, that such dignitaries ought to remain at their temples, receive visitors, and train students [15].

The old master would not have approved either. Imakita Kōsen, as huge, craggy, immovable, and ancient as the mountains surrounding Engakuji, had only recently passed away. Since Sōen first joined the monastery, Kōsen had been impressed by his dedication, the speed at which he grasped the subtleties of Zen philosophy and mysticism. But he never fully understood or appreciated his young disciple's waywardness. Sōen had received his *inka*—the official certification of his experience of enlightenment—in five years, a fraction of the time it took others if in fact they ever achieved it at all. Most did not. Having completed his training, the customary course of action was to become a temple priest and settle into a routine of performing funeral and commemoration rites. Sōen bored of this quickly. Instead he left for Tokyo. Enrolled in college. Studied "Western science." Learned English. It was an unorthodox course of action and the old master was unimpressed. Though a progressive thinker in his own way, the abbot considered study—even religious study—inferior to the experience of religion. "Even a million volumes of scripture are like the light of a candle to the sun when you compare them to the actual experience of enlightenment," he is remembered as saying [16]. If Sōen felt compelled to study, let it be in topics more pertinent to a Buddhist priest. "To learn English to meet foreigners is not the right thing to do," he bluntly told his disciple. "You have not yet learned all the *kanji* that you will need to know [in order to read and discourse on Buddhist religious texts], so it is useless for you to learn English" [17].

There was more that the old master might have worried about had he known how the secular atmosphere of Keiō University was influencing his young disciple. Sōen toyed with the idea of abandoning religious life for an active role in the modernization of Japan [18]. One of his mentors suggested that he instead study the roots of Buddhism in a country with closer ties to its Indian origins. Upon graduation Sōen left for Ceylon, following in the footsteps of a handful of other Japanese priests already there. While staying in the British colony he not only practiced his English, but also learned Pāli. Kōsen wrote letters recalling his wayward pupil. For three years Sōen defied the summons, explaining to his master that by broadening his understanding of

Buddhism to include its non-Japanese expressions he would be in a better position to propagate it [19].

When he received the invitation to attend the Parliament of Religions, Sōen defied his followers as he had once defied the old master. In the absence of their support, whether moral or financial, Sōen's first class berth in the Canadian Pacific steamer connecting Yokohama to Vancouver was arranged by Barrows. Anxious to ensure international representation at the event, the chairman had organized a private subscription to defray the travel costs of the Buddhist delegates [20]. A subscription was also taken up in Japan by 4,200 priests throughout the country [21]. It was rumored that Sōen raided the temple treasury—selling off a set of religious images—to cover other expenses [22].

PART 3

Following the daylong pageantry of the Parliament of Religions opening session, Sōen had a full week before he would deliver his address to the general assembly. In this time there were receptions to attend, Parliament sessions to observe, the expansive grounds of the World's Fair to explore. His inquisitive mind led him to the Hall of Machinery where a massive dynamo delivered electrical power throughout the fairgrounds. Japan's exhibit of historical art met with his approval. Lake Michigan did not: "It's huge, but not beautiful" [23]. Barrows, who was pastor of the influential First Presbyterian Church, invited Sōen and the other Japanese delegates to attend Sunday services. They were treated to a sermon, "Christ the Wonderful." Three Chinese laborers were then produced and baptized, a hint as to the hopes and expectations that Parliament organizers had for the Buddhist delegates. Subtlety was not always Barrows' strong suit [24].

Sōen and the other Japanese delegates brought with them a set of Buddhist sūtras, a gift for Reverend Barrows. They also brought a set of very specific objectives for their speeches at the Parliament.

First, they wanted to draw attention to the patriotic spirit of the Japanese people. This dovetailed with a larger agenda of Japanese participation at the World's Fair, which aimed at presenting their country as civilized, industrialized, modernized (or least modernizing), and therefore worthy of inclusion into the family of nations [25]. Second, they wanted to demonstrate Buddhism's positive influence on Japanese spirituality. Since the Meiji Restoration and the opening of Japan to trade with the West, Japanese Buddhists were threatened on two fronts. Shintoism had eclipsed Buddhism as the religion favored by the government. Additionally, Christian missionaries were making regular incursions into the country, depriving temples of membership and income. With the two rival faiths curtailing Buddhist influence over politicians and populace, it was feared the religion was in decline. Third, the Japanese delegation wanted to promote Mahayana Buddhism (that is, the *Daijō*, the Buddhism to Japan, China, and Tibet) as worthy of academic attention. With Western scholars favoring Theravada (the Buddhism to Southeast Asia) as the earlier, purer form of Buddhism, they tended to view the northern branches as a corruption. It was a conception the delegates were eager to dispel. Finally, they would promote Buddhism as a "universal religion" that corresponded closely to modern science and philosophy. This would be the topic that Sōen would address in his only presentation to the general assembly.

Just as noteworthy is what was not considered a primary objective among the Japanese delegates. Sōen and the others were less interested in presenting the specific tenets of their respective sects. Sōen, for example, would refrain from any mention of meditation. This is significant since seated meditation is the hallmark of the Zen sect, the means by which practitioners might share in the Buddha's experience of enlightenment. It is this emphasis on meditation that sets Zen apart from many other forms of Buddhism. Sōen also avoided reference to *kōans*, which are often viewed as paradoxical anecdotes or questions that have no logical answer and are meant to bring the rational mind into sudden experience of an enlightenment that transcends rational thought. The Rinzai school of Zen to which Sōen belonged is characterized by the use of *kōans* as a way of determining whether students are progressing in their practice. *Kōans*, however, are essentially non-rational and—to the unenlightened mind at least—apparently nonsensical. With nineteenth century America barely able to grasp Buddhist philosophy at its most rational, it would serve Sōen to steer well away from these subtle devices. He would make no reference to them, to meditation, or even to Zen in any of his Chicago discourses.

The other benefit of such a strategy was that it dovetailed with the intent of his fellow delegates. They hoped to present Japanese Buddhism as a unified group of sects—much like Christianity with its various denominations—rather than as rival factions rife with backbiting [26]. Parliament organizers were equally concerned that the Buddhist representation not dwell on the subtle distinctions between its various branches, but rather help the audience "to learn what universal Buddhism teaches of the great subjects of human life, duty, and destiny" [27]. Sōen and the other Japanese delegates also avoided overt proselytism while in Chicago. They would deliver their papers, answer questions, and distribute thousands of pamphlets brought from Japan. But no overt attempt was made to win converts. They wanted simply for Westerners to gain an appreciation for their religion.

Assisting Sōen throughout the event was Nomura Yōzō, a layman who regularly visited Engakuji to sit in meditation with the monks. His English was self-taught, honed as a teenager running errands for American guests at Kyoto hotels. Not so many years before, Yōzō had briefly represented a tea exporter in San Francisco before returning to Japan with only a dollar to his name. He resumed Zen practice at Engakuji, keeping his eyes half open to his next opportunity to travel abroad. This happened when Sōen, who had never directly spoken with the layman, asked if

Yōzō would accompany him to Chicago as his translator. Despite his years studying English, Sōen was never comfortable speaking the language [28].

On the day of Sōen's speech, Nomura Yōzō—whether due to illness or stage fright—did not feel well enough to read his paper, "The Law of Cause and Effect According to Buddha." Reverend Barrows, who was presiding over that morning's session, took the podium for Yōzō. Sōen greeted his audience with a formal bow, then took a seat to Barrows' right. The auditorium was like a sauna, Chicago's lingering summer deciding to produce its sweltering best for the occasion. Sweat beaded down from the shaved forehead of the mute abbot, forming pools at his feet [29].

The paper introduced the Parliamentarians to dependent co-origination. A central teaching in Buddhism, it explains how suffering arises and ceases on its own accord without the involvement of a punishing or forgiving, destroying or creating deity. Natural phenomena were presented as the result of a multitude of causes and conditions that are in fact interrelated with one another. If he could speak to his audience spontaneously, Sōen might have noted that the unwelcome trickle down his torso resulted from perspiration that in turn resulted from his presence in the stuffy auditorium. This was caused from his presence in Chicago, which itself resulted from his eagerness to travel 7,000 miles to address a crowd generally unprepared for a Buddhist philosophy lesson in such uncomfortable conditions. It was futile to attempt tracing the origin of a cause back to a "First Cause" since any given cause is but the effect of an earlier cause which is itself preceded by others, *ad infinitum*. For this reason Buddhism posits a universe without beginning, without end. The foundation laid, Sōen applied the notion to the human condition:

> It is not education nor experience alone that can make a man wise, intelligent and wealthy, but it depends upon one's past life. What are the causes or conditions which produce

such a difference? To explain it in a few words, I say it owes its origin to the different qualities of actions which we have done in our past life, namely, we are here enjoying or suffering the effect of what we have done in our past life. … We enjoy happiness and suffer misery, our own actions being causes; in other words, there is no other cause than our own actions which make us happy or unhappy. … Thus [the] various attitudes of human life can be explained by the self-formation of cause and effect. There is no one in the universe but oneself who rewards or punishes him. The diversity in future stages will be explained by the same doctrine. This is termed in Buddhism the 'self-deed and self-gain' or 'self-make and self-receive.' Heaven and hell are self-made. God did not provide you with a hell, but you yourself. The glorious happiness of future life will be the effect of present virtuous actions. … We are born in the world of variety; some are poor and unfortunate, others are wealthy and happy. The state of variety will be repeated again and again in our future lives. But to whom shall we complain of our misery? To none but ourselves! We reward ourselves; so shall we do in our future life. [30]

There is no report on the response of the audience, which could be quite lively—shouting, waving handkerchiefs, and rushing the stage when appreciative of the sentiments in a particular address, booing and crying "Shame!" when disapproving. On one occasion, following the presentation of a Japanese delegate a person sitting near Yōzō asked if he had understood the lecture. "Certainly," Yōzō replied. "Didn't you?" Receiving a negative reply, Yōzō explained that the speech was about the essence of Buddhism. However, it lacked the technical terminology that would have made its points more explicit, but at the same time it had gone over the heads of the Parliamentarians unprepared for such an in-depth discussion of Buddhism. "The reason why you do not understand is your lack of knowledge [about Buddhism]. Given time this will clear up as we talk more about this truth with you" [31].

It seems to have been a common experience for the Japanese delegation. They faced numerous obstacles to making themselves heard. Chief among these was the inability of the priests to make forceful presentations directly to the audience in English. Instead they relied on translators less familiar with the subject matter or, in Sōen's case, a Protestant missionary antagonistic to his goal of building an appreciation for Japanese Buddhism in America. Additionally, the translations of the Japanese representatives' speeches, while carefully prepared, either oversimplified complex theological points or incorporated Theosophical language that did not do justice to the original [32].

Problems were not just linguistic. For the past generation Americans had been conditioned to associate Japanese culture with the picturesque, rather than the philosophical. The Japanese priests at the Parliament of Religions, with their polite bows, gorgeous robes, muted voices, and mild countenances, only contributed to this image. Throughout the event they were regularly upstaged by other Asian delegates with a fluent command of English and considerable personal charisma. These included one of their own number, Hirai Kinza, a lay Buddhist. His oration was a stinging rebuke of Christian missionary activity. It flouted the Parliament's rules to avoid controversy and effectively fired the first volley of an ensuing battle of words between the envoys of the Orient and the Occident. When it was delivered, Hirai's address received a lively response from an audience quick to denounce the practices of "false Christianity" [33]. Swami Vivekananda of India earned standing ovations and set a "sea of white handkerchiefs" waving appreciatively when he spoke on religious brotherhood. The mere promise that he would make a few impromptu remarks at the end of a session was enough to prevent the audience leaving early from an otherwise dull session. And Dharmapala, the young Buddhist firebrand from Ceylon, electrified spectators with his talk of 475 million Buddhists in Asia and the world's debt to his religion [34]. His evening lectures at the Athenaeum building prior to the Parliament's close drew crowds too large to be contained in the hall [35].

Dharmapala drew additional attention when, at the end of his Athenaeum lecture, he officiated over a ceremony for Charles Strauss' conversion to Buddhism. Strauss, a well-educated New Yorker, had been raised Jewish, converted to Christianity, and subsequently turned to Theosophy. The Theosophical Society provided many Americans with their first introduction to Buddhism, and it was through the organization that Strauss discovered the writings of Dharmapala, a rising star within the organization. He had been in correspondence with the Singhalese ascetic for the past year. So eager was he to meet him, Strauss offered to personally defray Dharmapala's travel expenses to America [36]. It was the first known conversion to Buddhism within America. Strauss apparently remained Buddhist for the rest of his life [37].

Shaku Sōen considered Strauss' conversion a victory for the Buddhist delegation [38]. He and his fellow Japanese delegates did not expect, did not attempt to achieve similar results. Their goal, as noted, was not to win converts, but to educate Westerners on the significance of Mahayana Buddhism, to demonstrate that Buddhism was a living religion able to stand alongside the most respected of Western religious traditions. Yet even in this Sōen left Chicago mostly discouraged. He lamented that Westerners would need a lot of basic education before Buddhist missionary activity could be accomplished among them [39].

2

THE SPIRITS OF BELMONT HALL

1894-1897

PART 1

WHILE Shaku Sōen lamented that Americans were unprepared to appreciate Buddhism when he was in Chicago, he would have been surprised to learn that far to the west a community was being formed that placed high value on the seated meditation that so characterized his sect. One of its guiding lights was a slightly-built woman with sharp eyes, eloquent speech, and refined tastes. Her name was Ida Evelyn Russell.

In December 1894, barely a year after Sōen had left America after a stay of only three weeks, Ida had just moved into Belmont Hall [40]. The facility operated as a boarding house for girls only months before its lease became available. It was taken up by Dalton Wheeler, a local businessman and Ida's personal friend. When Wheeler, his wife, and children moved into the seminary, situated on the western border of downtown Los Angeles, they were not alone. Ida arrived to claim a room for herself and another for her mother. Ida's husband, Alexander, would stay at the hall when his work as a traveling salesman brought him to Southern California. There were others as well: Mark Hopkinson, newspaper compositor; George Hoffmann, barber; George Baisley, oil well driller; Lottie Farnsworth, school teacher; Dr. Wallace, physician; Robert Mikkelson, pattern maker. There were more than a dozen residents in all, with Josephine Holmes the commune's centerpiece.

Ida had met Josephine in San Francisco, perhaps as early as 1889. An immigrant from Norway, Josephine made her way west via Sioux City and Omaha. She was conversant in English, but could only write the language phonetically. Josephine had worked as a laundress until recently, but it was not the details of her background that fascinated Ida. It was her words. "She spoke of peace, contentment and gratitude to God for his bounties as being essential to a higher standard of character," Ida would explain [41]. Josephine taught "that people's lives were too restless, and that a quieter mental condition was requisite. All of the worry, anxiety, discontent, anger and the memory of the past with its sorrows and anguish ought to be fought by people and they ought to live in the present while trusting God for the future" [42].

Such sentiments appealed greatly to Ida. In college she had been exposed to a wide range of philosophies, both ancient and modern. She immersed herself in Plato, leafed through Marcus Aurelius, pursued the imitation of Christ with Thomas à Kempis, pondered the marginally orthodox mysticism of Madame Guyon, and nursed a decided appreciation for Emerson and the Transcendentalists. There was something about the teachings of this simple peasant woman that resonated with Ida's intellectual exploration of Quietism throughout the centuries. To her, Josephine Holmes was "one that rested upon God's will more closely" than herself [43]. She possessed a greater sense of inner peace, a quality that Ida very much hoped to acquire. Ida may also have felt a personal connection. The two women were roughly the same age: Josephine 38 to Ida's 37. Like Josephine, Ida came from humble origins, born into a working-class neighbourhood of carpenters, carriage makers, and shingle bunchers in Bangor, Maine. While she was still a child her father, a sailmaker, emigrated to California, braving the long journey with his wife and daughter years before the intercontinental railroad was completed. They settled in San Francisco near the city docks, where men sewing sails did swift business despite the increasing number of steamships moored in the harbor. Ida's father died seven years after his arrival in the city, aged 42. He could not have left much money to his widow since Elizabeth's personal property amounted to less than $1,000, perhaps much less [44]. To make ends meet Ida's mother rented out furnished rooms.

Ida became a follower of this strange, semi-literate foreign teacher with whom she shared much in common. She left San Francisco, her home since childhood. In the company of her mother and perhaps her husband she relocated to Southern California where Holmes had begun to gather others to her beliefs. Holmes recommended a vegetarian diet to those who followed her. Though meat was served to community members who wished it, Ida consistently refrained and would maintain a strictly vegetarian diet her entire adult life. Josephine turned to art for spiritual guidance. She filled the parlor with paintings—original works by her infirm sister suffering from consumption. The dying woman found inspiration in nature—storm and cloud, mountain and volcano, foliage and sunset. All were rendered in brilliant, some said gaudy, colour. The paintings were allegorical, meant to signify the various spiritual conditions in which people find themselves. From these Josephine would draw inspiration for the lectures she delivered to her community. Later in her life, Ida would likewise surround herself with art whose purpose was not decoration but the uplifting of the soul. Josephine and Ida, though both without children, both maintained well-defined thoughts on child education. Public schools were not to be trusted. Children should be educated at home, but not given formal lessons until their minds had sufficiently matured, preferably after the age of nine.

Both women also considered themselves pious Christians, though neither was a member of a specific church or congregation. Josephine identified with Lutheranism, considering it to be "perfectly correct, excluding the creeds" [45]. Ida, for her part, had been born and baptized Roman Catholic. Though later in life she became reacquainted with the ancestral faith of her Irish ancestors, Ida was not particularly close to Catholicism at this time. She is remembered as having attended Baptist services, her wedding was Presbyterian, and she may have attended a Methodist preparatory school [46]. Josephine and Ida did not restrict their religious interests to Christianity, but rather sought what they believed to be expressions of truth in other religions. They looked to Judaism and Hinduism for guidance, read the *Analects of Confucius*, and followed Emanuel Swedenborg's mystical flights to heaven and hell. The doctrine of reincarnation seemed to be taken for granted among the Belmonters, as they came to be known [47].

Meditation was also highly valued and practiced on a daily basis. Years later, Ida would refer to an assembly of sixty or more people with whom she would sit in meditation on a regular basis starting in the early 1890s. She never clearly identified them, but she clearly meant her friends in Los Angeles. Unfortunately, the only allusions to the practice are from sources extremely hostile to the goings-on at Belmont Hall. "The main point of her [Josephine's] teaching is the complete paralysis of the brain," noted one antagonist. "All reasoning and speculation are tabooed, and every effort is made to keep the mind a blank. … Only by cutting himself [off] from all 'earth[ly] conditions' and annihilating reason and memory can man attain his former state of innocence and purity" [48]. It is impossible to reconstruct precisely how meditation was practiced or the exact benefits Ida, Josephine, and the rest hoped to derive. It was certainly a communal practice, Ida's community gathering together for a prayer and a hymn, then sitting silently together in a manner that might not be foreign to a Quaker.

Finally, with her followers made up of both men and women, single and married, all living under a single roof, Josephine encouraged abstinence among all her followers. Abstinence included not only refraining from sex but also extended to choice of food, topics of conversation, and types of reading materials. Spiritualism and ghosts were taboo topics, presumably because a number of community members had backgrounds as mediums and Josephine frowned on this sort of activity. Newspapers were also not appreciated—a continuous influx of miscellaneous information being detrimental to clearing one's thoughts. Yet there was nothing overly rigid with these rules. Non-vegetarian meals were served to those who wanted them when they wanted them. Newspapers could discreetly be perused in the privacy of one's own quarters, and the odd séance was clandestinely arranged from time to time.

It was the recommendation of abstinence that led to the downfall of Josephine Holmes' initial community, before its move to Belmont Hall. "She said that married ought to live as if unmarried, save for the bearing of children, and unless that was observed perfection could never be reached," recalled Mary Van Auken, one of Holmes' first devotees, president of Los Angeles' first Spiritualist society, and owner of the boarding house that was the commune's first headquarters [49]. The landlady broached the subject with her husband. This burly carpenter was enamoured enough with Josephine's ideas to lay aside his saw for about a week when she suggested that he concentrate more on improving himself mentally and spiritually. But when spirituality infringed on connubial privileges, that was where the line was drawn. Expelled from the Van Auken boarding house, Josephine Holmes, Ida Russell, and the rest of the small community removed themselves to the home of another follower and then to Belmont Hall. It was here that Ida was to come into her own as a speaker on religious topics as she immersed herself in meditation.

The meetings at Belmont Hall were simple affairs, according to Elder M. Mays Eshelman of the Baptist Brethren of Dunkards. "Miss Holmes had the faculty of stating in few and simple words what might be found in the philosophies regarding the human will in relation to the divine will, and answered questions along this line" [50]. As early as the pre-Belmont Hall days Ida would also respond to auditors' questions [51]. Despite the participatory nature of the Belmont Hall gatherings, it was always clear who set the rules. Josephine Holmes was the guiding light, the ultimate authority in doctrine and lifestyle. Once when a preacher entered into a heated discussion with her over a biblical question Josephine declared her oratorical opponent an upstart, "addressing other forcible language at him" [52].

Besides the dozen or so residents of Belmont Hall, forty to fifty others would arrive from their homes throughout Los Angeles. Meetings were held daily. They would generally open with a hymn such as *Nearer My God to Thee*, accompanied by piano in the old school hall. Following this would be a period of prolonged silence in which attendants sought to clear their minds of all miscellaneous and superfluous thoughts. In a mental state considered more receptive to communion with God, Josephine might briefly address the group. On many occasions, this would be the responsibility of Ida who was generally recognized as Josephine's lieutenant and second in command of the community. Though small in stature, Ida was a force to be reckoned with, both on the podium and off. Highly articulate and self-confident, she could easily rebuke any who opposed her. She dressed stylishly and expensively, giving her an air of professionalism. Adopting European fashions provided an added air of the exotic. When speaking, she scanned the audience, gauging response and receptivity. Forceful gesticulations drove home points and precise—some said stilted, overly dramatic—diction made her thoughts clear.

When first speaking at the Belmont Hall gatherings, particularly in its early days, Ida relied on Josephine for encouragement when facing an audience. It wasn't that she completely lacked previous speaking experience. At both regional and national conferences of the Women's Christian Temperance Union she would speak on Sunday school work and other activities regarding children. As Most Exalted Chief of the local Pythian Sisters lodge she would also have regularly addressed at least small gatherings [53]. Perhaps it was expounding on religious or philosophical matters that made Ida initially nervous. One of her earlier addresses was on "Forms and Customs." In it she decried people's tendency to blindly follow in the footsteps of their predecessors rather than to strike out into new directions better suited to them [54]. During this early address Ida made sure Josephine was nearby. When unsure of herself she would place a hand on her mentor's shoulder or slip a hand into one of Josephine's, who would gently squeeze it by way of encouragement. When biblical authority was needed to back up one of Josephine's or Ida's statements, Reverend Eshelman or another man of the cloth would be consulted. Following the lesson, participants would either retire to their rooms for an evening of quiet contemplation or break into small groups to discuss the meeting.

PART 2

Despite the pursuit of truth and tranquility among the Belmonters, the community was beset by trouble from its beginning. Teenaged Arthur Taylor, his face pale and vacuous, struggled to recover from a bout with typhoid fever that nearly claimed his life. For months, Josephine and the other women in the Hall nursed him nightly. Two men of the commune were suicidal. One would leave the property in the middle of the night, walk to nearby West Lake Park, and grimly contemplate a watery grave. One young woman claimed clairaudience, saying she could literally hear the voice of her conscience speaking to her. And Anna Wilkinson, for eighteen months Josephine's follower, was gradually beset by what her doctors called "religious mania." In her ravings she would cover her eyes and run backwards as if pursued by demons. She would moan and mutter to herself, sometimes about killing her two children. At one point, as Mrs. Wilkinson dashed from her house "she tore her clothes from her body as she ran and finally reached an electric-light pole in a state of nudity, and, placing herself against it, raised her arms aloft and declared that the pole was a cross." Her husband ultimately committed her to an asylum [55]. Josephine and Ida soon ventured out to the institution to formally disavow responsibility for her condition [56].

The arrival of Charlotte Farnsworth, a refined, educated woman of 28, had repercussions for the Belmont Hall devotees that would ultimately drive Ida Russell from their midst. When Ida first met Charlotte she was an overworked school teacher on the verge of nervous collapse. Ida took an interest in the pathetic young woman, spending long days with her in the rural Ojai valley where she offered some practical advice on how she might recover. Ida also introduced the distraught schoolmarm to Josephine Holmes. Ida diagnosed Charlotte's mental anguish as stemming from her worrying too much over past mistakes and a future she could not possibly predict. "She advised me to close up the channels of my many imperfections and that would end my sufferings. I followed the advice and was much relieved," she later recalled [57]. Two months later Charlotte numbered among the first members of the Belmont Hall community. There she was tasked with contemplating "on our imperfections of character that are holding us back and that [are] the channels through which we suffer. When we close them our suffering ceases" [58]. On a more practical level, Charlotte was also required to wash up the dishes after meals and otherwise look after the kitchen.

Charlotte responded to this personal attention to her anguish. It was something that her family failed to offer her. "Such sad, lonely days as I passed in the midst of you when I first went to Ida for instruction. She was the only friend I had," Charlotte wrote in a scathing letter to her mother. She both chided her mother and beckoned her to Los Angeles. "When you went East one of the reasons I did not go with you was because I would not leave Ida and her teachings. … You must decide whether you will let me go on with this life without you, or whether you will come here to

Belmont Hall and learn what many a poor, hungry soul would give all that it had for the opportunities so freely offered you" [59].

Charlotte's mother never responded to the summons but her brother-in-law, Theodore Gray, did. Rather than attempt to join the confraternity, however, he arrived to extricate young Charlotte from it. He briefly queried Ida as to the religious teaching she promulgated. During this interview the pious Episcopalian in him was distressed to learn that Charlotte had not stepped inside a church since taking up with Ida. The thought that this talented college graduate was now performing kitchen work also irked him. Gray demanded that Charlotte disassociate herself from Ida and return with him at once to San Francisco. Charlotte refused. Alexander Russell—in one of the only indications of his active participation in life at Belmont Hall—offered to intervene. Gray declined this invitation to a man-to-man chat. Instead he spoke man-to-man with George Insley, director of a local detective agency. He also approached Harrison Otis, publisher of the *Los Angeles Times*. Gray's story deeply impressed General Otis, who vowed to do his part in either liberating his relative or preventing others from being duped by the "cranks" of Belmont Hall. Insley dispatched one of his agents and Otis one of his reporters to infiltrate the community, determine the nature of life there, and publish their findings.

In early February 1895 there arrived at the doorstep of Belmont Hall detective Howard Dodd, using a false name and professing to be a truth seeker with plenty of money to invest in the right kind of establishment. Muriel Irwin, a master of the purple prose and yellow journalism that characterized the *Times* in this period, appeared a little later, handing over a five-dollar gold piece for one week's room and board.

Exactly what happened over the next few days is difficult to determine. This is not for lack of testimony, for in the exposé and legal action that followed a considerable amount of testimony was recorded. But the statements made under oath are so at odds with one another as to paint completely contradictory pictures of life at Belmont Hall. The Times-Mirror faction presented Josephine Holmes as a "snaky abomination" [60], a conniving illiterate with messianic pretensions. Ida was depicted as a skilled hypnotist who colluded with Josephine to delude and dominate their weak-minded followers. The beliefs promulgated by the duo were to the *Times* "a disgusting mixture of blasphemy and absurdity, which could gain credence only with the ignorant and superstitious" [ibid.].

The night before the exposé was published Theodore Gray once again implored his relation to abandon Ida Russell and Belmont Hall. It was arranged that she not be mentioned in the article. Even one that followed it up a day later and contained a list of Belmonters that Irwin stole did not mention Charlotte Farnsworth. Nonetheless, Gray tried to impress upon his sister-in-law the untenable position in which she was about to find herself. She must return with him to San Francisco or face social disgrace. Charlotte chose embarrassment and disgrace over abandoning Ida Russell. She rushed from the rendezvous with her in-law to prepare her coreligionists for the worst the *Times* could offer.

A QUEER LOT—"THAT'S WHAT!"

Belmont Hall and Its New Breed of Fakirs

Josephine Holmes, Boss Fakir,
Ex-Washerwoman, and
Her Grand Inspirations

An Extraordinary Hodge Podge
of Bosh and Blasphemy —

Impious Pretensions—
A Pretender and Her Dupes

In the western part of the city, on the corner of First street and Belmont avenue, is a large building, set in the midst of extensive grounds. This building was formerly used as a college and is known as Belmont Hall. Here dwells a small community of choice spirits, who are busily engaged in constructing a new heaven and new earth on what they appear to think an entirely new plan, and one much superior to the old-fashioned method used for some ages by the Creator.

The controlling spirit in this aggregation of saints is a woman, who goes by the name of Josephine Holmes, a Norwegian of the peasant class, and an ex-washerwoman. As this woman can barely read and write, and speaks only broken English, she is assisted by one Mrs. Alexander Russell, the wife of a drummer connected with the Bowers Rubber Company of San Francisco. Mrs. Russell possesses some education and ability, and, having been trained for the stage, she is a valuable adjunct to the Holmes woman, in capacity as mouthpiece, or "lecturer."

… As long as pure crankiness was believed to be the only characteristic of this queer institution, it aroused but little curiosity or interest, but certain events of late have gone to indicate the presence of some crookedness beneath the outward show of decency and order, which imperatively demanded investigation. … This business has gone on long enough, now the victims may be deluded

> into the degrading slavery imposed upon the
> disciples of Miss Holmes, and it is fully time to
> show the place in its true colours, as an
> establishment ruled upon principles inimical to
> the laws of God and man, and dangerous to
> society…. [ibid.]

Josephine, Irwin wrote, claimed to be a sinless spirit incarnated to complete the failed mission of Jesus Christ. In order to receive her message, followers were required to renounce independent thought, clearing their minds of all activity. She was a medium who pretended to be possessed by an array of spirits, from a comic trickster called Abel to an African serpent that would cause her to slither along the floor. The aims of this occult priestess were plain and simple: to defraud her victims of their money. According to Irwin's initial exposé and the many newspaper articles that followed, Belmonters were charged board on a sliding scale from $5 to $35 a week—up to six times the going rate of standard boarding house accommodations. Josephine was said to have laundered enough money from her hapless victims to engage in sizable real estate transactions that served only to increase her personal wealth. Both Ida and Josephine were presented as being in league with Thorvald Holmes, Josephine's brother, "whose business it is to attend to outside affairs, gather in as much filthy lucre as may come within reach of the faithful" [61].

Belmont Hall benefited Josephine in other ways, according to the *Times*. While she demanded abstinence from her followers, Josephine kept the Hall filled with a veritable stable of virile stallions. One was the young Arthur Taylor, who could be observed at public meetings with an arm around Miss Holmes' wasp-like waist. The pair would last be seen in evenings walking together toward her bed chamber, emerging in the morning with Arthur carrying Josephine's shawl. The young man's pale complexion was attributed not to his battle with typhoid, but to

Josephine not letting him get a wink of sleep at night. George Van Auken, brother of the boarding house keeper who was formerly Josephine's disciple, was also in the harem, according to the *Times*. Josephine was once caught sitting on his lap and it was said that when traveling by train the two shared a sleeper cabin. Van Auken, incidentally, had a wife and four children in New York.

Residents of Belmont Hall were presented as "an aggregation of fools … whose mental equipoise has been badly disturbed" [62]. They were weak-minded dupes, victims of this "evil genius" who easily controlled them all. Except for Ida Russell, "who bears a close resemblance to a tenth-rate actress of the vulgar sensational type." (The reporter initially confused Ida Russell with a nationally popular vaudeville performer of the same name.) Ida was co-conspirator. During periods of group meditation the *Times* reported that Ida would gaze down from her elevated platform, meet the eyes of any who dared, and extend her hypnotic power over them. When she tried to gain control over the reporter a battle of wills ensued. "They gazed at each other for a long time, when, to the amazement of Miss Irwin, Mrs. Russell showed signs of confusion and distress, and faltered as she arose and attempted to speak. She was able only to stammer out a few broken sentences, when she sank back into her chair. … The meeting broke up in great confusion after this display of the power of evil" [63].

PART 3

The reaction of the "queer lot" was swift and, as it turned out, rather queer.

Within days of the article's publication Ida Russell, Dalton Wheeler, and a handful of other Belmonters stormed the office of the attorney general. They demanded that he issue a complaint against General Otis on the charge of criminal libel. The assistant district attorney agreed that portions of the article appeared libelous. Even if there were a way to prove Josephine Holmes' religious doctrines as false, there was little warrant for describing her in terms like "snaky abomination." He declined, however, to issue the complaint. A civil suit would be the more appropriate course of action. The petitioners returned a little later to jawbone the district attorney himself. When he reiterated his assistant's conclusion Dalton Wheeler and a couple of the other men advanced on him in a menacing fashion. The assistant quickly entered the room and defused a situation that seemed to be heading toward violence. At this point, fury blinded the Belmonters and they lost sight of the correct target. They hired lawyers to launch proceedings against Major John Donnell, Los Angeles District Attorney, claiming that he should be removed from office due to neglect of duty. To the amazement of the local legal community a judge agreed to hear the case, but decided in favor of the defendant. The Belmonters requested a retrial. Denied. They appealed to the state supreme court. Dismissed.

With that avenue blocked, they reconsidered the path Major Donnell initially suggested. The civil suit against General Otis and his Times-Mirror Company claimed $25,000 in damages. The Belmonters finally had the right target, but the enterprise was doomed from the start. Otis was among the most powerful men in Los Angeles. Access to some of the state's most effective attorneys had freed him from the libel hook on more than one occasion in the past. In this case he was represented by Stephen M. White, who was also serving as U.S. senator at the time. The prosecution, through a series of handpicked witnesses, presented Belmont Hall's version of events covered in the exposé. Josephine testified that she was not and never had been a medium. Ida said that, before the *Times* reporter demonstrated Holmes' alleged snake slithering routine to the general hilarity of the jury, she had never before seen such a performance. The residents of Belmont Hall were not a commune, as reported, but a family, or rather a gathering of several distinct families no different from those living in boarding houses across the country. Josephine was no autocrat;

rather, everyone did pretty much as they pleased. She claimed no divine authority, no ability to travel to different spheres of existence. Rather, she was a devout Lutheran, a simple subject of King Otto II. No "services" were conducted in the hall, just informal discussions on religious subjects for those who wished to participate. And absolutely no money changed hands except to pay for room and board. Ida, for her part, exercised no hypnotic powers. The dramatic sequence with Irwin was explained away as stage fright. While preparing to speak that evening "I saw Miss Irwin looking straight at me with a face that was filled with malice, and the restless eye of the man by her side wandering around," she testified. "The expression upon her face intensified. I turned to Miss Holmes and said that little lady and gentleman are deadly enemies and have [conceived] a deadly hatred to me." She sat down and refused to address the gathering.

There is little doubt that during the time the *Times* reporter and Detective Dodd stayed in Belmont Hall they saw exactly what they chose to see and reported what they were paid to report. General Otis wanted an article that would shame Charlotte Farnsworth from the community and that is what was delivered, both in the press and in the court. However, the inmates of Belmont Hall also had a carefully-groomed image they wanted to present to the jury—an image, unfortunately, that was difficult to maintain as the Belmonters contradicted one another, refused to answer direct questions, attempted to coach witnesses, and very likely perjured themselves.

Ida contradicted herself by first stating she had never addressed a gathering of any sort since reading her graduating essay to an assembly at college, but later testifying that she spoke regularly at Belmont Hall under the tutelage of Josephine. In fact, Ida had been addressing large gatherings at the Woman's Christian Temperance Union since at least 1890. She claimed to have never before met a Spiritualist despite the fact that a number of Josephine's followers were known mediums. The defense produced a letter in Josephine's hand in which she talks quite plainly about spirit "controls" that direct the actions of her followers. She also described an instance when she banished the unwelcome ghost of Swedenborg who had decided to disrupt a meeting. The same letter contradicted Josephine's claims that she never received money for giving spiritual advice. In it she discusses a recent trip where her addresses on religion were part of a clearly profitable enterprise. "They have writen three letters to me sins I am back offeing me anny thing I will ask if I only come back and speek for them," she wrote in her phonetic spelling. "There is lots of Money among them" [64].

The strategy of the Belmonters—to generally deny the allegations made in the exposé but provide no detailed insights into their actual beliefs and practices—failed. The jury decided in favor of the defendant. What's more, the trial gave General Otis repeated opportunities to continue his typeset crusade against the "pseudo-religious cranks" of Belmont Hall. From the publication of the initial article in February 1895 to the conclusion of the civil trial three years later the *Times* produced page after page of hostile copy. The three other daily papers in Los Angeles took up the story as well, though the *Examiner* gave it as little space as possible, perhaps because one of its editors was among Josephine's followers.

The Belmont Hall community held tight throughout this period of persecution. Ida continued to hold forth on religious topics. Groups of sixty to seventy sympathizers would convene in the cavernous hall to sit silently together in meditation. Charlotte Farnsworth remained steadfast, refusing to leave Ida's side and return to her family. But in the wake of the trial's disappointing conclusion Ida Russell left the community. It is not known if the evidence and testimony against Josephine Holmes—her mentor for nearly a decade—drove a wedge between the two. Perhaps she was alerted to a subculture of Spiritualism that she was not aware existed at Belmont Hall. There is no evidence to indicate that

Spiritualism ever interested or influenced her. Or maybe the prolonged public exposure made her own stay in Southern California socially untenable. Alexander's name came up repeatedly in the articles. He certainly resided at the Hall from time to time and evidently participated in life at Belmont Hall when in town. Throughout the proceedings he maintained a low profile, and most likely a far distance from court functionaries serving subpoenas. It may have been at his urging that Ida finally abandoned the community. There is no evidence to suggest she ever again associated with Josephine Holmes or anyone else from Belmont Hall.

By late 1897, just months after the conclusion of the trial, Ida traveled north. Along with her expensive gowns and polished jewelry she also took her convictions about diet, communal living, the spiritual value of art, and—most notably—the importance of meditation in spiritual development. She would be quick to share these convictions with others in her new neighbourhood.

3

CHAMPIONS OF BUDDHISM

1897-1901

PART 1

C OMMUNITY, teaching, and meditation were also on
Shaku Sōen's mind in 1897. Three years had passed
since his return to Japan from the Parliament of Religions. Such a
diverse representation of different faiths, combined with
aggressive promotion on the part of the organizers and the
attention of reporters around the country, had made the event
world famous. Back home, Sōen no longer found himself the
obscure young bonze who had set out to Chicago. He was now a
"champion of Buddhism," as the Japanese press hailed the
returning delegates [65].

> These five have journeyed to the Parliament to present
> Mahayana Buddhism, to stand amidst heterodox and
> barbarian teachings and to learn the subtle aspects of each.
> Clearly no easy task. All subsequent priests who journeyed
> [sic] to the Occident will be judged by their standard. ...
> They have placed the brilliant light of the Mahayana in the
> heavens over the Occident and have provided for the
> salvation of all believers of foreign religions. [66]

Though their addresses had by and large been drowned out by
other, more forceful presentations, the Japanese Buddhist
delegation had stood shoulder to shoulder with Christians of the
West and presented their religion on equal terms. It was an

unprecedented event. In his exuberance, one of the "champions," Toki Hōryū, told a gathering of two hundred Buddhist priests that Christianity was in decline in both Europe and America, that the Parliament "only served the purpose of displaying the glory of Buddhism over Christianity." He recommended the immediate establishment of Buddhist temples in America, particularly along the Pacific coast [67]. It was suggested by another attendee that if Buddhist missionaries were sent to America they could easily establish temples and win converts [68].

Now among the more recognizable figures in Japanese Buddhism, Sōen embarked on an aggressive schedule of teaching and publishing. An account of the Parliament and an exposition on meditation were followed up by an overview of early Zen patriarchs and a presentation of the Ten Ox-Herding Pictures, a series of images that provide metaphors of the Zen practitioner's search for his true self. They communicated his thoughts not just on Buddhism in general, but on specific elements of Zen practice omitted from his presentations in Chicago.

These writings were mainly compilations of his public addresses. Sōen, as his old master noticed years earlier, was not of a scholarly bent. He was a natural teacher and an able administrator. This was just what Engakuji needed to attract new members, both clerical and lay, and accommodate itself to the modern world. In addition to beginning to build a corpus of literature that could communicate his thoughts to the widest possible audience, he began publishing a monthly journal, *Engaku*, "Perfect Enlightenment." He revised the regulations governing his sect [69], assumed the presidency of a local Buddhist school, and was reelected abbot [70]. As Sōen began teaching regularly, his addresses were written down and reported—either word-for-word or in summary—in Buddhist magazines across the country. Graphophones were employed to record his speeches and distribute them throughout Japan [71]. Before long, new students began to arrive at Engakuji, eager to learn from its very visible abbot. These not only included monks from other abbeys, but also the laity: novelists, journalists, high school teachers, professors, university students, and government workers.

During this period Sōen reinstated a society for laity in Tokyo interested in practicing Zen without venturing out to Kamakura on a regular basis. Initially founded in 1875 by Kōsen, it included a number of professors, military men, and minor nobles who had kept the old master informed on the rapidly changing Japanese government and also promoted his political and religious sentiments through secular channels otherwise closed to him [72]. The deaths of its more prominent members seem to have led to its closure in the 1880s. Sōen appointed Shaku Sōkatsu as the superintendent of the newly opened Ryōmō Kyōkai, or The Forgetting Both Society, a reference to a lesson taught through the Ten Ox-Herding Pictures.

Sōkatsu, whose religious name means "Energetic," had an enviable pedigree. He had been born into an impoverished branch of an otherwise wealthy family tracing its samurai lineage back to the Hōjō clan shōgun who founded Engakuji 600 years earlier. Sōkatsu started his Zen studies under Kōsen, completed them under Sōen, then traveled to Burma and Siam in emulation of his new master's own interest in the Buddhism of southeast Asia. Upon his return, Sōen summoned this disciple and, in words that were hopefully not as theatrical as later recalled, put him in charge of the lay society: "You acquired the great wisdom of Buddhism. Now you must complete the Four Great Vows which you made and turn the wheel of supplication for the benefit of others. The assemblage which Kōsen Oshō called Ryōmō Kyōkai has dispersed, Sōkatsu. You must go to Tokyo for the purpose of reviving it, blowing once more the bellows and rekindling the flame to forge those laymen who wish to attain enlightenment" [73].

Sōkatsu reopened the society in a renovated farmhouse surrounded by rice fields, just beyond the furthest suburb of

Tokyo. It was a district popular among students, where rented rooms were inexpensive and the commute to the university tolerable. It is little wonder, then, that many of Sōkatsu's disciples were college students, in addition to some young doctors and the odd minor noble.

Sōen visited Sōkatsu's temple on occasion, such as when he was invited to celebrate the day commemorating the Buddha's birth. Saké was served and Sōen was entreated to paint a giant calligraphic banner on an eight-foot length of canvas. One of the students—Sasaki Yeita, a young sculptor with aspirations for the stage and a day job in the post office—then entertained the abbot with an imitation of a comic monologue popular at the time. Sōen is remembered as having laughed out loud—a difficult image to conjure up given the severe face he always presented to cameras [74]. Earlier, when first introduced to the amateur entertainer, Sōen asked Yeita what he wished to do in life. He replied that he was studying art, that his specialty was carving dragons for temple gates. Sōen looked at him sternly and replied, "Carve a Buddha for me when you become a famous artist." Later, through Sōkatsu, he would realize that the Zen master did not actually want to receive a statue, but desired the young man to carve a Buddha within himself [75]. Sōen would be surprised to learn exactly where Sasaki Yeita would wind up carving Buddhas in the upcoming years.

This combination of severity and sociability was part of a complex personality that fascinated those who met Sōen. He was a contemplative monk, yet a man of action; head of an ancient priestly institution, but open to modern methods and ideas. He embraced some monastic proscriptions—such as those against eating meat, growing out one's hair, and marriage—yet disregarded others—such as those against tobacco and alcohol. In another anecdote, this one dating back several years earlier, after striving for five years to attain enlightenment under Kōsen, Sōen celebrated his achievement by disappearing for a week into the Yoshiwara gay quarters (*yūkaku*). When he was ready to leave, the madame of the establishment discovered that her enlightened guest did not possess the funds necessary to settle his account. Sōen was detained at the house while a messenger, dispatched to Engakuji, returned with his payment. Kōsen was perplexed, not just because of the scandal his protégé had caused, but more importantly because the monastery's monetary situation was tight and he was unable to pay his student's debt. Kōsen had to collect money from outside sources in order to obtain Sōen's release [76].

Sōen's religious name translates roughly as "Teaching religion" [77]. This he did vigorously throughout his life, sometimes at the cost of his health. Upon waking in the morning Sōen would light a stick of incense and sit in meditation until it burnt out, only then changing his clothes and starting his day. He ate frugally, never filling himself at a meal. He was an iconoclast who could playfully deride fellow Buddhist dignitaries for standing on ceremony, yet when representing his own office he projected solemn dignity. It was his eyes that were most commented on by those he met. They could project the cold light of the full moon, sending a chill into unnerved students as he seemed to stare into their souls. The Zen master was strict with pupils, not sparing the rod when he felt sense needed to be beaten into them. Passing his room at night students would instinctively bow, even though the door was closed and the revered teacher mostly likely asleep [78]. Yet—as shall be seen—he could be deeply sentimental at the loss of a friend, feeling the absence as if a member of his own family were taken away.

PART 2

In the years following the Parliament Sōen maintained an active correspondence. This included Dr. Paul Carus, publisher of philosophical books and journals from a small mining town on the outskirts of Chicago.

December 16, 1893

Dear Dr. Carus:

It was certainly good fortune that through the light of Buddha we met together [when] I sojourned at Chicago to attend the Parliament of Religions. … As for my part, I am a Buddhist, but far from being a conservative religionist, my intention is rather to stir a reformation movement in the religious world. In other words I am one who wishes on the genuine and spiritual Buddhism to renovate that formal and degenerated Buddhism. And I believe that if the present Christianity be reformed it will become the old Buddhism, and if the latter be reformed it will become the future religion of science which is still in the womb of Truth.

March 8, 1894

My Dear Sir:

Lately I took great pleasure to receive your kind letter again which informed me that you have almost finished a work about Buddhism—you may imagine what a joyful information it was to me. I think you may well be said to be a second Columbus who is endeavoring to discover the new world of Truth.… .

May 17, 1894

My Dear Friend:

Buddha who lived three thousand years ago, being named Gautama, now lies bodily dead in India; but Buddhism in the twentieth century, being named Truth, is just to be born at Chicago in the New World. …

Prior to the Parliament of Religions, this "second Columbus" entertained a passing interest in Buddhism, which impressed him as a religion that "does not prescribe any dogma to be believed in" [79]. Within days of the Japanese delegation's arrival at Chicago he arranged for an intermediary—a comparative religion scholar who was on the committee that selected the Asian delegates—to distribute gifts to the priests. The liaison impressed upon Sōen that the gentleman with the black straw hat and crop of hair that "seemed for a long time to have been strangers to the barber's scissors" desired to make their acquaintance [80]. With Nomura Yōzō helping clear up the initial language difficulties Sōen and Carus developed a rapport. For a full week after the Parliament they discussed Buddhism and Carus' philosophical pursuit of a religious system not dependent on the miraculous, wholly compatible with modern science and rational thought. Carus felt Buddhism fit the bill nicely. To him it seemed a "religious mythology explained in scientific terms; it is the esoteric secret of all exoteric doctrines. It is the skeleton key which in its abstract simplicity fits all locks …. It offers food for thought to the philosopher, comfort to the afflicted, and affords a stay to those that struggle. It is a guide through the temptations of life and a lesson to those in danger of straying from the right path. And yet it demands no belief in the impossible" [81].

Buddhism did not only present Carus' very active mind with a new intellectual pursuit. It was also a business endeavor. Within months of the Parliament's closing ceremony he authored *The Gospel of Buddha*, essentially a compilation of Buddhist writings presented in an approachable, non-scholarly format. It was well received, translated into a number of languages, and brought in returns impressive enough to warrant additional books on the subject. In 1896 he wrote and published *Karma: A Story of Early Buddhism*. When Leo Tolstoy translated it into Russian the celebrated count said he wished he had written it himself [82]. *Dharma, or The Religion of Enlightenment, and Nirvana: A Story of Buddhist Psychology* issued from Carus' pen in the same year. *Buddhism and Its Christian Critics* followed in 1897. With few authors presenting Buddhism in such a popular format and with American interest in Asian religions piqued by the well-publicized Parliament of Religions, the publisher soon realized he had tapped a new market. Books on Buddhism soon made up one-quarter of Open Court's sales figures [83].

For Sōen, the Open Court's monthly journal let him continue communicating to an American audience long after the Parliament had ended. In its pages he presented poetry that was published in Chinese characters, transliterated and translated. He also authored articles on "The Doctrine of Nirvana" and the "Universality of Truth." But Carus was not simply an outlet for his own writing. Sōen believed the publisher to be providing Americans with the "basic education" he believed they needed before they could grasp the gist of Buddhism. "As both an eminent philosopher and a scholar of comparative religion, Carus is a beachhead here for us," Sōen wrote in the introduction of the Japanese translation of *The Gospel of Buddha*. "If he could be brought to understand the true meaning of Buddhism, it would be better than converting a hundred thousand ordinary people" [84].

In early 1897 Sōen landed one of his students on this beachhead. As Ida Russell and her friends at Belmont Hall prepared for their day in court, Suzuki Teitarō was killing time on the steamer *China*, quarantined for a week in San Francisco for fear of smallpox. Carus knew him as the translator of his *Gospel of Buddha* into Japanese. Suzuki also translated Sōen's *Open Court* articles and correspondence into English, responding to Carus' neatly typewritten, efficiently carbon-copied letters in a barely legible scrawl. Though Suzuki was and always remained a layman, Sōen introduced him as "my ordained disciple." Known also by his religious name Daisetz, 'Great Simplicity,' Suzuki may have momentarily considered becoming a priest at about this time. In one of his first letters to Carus, Daisetz wrote cryptically, "I intend to visit [America] as a Buddhist priest, though I am not worth while to be entitle [*sic*] so" [85].

Daisetz had been patiently practicing Zen at Engakuji since the late 1880s, initially under the tutelage of Kōsen. He sometimes walked from Tokyo, a distance of thirty miles, for the privilege. Daisetz had wanted to travel abroad, to Ceylon in emulation of Kōsen's successor and his new teacher, but lacked the funds for such an endeavor. Though his family had been relatively well off and enjoyed samurai rank in previous generations, it was now impoverished. An older brother provided an allowance that helped pay for classes at the Imperial University. Though Daisetz never received a degree he acquired a working knowledge of English and an ability to read Chinese, Sanskrit, and Pāli.

Despite his religious training, Daisetz did not embark for America as a Buddhist missionary. Rather, he went to continue his education under Carus. "Now I have something to ask your kind consent relating to the person of Suzuki Teitarō," Sōen wrote to Carus the previous year. "He tells me that he has been greatly inspired by your sound faith which is perceptible in your various works, that he earnestly desires to go abroad and to study under your personal guidance. If you will be kind enough to consent to take him under your patronage, he will willingly do everything you may order him, as far as he can." Sōen added it was his hope that through Daisetz's presence in America "your country may have also a good opportunity to know what the Japanese Buddhist would say" to the various intellectual and religious discussions of the day [86].

As it happened, Carus was struggling with a translation of the *Dao De Jing* and readily accepted the help of this young scholar. When health inspectors cleared his ship, Daisetz lingered in San Francisco for a week before clambering onto a train bound for LaSalle, Illinois.

PART 3

Sōen may have lost one disciple with the departure of D. T. Suzuki, but in the mid-1890s he was regularly gaining others. As the decade progressed and his reputation increased, seventy to eighty students—both monks and laity—would visit Engakuji to sit in meditation and attend his discourses [87]. Representative of these is a lecture he gave at this time on the day commemorating the Buddha's enlightenment.

> To study Zen is not a difficult task. Just stop your hankering for anything and make yourself [sit] erect like a great iron wall. If there are three thousand worlds in the universe, as the old scriptures say, consider them all as your own temple. If there are countless sentient beings in each of these worlds, consider them as living in your own belly and therefore seated with you.
>
> Ask yourself what this mind and body are. Consider them thoroughly, down to the very depths. Your body is not your body, but one part of all sentient beings' body. Your mind is not your mind, but one part of all sentient beings' mind. Your eyes, ears, nose, tongue, hands, and feet are not your individual belongings; you are sharing them with all sentient beings. What you call "self" and "others" or when you make the distinction between "same" and "different"—these are your dualistic ideas. If you cling to self, which is empty by nature, you are planting seeds of delusion. Living constantly with this understanding, your point of view will expand to the limitless extents of the universe. Relative and absolute, differentiation and equality, and all other dualistic thoughts will melt away. In Zen we call this the "great death." It is not real realization, but you are on the way to the palace... [88]

Among those on the way to the palace with Sōen was Nomura Yōzō. After the Parliament of Religions, Sōen's translator did not immediately return with him to Japan. Instead he accompanied one of the other delegates to Europe, translating for him in several countries. When the two separated, Yōzō continued on his own to Italy, then on to Britain's colony in India. Along the way he made mental notes of western business practices, as well as the fad for Japanese curios throughout America and Europe. Returning home, Yōzō picked up a job with a Yokohama silk merchant and resumed his study at Engakuji. Conversations with his mentor and onetime traveling companion were not restricted to matters of religion. Yōzō envisioned a career built around selling Japanese goods to foreigners, and he asked his teacher's opinion on the matter. Sōen approved of the idea but, recognizing the independent streak that caused Yōzō to quit jobs almost as quickly as he found them, recommended that he not be dependent on anyone else. He should start his own business. Returning home, Yōzō had much to meditate on [89].

Also among Engakuji's swelling membership at this time were Senzaki Nyogen and Uemura Sōkō. Their experiences at the monastery could not have been more different. Nyogen was not at all well when he stood before the wooden gates of Engakuji the year before Daisetz Suzuki embarked for America. The two had met in Tokyo where they attended the same Sanskrit class. Nyogen was nearly twenty years old and had spent the past year traveling Japan as a penniless mendicant visiting the masters of different Buddhist schools [90]. He was already a priest twice over, having been ordained in both the Sōtō school of Zen and more recently in the Shingon sect. It was probably Daisetz who invited Nyogen to one of Sōen's public lectures. Though unable to speak with the Zen master directly, the encounter for Nyogen "was the true turning point of my life." He immediately wrote the charismatic abbot, asking to join the ranks of his followers [91]. On his arrival Nyogen noticed the abbot possessed "severe penetrating eyes and a stern mouth … all very different to the kindness he had displayed in his letters." What Sōen noticed was that his newest charge was quite ill. In fact, Nyogen, whose religious name means "Like a fantasy," was in a very real predicament. He had tuberculosis. The abbot directed that he be isolated in a small hut within the monastery precinct. Once, during one of Sōen's occasional visits to the hermitage, a distraught Nyogen asked, "What if I should die?" Sōen's response was as severe as the eyes that Nyogen met on his arrival to the monastery: "If you die, just die" [92].

It was a full year before Nyogen was finally allowed to participate in the daily life at the monastery. To a newcomer it could be as delightful a place as it was frightening. Years later he would recall a vivid memory he retained from this time: "The fog was heavy in the mountains, and the temples had entirely disappeared out of sight. Neither trees nor towers were in view. Everything seemed to have vanished away. But, through the fog, I heard my teacher's voice far above in the shrine, [and] while I was ascending the stone steps in the fog, I joined in his recitation—a chapter of the Sanskrit canon."

Every other day the monks would assemble for Sōen's lecture after which they would meditate together. To Nyogen, "it was as if many silent stars had gathered around that brilliant North Star" [93]. In mornings and evenings each monk was allowed to enter Sōen's private quarters for personal instruction, known as *nyūshitsu dokusan*. In these sessions the master would evaluate his disciples' spiritual progress. To do this, he assigned each a *kōan*, used to focus meditation and aid the student in transcending dualistic thinking and rational thought. A *kōan* Kōsen was fond of assigning was the classic "What is the sound of one hand clapping?" If the student provided a response acceptable to the master, another *kōan* was assigned until he was convinced of the pupil's progress. If the answers were unacceptable, Sōen's response could be quite different. "At midnight we entered the master's room, one after another, to receive his personal guidance," Nyogen would recall. "The master would hit us with his stick, and scold us like a thunderstorm. We repeated the Buddha's words in our heart, 'I am the one who accomplished *Zazen* (meditation), and you are all on your way now. Someday, every one of you will become a Buddha, as I am now.' Thinking thus, we smiled under his whip, and encouraged ourselves after our stormy visits" [94]. Such aggressive teaching techniques were by no means reserved for Nyogen. Daisetz Suzuki remembered being so frustrated with his *kōan* that he gave up attending personal interviews except when they were compulsory during the annual retreat. "And then all that usually happened was that the *Rōshi* (the teacher) hit me" [95].

It is little wonder that newcomers to the monastery often delayed practicing *dokusan* as long as possible. Those too timid to walk to the master's private quarters might be forcefully removed from the meditation hall by senior monks who would carry them to their dreaded interview [96]. Nyogen, it seemed, had no such superiors willing to tote him into Sōen's quarters, which he compared to a lion's den. He soon gave up trying to answer his *kōan*. As a result, his training under Sōen's supervision seems to have come to a standstill and his ability to understand Zen, at least Zen of the variety that Sōen taught, seems to have been stymied. "I am positive he didn't practice *sanzen*," Daisetz recalled much later, using the synonym for *dokusan*. "I suppose Senzaki knows only a little about Zen, though he and I have been good friends all the time" [97]. It was perhaps because he was frustrated with his religious life that Nyogen started reading up on other subjects— among them the educational theories of Friedrich Fröbel, inventor of the kindergarten system.

Uemura Teizō was having a very different experience of Engakuji at this time. Whereas Daisetz's family was impoverished, the Uemuras were among the more prominent families in Tokyo. Whereas Senzaki's maladroit religious pursuits were leading to frustration, Teizō was proving himself both dedicated and talented. He had been introduced to Engakuji by one of his high school teachers who practiced there himself. While still a teenager, Teizō attempted to meditate for an entire week, sustaining himself only on a small bag of sweets. On the first morning of the fast he consumed the bag's entire contents. By the second day he was so weak that he could not walk to the toilet without having to support himself along the way. On the third day he could not maintain a seated position while meditating, needing to support himself with one arm on the floor. A breakthrough came on the fourth day. No longer weak and unable to concentrate, he completed his week-long retreat. This type of dedication earned him Sōen's special attention. He proved an apt pupil and developed an especially close bond with his master. Fellow students teased him about this close relationship with Sōen, saying he had "jumped into the master's *futokoro*," that is, the inner part of the kimono [98].

After high school, Teizō entered the Imperial University where he took classes with Daisetz Suzuki and mastered the English language [99]. He disentangled himself from his studies at least once a month to visit Engakuji, also spending summer breaks at the monastery to continue his Zen training. After graduation the able young man enlisted in the prestigious Imperial Guard. Decommissioned after a year, he formally joined Engakuji as a monk. It was a coup for Sōen. Not only was this newest of his students quick to pick up the intricacies of Zen philosophy and practice, the addition of an Imperial University graduate to the ranks of his followers would add to the prestige of Engakuji [100]. The abbot gave his newest charge the religious name Sōkō, special to Sōen since years earlier it had been his own religious name before he was compelled to change it [101].

Like his master in his youth, Uemura Sōkō possessed a wanderlust that, ironically, started to manifest itself after he took monastic vows. It was not only Engakuji's secluded valley that felt confining as the last years of the nineteenth century waned. "I don't want to live on such a small bean as Japan," he wrote to Daisetz in the far away and exotic land of Illinois. Sōkō compared himself to Robinson Crusoe, stranded on a tiny island. "I am ready to breathe the air of the larger countries right away" [102].

Uemura Sōkō would have his wish granted, though he would remain overseas longer than he could ever have imagined.

4

To Heed the Admonitions of All Buddhas

1897-1901

PART 1

S INCE leaving Belmont Hall Ida Russell had changed addresses twice. From Los Angeles she and Alexander traveled to the island of Alameda just off the eastern shore of the San Francisco Bay. They stayed there nearly two years before moving back to downtown San Francisco, into a sizable house on a fashionable stretch of Gough Street. Another two years passed and they were preparing for a third move.

Details from this period of Ida's life are limited. To her, San Francisco was home, so it makes sense that she would return there. It was where she had romped as a child, where she would have explored Chinatown—perhaps acquiring her first taste of a budding appetite for Asian culture—when her parents moved into a neighbourhood just beyond its southern border. It was where her mother, Elizabeth Conner, rented furnished rooms to money brokers, post office night clerks, and an up-and-coming salesman. Alexander Russell cut a dapper figure in the city, with his waxed handlebar mustache and slicked-down hair, confident gaze and East Coast manners. He had arrived from his native New Jersey in 1877, aged 22. His family had been active in the rubber trade until the Panic of '57 and bad credit brought that line of business to a close. Kerosene lamps and steam engines were his father's latest business interests before a stroke ended his life at the age of 55. After the funeral Alexander headed directly to San Francisco.

He was immediately employed as a clerk for Goodyear Rubber, perhaps suggesting that former colleagues of his father were making sure the young man had a fair start. After marrying his landlady's daughter, the newlyweds continued to reside at Elizabeth Conner's boarding house. Over the next three years Alexander rose through the ranks, eventually being promoted to salesman, peddling rubber gloves, boots, and hoses locally. In 1888 he ran for public office and soon found himself county recorder. The post brought an income of $4,000—roughly $120,000 in today's currency—until he returned to the rubber trade when his two-year term expired. Through much of this time Alexander and Ida lived in the Conner boarding house alongside the farriers and other working-class lodgers there. When Ida was called away to Josephine Holmes' community Alexander's business travel often brought him back to San Francisco. Sometimes he would keep rooms at the Grand Hotel, other times at a house that Ida would presumably visit when not in Los Angeles.

What drew Ida to Alameda immediately after Belmont Hall's legal debacle is less certain. One possibility is the existence of the Home of Truth on the island. It was one of a number of spiritual associations that emerged under the umbrella of New Thought. Main branches in Alameda, San Francisco, and Los Angeles—all places Ida called home in the 1890s—were in fact communes where religious seekers could benefit from close fellowship with their peers. Members were treated to an eclectic fare of religious, ethical, and "therapeutic" teachings based partly on Christian Science but liberally peppered with Hindu and Buddhist ideas. The truth housed in Alameda included the belief that each individual's "Real Self" is in fact God, and that this divine immanence could be encountered in meditation [103]. Given the similarities between Home of Truth beliefs and those of Ida she may have been seeking the comfort of likeminded religionists after the downfall of Belmont Hall. Ida, however, was not looking to join an existing community at this point in her life. She was ready to found a new one.

It was probably in Alameda that Ida first met the Crossleys. Like the Russells, Clarence Crossley arrived in Alameda in 1897, bringing with him his wife Grace. Like Ida they were religious liberals, members of San Francisco's First Unitarian Church. They had been married six years earlier by its head minister, Horatio Stebbins, who fostered an active interest in the Brahmo Samaj, an Indian society devoted to the revitalization of Hinduism. Like Charlotte Farnsworth of Belmont Hall, Grace Crossley turned to Ida for guidance and consolation, in this case at the loss of a child [104]. When the Russells returned to San Francisco the Crossleys went with them—not just to the same neighbourhood, but to the same Gough Street address. Joining them were three other women: Mary Keeler, an artist who worked at the same printing company as Clarence; Bertha Christofferson, a Norwegian immigrant of no known relation to Josephine Holmes; and Elise Drexler. All were in their mid-thirties. All were unmarried (or recently widowed in the case of Elise) and would remain so for the rest of their lives. For nearly twenty years, they formed the nucleus of Ida's new community.

Life at Gough Street was organized along lines recognizable to a Belmonter. Men and women, whether single or married, shared a common dwelling. Women were in the majority and occupied the posts of power. Children were welcome, the only one at the time being the Crossleys' only surviving daughter Katherine. Members were by no means confined to the house. However, they had specific responsibilities to the community that tended to preclude outside jobs. Bertha kept house, did cleaning and washing—the same position that had been occupied by Charlotte Farnsworth at Belmont Hall. Mary Keeler acted as Ida's private secretary, taking dictation and making appointments. Clarence Crossley was a skilled lithographer and was sometimes employed as a book illustrator. But unlike Mr. Van Auken—the Riverside carpenter Josephine Holmes induced to lay aside his saw and follow her—Clarence only worked sporadically while with the Russells. His responsibilities to the community varied. Sometimes he chauffeured members in a horse cart, other times he doubled for Mary Keeler as Ida's amanuensis [105].

Simple vegetarian meals were eaten communally, with a period of silent prayer preceding and following each meal. Alcohol was of course taboo, and not just within the residence. Shortly after moving in Elise Drexler issued a warning to all businesses on properties she owned. In order to maintain their lease they were not to serve or sell alcohol on their premises. Her husband, twice her age when they married, left her a sizable fortune upon his unfortunate but not entirely unexpected death in 1899. The estate was conservatively valued at $4 million—a figure that in today's currency amounts to more than $100 million. Most of the estate went to his young bride. It included not only an expansive mansion on the most fashionable stretch of Van Ness Avenue, but also a number of business concerns, agricultural enterprises, and tracts of downtown real estate. Her properties included a number of saloons, some of them well established and occupying the same site since the Gold Rush. The barkeeps protested their eviction to their new landlady. Elise stood firm. They demanded an explanation, hoping perhaps to appeal to her business sense. Business was not on her mind in this matter. "I am trying to better myself, to uplift myself, to be true to myself. That is one of the reasons why I allow no intoxicating drink in my home and feel I have no right to permit it to be sold or served in properties that I own," responded the heiress who had been receiving Ida Russell's spiritual guidance for more than a year at this point. "I know I can get bigger rents from liquor dealers than from any other class of tenants. In refusing to accept them I am sacrificing myself financially." When pressed for details, her responses went from vague to cryptic: "It is premature to discuss the question at present.

I fear that the publicity at the present state of my plans may harm the cause I would serve" [106].

Art, too, was held in high regard in Ida's new community. It was a more sophisticated pursuit than at Belmont Hall, where the amateurish paintings of Josephine's sister cluttered the parlor. Replacing this was a serious, disciplined study of art in all its forms—visual, musical, literary, theatrical. For the past few years Elise Drexler and Mary Keeler were among a select coterie of society ladies making a systematic study of the philosophy, psychology, and spirituality of art. Lectures were held twice a week; attendance was by invitation only. The topics so engrossed the privileged set, one gossip columnist explained, "that society has become a secondary consideration, and they are willing to forego even afternoon teas if there is lecture on the tapis."

Discussing painting, sculpture, music, poetry, and literature, speakers sought to awaken a "spiritual art of the soul… that not only sees the beauty of the eye, but recognizes the beauty of the soul shining in it." Applying the lessons to everyday life, participants used musical and poetic principles to develop lyrical styles of conversation. Sculpture was scrutinized to improve their posture. They developed a style of art criticism they believed could as effectively analyze a still-life as reveal the moral character of people around them. Using this system of character study, attendees of the artistic soirées, like readers of the popular psychology books of a later generation, said "they unconsciously find themselves analyzing friends and strangers alike, and that there is an irresistible fascination in trying to fathom people by the principles" they learned. Finally, they practiced something the uninitiated journalists described as "mental self-control"—very likely a reference to meditation [107].

PART 2

Exactly how much of these lessons on the philosophy of art found their way into Ida's little community is uncertain. As shall be seen, art played a central role in her spiritual pursuits. If she wrote a treatise, delivered a lecture, wrote a letter spelling out her thoughts on this—or most any other—matter it has not survived. In fact, almost nothing from her pen seems to exist. It is highly disappointing since the little material that has survived—a pair of letters, a newspaper editorial, some maxims in a child's scrapbook, the reminiscences of Japanese friends and acquaintances, quotations jotted down by journalists concentrating more on sensation than accuracy—reveals a highly articulate woman of well-considered opinions and heartfelt convictions. Considering that for more than a decade she employed a private secretary whose duties included taking her dictation and that community members were in the habit of quoting her original aphorisms, a collected body of work must have at one time existed. But the years following her death were characterized by confusion and turmoil. When she passed away any corpus she might have developed seems to have disappeared as well.

Fortunately, the articles by and about her are consistent enough to reconstruct a general overview of her thoughts on spirituality. There are also telling similarities between what we know of her beliefs and those of several local religious groups. As noted, Ida's approach to religion was eclectic. This is not entirely surprising given San Francisco's diverse and avant-garde religious milieu. "Institutes of Metaphysical Science have been started which include the teaching of mind-cure, animal magnetism, mesmerism, spiritualism, clairvoyance, and mediumship; while we, as Christian Scientists, are denounced for having our jacket[s on] too straight," complained one perplexed missionary [108].

Ida was certainly familiar with one or more of these metaphysical institutes—Annie Rix Militz's Home of Truth and perhaps Malinda Cramer's Institute of Divine Science. These New Thought groups, borrowing on their Christian Science roots, tended to conceive of spiritual development in terms of illness and cure, needs and remedies. This was also the case with Ida. She would not recommend a specific spiritual path to any particular individual without first getting to know the person quite well. Once she diagnosed the person's spiritual state, she prescribed a set of moral and religious practices best suited to removing the unwanted tendencies and advancing him or her along the spiritual path. The first evidence of this was Ida's tutelage of Charlotte Farnsworth, the Ojai school teacher approaching nervous breakdown. Much later in her life, Ida clearly retained the practice. When asked by a complete stranger what spiritual advice she would give him, Ida replied, "I would advise you as a commencement, *not knowing your spiritual needs*, to think and meditate on the fact that there is a good and just God" [109], emphasis added]. At another time it was commented that Ida never asked for any sort of payment for her "services," "except the thanks of the people when they told her that she had helped them to try and lead a better life" [110].

In other respects her religious thinking could be more conventional. From Christianity, she maintained a reverence for the Bible which remained a primary source of inspiration throughout her life. She also appreciated certain traditional Christian doctrines, such as that of redemption. She held the figure of Jesus Christ in high regard throughout her life and never ceased to identify herself as Christian. A belief that angels in some way looked after people's well-being is also a vague but recurring theme [111]. Ida's Christianity, however, was generally not the stuff propounded from the pulpits of most denominations. Christ was for her more of an abstraction than a historic figure, an ideal to realize in one's own self rather than an individual to whom one pays homage. It is much the same position taken by many of the metaphysical institutes of the New Thought variety. As such, Ida did not regard the title of Christ as the sole property of Jesus and placed the luminaries of other, non-Christian religions on equal footing with the founder of Christianity. It was her vow, she once said, "to heed the admonitions of all Buddhas, of all Christs, of all Enlightened Ones" [112].

Another source of Ida's religious thought was the Theosophical Society. In 1901, just as she was preparing to transfer her Gough Street community to quarters more conducive to their spiritual pursuits, Ida and Alexander formally joined the Society. That spring its white-bearded patriarch—Henry Steel Olcott, whose *Buddhist Catechism* Shaku Sōen had perused in Ceylon [113]—stopped briefly in San Francisco. He had met with the Russells and was impressed enough to admit them as members at large [114]. Theosophists held a fascination with hidden doctrine, esoteric truths that could be discovered in and coaxed from exoteric religious expression. Esotericism was also core to Ida's religious musings and, as shall be seen, it did not endear her to all of her acquaintances. The Theosophical Society provided many Americans with their first introduction to Buddhism. Its publications and local lodges had been discussing the religion in detail for more than a decade. San Francisco's multicultural atmosphere, however, was to give her more direct exposure to the religion.

Perhaps taking some of the $30,000 set aside back in 1893 for the propagation of Buddhism in France, the Pure Land sect sent two priests to San Francisco to attend to the spiritual needs of the city's growing Japanese immigrant population. By 1901 five hundred people attended the services of "The Buddhist Mission," including about twenty Caucasians who formally converted to the religion [115]. They met together regularly, sang from hymnals composed and published by Paul Carus, and received instruction from the Pure Land priests in their broken English. They also produced their own publication, *Light of Dharma*, to which Ida Russell subscribed [116].

This would not have been Ida's first direct contact with Japanese Buddhism. While in college, as she pursued her curriculum of Quietist and Transcendentalist philosophy, she also encountered texts on Buddhism that detailed its emphasis on meditation [117]. The exotic creed would fascinate and inspire her for the rest of her life. But she never held Buddhism—or any other religion for that matter—higher than other spiritual traditions. Nor did she ever attempt to synthesize Buddhism, Christianity, or other faiths into a single system. In her own words, "I have studied all the religions and have taken what seems to me to be the best from all. ... Each individual requires the spiritual philosophy which suits his individual needs to attain happiness" [118]. From Buddhism Ida may have gleaned the concepts of reincarnation and karma, which are sometimes implied when she briefly overviewed her religious thoughts. Also, Buddhism's focus on meditation clearly dovetailed well with the quietism she had long valued. Ida may have also borrowed some of these ideas from Hinduism as well. Vivekananda, the swami who caused a great stir at the Parliament of Religions, was temporarily residing at the San Francisco Home of Truth at the same time that Ida moved back to the city [119]. It is not inconceivable that she audited his lessons in "Concentration and Breathing" [120]. Other evidence of appreciation for Hinduism is found in her possession of a Sanskrit dictionary (there is no evidence that she ever studied Japanese or Chinese), her elaborate Hindu shrine imported from India [121], and her voiced admiration for "the highly developed esoterics of India" [122].

To add substance to what might otherwise have become an unappealing gallimaufry of religious beliefs, Ida championed a trinity of guiding principles that she referred to as purity, quietude, and sympathy. She summarized her thoughts on this in the following manner: "Whatever happens to us in life, we must comport ourselves ... in a pure manner. Though we live in a world full of strife, we must strive to maintain our hearts in a state of imperturbable quiet. Instead of saying we are part of the Universal Spirit or the universal leader, it is better to manifest a heart of compassion and charity" [123].

The purity that Ida promoted encompassed both body and mind. Abstemious and vegetarian for much of her life, Ida maintained that physical purity could be attained, at least in part, by eschewing alcohol and meat. Ida might also have included ritual bathing as a means of corporeal purity, for local quidnuncs curious about Ida's daily life would later recall that she and members of her household immersed themselves in the ocean at dawn each morning [124]. Purity would certainly not have been restricted to corporeal matters, however. Unfortunately, little indication has survived that provides insight into how she would have characterized spiritual purity. Perhaps the best clue lies in an axiom about thoughts and actions producing positive karma, that belief that we reap what we sow on a cosmic level both in this world and the next. In a charming note to her eleven-year-old niece, Ida revealed how she had blended aspects of Buddhist and Christian concepts to create a mélange palatable to children: "Dear Janet— We make our blessings and our sorrows. Good thoughts and good actions become Guardian Angels to protect from harm" [125].

Sympathy, to Ida, involved an approach to religion that was not just idealistic but practical. Able to comprehend abstruse philosophies and present them in a manner that was at once approachable and personal, Ida was by no means content to let spiritual pursuits stop short at the door of intellect. She was impatient with religious societies that only preached doctrines and endlessly discussed abstract concepts. When on the witness stand during the libel trial, Ida was questioned by a lawyer about her vegetarianism. He hoped her to say that animals possessed souls so that he could lampoon her religious beliefs. He was to be disappointed. Ida reprimanded him for thinking she wasted time pondering "things impossible to fathom in this life." Instead, "keeping malice, anger, and other evil qualities in subjugation is much better than speculating about things that cannot do one any good" [126]. Rather than contemplate abstractions that cannot be proven and have little practical bearing on life, Ida felt it more important to practice the charity and compassion promoted by different religions. The sentiment was reflected in her aphorism, "Why should we be contented to worship saints and not become one?" [127]. Ida's path to sainthood involved the active practice of charity toward those less fortunate than oneself. The welfare of refugees and, more particularly, orphans would occupy more and more of her time in the years to come.

Quietude, the third palmary element of Ida Russell's spiritual triumvirate, was intimately related to the pursuit of purity and the practice of sympathy. A tranquil spirit, she explained, is one not controlled by base, impure instincts; it is not distracted by selfish desires. When this tranquil state is achieved, she explained, mind and body, thought and action become one [128]. It was the pursuit of tranquility that led Ida to take up the practice of meditation. "By what means can we go through life quietly and purely to nurture a heart moved by the mystery of life?—this was the question they came to ask themselves in time," wrote a friend, recalling conversations in which Ida remembered her friends at Belmont Hall. "Seeking a means that was simple enough for all people to practice, a means that could be practiced anywhere, they ultimately struck upon seated meditation as the only possible practice. The state of mind of quiet and purity is the feeling that arises when body and mind become one. To maintain that state of Quietude they began to sit in meditation" [129]. In Ida's own words: "I believe in self-mastery and self-control, living true to the dictates of an illumined conscience. This illumination is gained in prayer, which may be termed meditation or communication between the soul and its source" [130].

It is not entirely clear where she first learned about meditation. It was certainly not through the Buddhist Mission since seated meditation is not among the practices of the Pure Land sect.

Moreover, there is no evidence that she had any direct contact with Zen Buddhists before the spring of 1902. However, by the 1890s the Theosophists were already familiar enough with meditation to be giving each other practical advice on it. "Exclude wandering thoughts, or any not strictly germane to the subject selected for thought, with the most painstaking care," experts advised. "Then, when the attention is fixed upon some interior subject, the clamor of the senses will quickly die away. For the attempt must not be made to hush their roaring by concentration upon the senses themselves, or upon the fact that we are endeavoring to still them. The way to forget a thing is not to think about it at all, either with satisfaction or regret" [131]. Theosophists at the San Francisco lodge provided formal instruction in meditation, which they referred to as "thought control" [132]. At the Home of Truth, on the other hand, it was called "concentration," and recommended as a way to awaken one to the "silent center of being where God is indwelling and which only can be experienced when the soul is in a state of quietude" [133]. It was recommended that beginners set aside thirty minutes each day, select a theme (such as love or peace) and dwell on it by repeating a mantra. Practitioners should then let their minds wander on the spiritual subjects that the theme inspired. People meditating alone were encouraged to keep a journal of their musings, while those practicing as a group should share their thoughts verbally [134].

In fact, the incorporation of meditation as a spiritual technique has deep roots in western culture, stretching through the American Transcendentalists to the French Quietists of the seventeenth century, back to the contemplatives of the Middle Ages and on to the Greek Stoics. Ida was in touch with all of these traditions. In her Gough Street community, meditation was no less important. "The most essential thing to have in carrying out your spiritual development is absolute tranquility of mind," she would say. "Only after obtaining this can you give yourself to perfect meditation" [135].

However, absolute tranquility was a rare commodity in downtown San Francisco. Horses clip-clopped along noisily. Newsboys cried out headlines. Salvation Army sergeants clanged bells and sang hymns on street corners. Everywhere was hustle and bustle and business in this commercial mecca of the American West. What Ida needed was a new address.

PART 3

The Oceanside House had stood on its lonely, wind-swept strand for more than forty years before Ida Russell rode past it in the first year of the new century. It was a handsome, if not entirely grand, edifice, its broad walls and modestly pitched roof conveying a boxy appearance. Rectangular windows, all equal in size and twice as high as they were wide, perforated the walls, filling the rooms with a warm and welcome light on the occasional days when fog did not enshroud the site. An ornate archway, through which both equestrians and the occasional motorist could pass, broke the white picket fence surrounding the property. Stone steps leading up to the imposing front door gave the place a respectable appearance, reflecting an upper-class environment to which Ida was becoming increasingly accustomed. But what appealed to her most was the isolation. The Oceanside House was about eight miles from San Francisco's hectic city center. The waves of the Pacific Ocean crashed on a beach just yards from the structure, filling the air with brine and constant maritime thunder. Behind the house, to the east, a long expanse of sand dunes rose and fell as the heavy wind added to and subtracted from their ever-varying forms.

There was no streetcar service to the area, no paved roads. Small single-family houses sometimes speckled the sandy plats. Larger homes with a dozen or more rooms—mostly weekend dwellings for moneyed San Franciscans—could be found here and there. One might occasionally encounter a small dairy farm. But the area was still remote, well beyond the westernmost fringes of the city's furthest suburbs. It was exactly what Ida was looking for. She purchased the building along with the two sand-covered city blocks that surrounded it for $21,500, probably paying cash.

At the time no one bothered to question the source of the money. A number of those who knew the truth wished they were mistaken. Later in life Ida embellished her humble origins, fabricating a fanciful tale that she had been wealthy ever since her father, a Forty-niner, struck pay dirt [136]. Despite her family's actual working-class background Ida was clearly accustomed to a fairly high standard of living by this time. In 1894 she was already following European fashions and adorning her imported gowns with jewelry conspicuous enough to elicit public comment. Alexander was certainly increasingly successful in his business endeavors. If his $4,000 salary in 1888 is any indication of later income, he would have been able to amply provide for his wife. But while his salary would be insufficient to support Ida's ambitious project, it would become Elise Drexler's unstated cause for which she was so willing to sacrifice herself financially.

While others held domestic responsibilities in Ida's community, Elise was different. She was Ida's close friend and confidant, a kindred spirit for whom Ida's message of purity and sympathy thoroughly resonated. Elise tended to be shy, even reclusive. She preferred Ida to do the talking and was undoubtedly impressed by what she had to say. As with Ida, San Francisco's avant-garde religious atmosphere broadened Elise's spiritual horizons. Together with her sister, Elise became an adept of the "metaphysical religions" derived from Christian Science, Theosophy, and other sources. Before long her family's library included *All Things Are Possible to Them That Believe* by Annie Rix Militz, *Divine Healing* by Captain R. Kelso Carter, and a collection of Max Müller's translations of Buddhist sūtras and Vedic hymns.

The library also housed a variety of books detailing the techniques of meditation, such as *The Hindu-Yogi Science of Breath* by Ramacharaka, *Just How to Concentrate* by Elizabeth Towne, and *The Way of Peace* by James Allen.

Unlike Ida, Elise had been born into privilege. Her father truly had been a Forty-niner. Surveying San Francisco—feral, fetid, and fire-prone—he found that the city did not glitter for him. He fled the boomtown, traveling north to establish a thriving lumber business and making himself Mendocino's largest individual landholder [137]. Elise grew up wealthy and well-connected, attending college in Benicia, California, embarking on a finishing tour of Europe, and remaining in Paris for months to refine her painting technique. When Elise visited San Francisco, society-page gossips eagerly commented on the fashions she wore. Her marriage to Louis Philippe Drexler, a recognized Croesus of frontier capitalism, produced no children. Rumor had it that it was never actually consummated, that "Elise was just as much a virgin when Drexler died as when they were married" [138]. When he did die, Elise had wealth independent of her family, money she could invest as she chose. Her initial investment decisions, however, were not to everyone's liking.

Elise "got interested in a woman, it was something like Christian Science," recalled a friend of the family years later. "This woman influenced [her and Elise] bought a big place out near the ocean and she made a Japanese garden and built a house over it. Then this cult—they went through some sort of service and this woman would tell Mrs. Drexler that she should give her some money" [139]. Katherine Crossley, Clarence and Grace's daughter, would recall that Elise put precisely $1 million at Ida's disposal, the equivalent of nearly $30 million today [140].

Ida, her Golconda, and the rest of the little spiritual community did not move into the Oceanside House immediately. A steady stream of contractors and laborers first descended upon the property to perform extensive alterations. Hired, as the property was purchased, in Ida's name, they built fireplaces and chimneys to protect residents from the chilling ocean breeze and persistent fog that tended to enshroud the district. They gutted the interior to produce cavernous halls with towering ceilings. There was a hothouse, a gymnasium, a ballroom with a small orchestra pit, and a chapel in which the community could sit together in meditation. The surrounding four acres were cleared and prepared for planting, for Ida not only envisioned an elegant garden on the property but a modest orchard as well. A fence—a towering fourteen-foot barricade—went up to encircle the entire property. Japanese architects designed it specifically to protect the enclosure from the wind, which howled continuously and filled the district with sand. Trees that grew above the defending walls would have their shoots burnt off by the brine in the air, but within the ramparts the garden was serenity itself. That the barrier also ensured the privacy of the little community was an added benefit.

It was not until October 1901, half a year after the purchase of the Oceanside House, that all was finally ready [141]. By this time, the erstwhile roadhouse was transformed into a spacious mansion: massive and squat, sitting like an alcazar on its low coastal promontory. It was able to comfortably house a dozen or more occupants. The Gough Street community filled its rooms. They prayed together in the chapel, the silence broken only by the squawks of gulls, the bellows of milk cows, and the rhythmic crashing of waves.

Ida regularly addressed the community, expounding on Plato, Emerson, and their quiet mysticism. Ida was not the only one to take the podium. She regularly invited guest lecturers. Katherine Ball, a local expert on Asian art, might discourse on silk paintings. At least once there was a visit from Dr. Annie Besant, the charismatic leader of the Theosophical Society whose previous incarnations she understood to include one of the Buddha's first disciples, an Indian holy man, and the son-in-law of a ruler of some unspecified kingdom in the second millennium BCE [142]. So when Nomura Michi arrived in San Francisco in the spring of 1902, it was perfectly natural for Ida to extend an invitation.

Michi spoke fluent English, having mastered it as a child while attending Catholic school in Tokyo. She was intelligent, cultured from both her upper-class upbringing and travels around the world. Upon her arrival in San Francisco she was the centerpiece *du jour* at the parlor room gatherings so popular among society women. Her topics ranged from international relations to womanly virtue. She also spoke on religion including the experience of her husband, Yōzō, who learned how to meditate from an eminent Zen master in Kamakura. Ida and Elise were intrigued. They plied Michi with questions. They invited her to speak with them again. But Michi was on the last leg of her journey. Shortly she would return home. If they were ever to visit Japan, she said, Yōzō could discuss the matter with them directly [143].

Ida Russell began making preparations immediately.

On May 1, 1902, about six months after moving into the Oceanside House and just weeks after meeting Nomura Michi, Ida and Elise drove out to the port of San Francisco. With them was Dr. Louis Philippe Howe, the 21-year-old nephew and namesake of Elise's late husband. In the years to come, he would remain closely aligned with her philanthropic activities and spiritual pursuits, both within the Russell mansion and elsewhere. Like his aunt, Louis lived at Ida's Oceanside mansion, participating in the community's life of vegetarianism and meditation. Endowed with remarkable physical strength (Louis is remembered as having entertained children by straightening horseshoes with his bare hands) [144], the young doctor was an effective chaperone for Ida and Elise. The trio boarded a steamer bound for Hawai'i and then to the Orient.

Interlude: Brooks' Folly

For more than a generation before Ida Russell and Elise Drexler moved into the Oceanside House, peace and tranquility could not have been further from the minds of its owners.

Operating as a roadhouse when gold fever still gripped the region, the building had a lively past, catering at times to San Francisco's rougher element. In the mid-1850s, a time when San Francisco was little more than a boomtown perched on the westernmost rim of the American frontier, the cargo of a shipwrecked lumber schooner washed onto the Pacific shore. The ship may have been the *Balance*, a vessel owned by Benjamin Sherman Brooks. A native of Bridgeport, Connecticut, Brooks set sail for California at the height of the Gold Rush. Rather than soil his hands in the mines, he established himself as an attorney specializing in property law. Not long after his arrival, he purchased a thousand acres of land, much of it blanketed in sand, along the Pacific seaboard. It was on this acreage that the lumber chanced to wash ashore. Not one to let an opportunity pass, Brooks hauled in the catch and with it built a moderately sized inn that he named the Oceanside House.

Like so many creation myths, this account of the caravansary's genesis contains measures of both fact and fancy. There are numerous narratives of the origin of the Oceanside House, each different in its details but all variations on an accepted theme: a foundering ship, waters abob with lumber, and an enterprising Forty-niner. Benjamin Brooks is occasionally dubbed "Bela," and at other times identified as Morton. The date for the house's construction varies, though there is no doubt it was standing by

1857 for this is when its services were first advertised in local publications. The material from which the house was made is sometimes identified as lumber from a cargo ship or the hull of the argosy itself. One colourful variant has the structure built from a "palace of the seas" whose ornate interior was gutted to provide the building its lavish trimmings. The less fanciful account involving the lumber schooner is supported by Bickford Brooks, Benjamin's great-grandson, who seems to be drawing on reliable family tradition [145].

Brooks' tavern was among San Francisco's first beach resorts to serve refreshments to day-trippers temporarily escaping their toil in city center. A high porch encircled the handsome building. Beveled plate-glass windows, a luxury at the time, flooded the interior with light. Several chimneys perforated the pitched roof and a balcony stretched around the second story to let people take in the invigorating ocean air. A long white fence led visitors, arriving on foot, horseback or carriage, from the sand-strewn road to the doorstep. San Franciscans willing to make the trip to the remote roadhouse in the 1860s described it as refined, with a "well-stored larder and elegantly furnished table." "All the luxuries of the market as well as the most choice liquors and wines will be found constantly on hand at the Ocean House [*sic*], served up in the most approved manner," noted a contemporary [146].

On less festive occasions, the Oceanside House is said to have had a darker side. It was remembered as distant enough from the authorities to serve as a den for some of San Francisco's shadier characters, a place where miners paid for their whiskey with gold dust, men lost their lives in duels, and gamblers won or lost fortunes at poker games that ran until dawn.

In its early years, the Oceanside House seems to have brought Benjamin Brooks a modest profit. This was no thanks to managers who surreptitiously auctioned off its plush furnishings one piece at a time. But Brooks had anticipated much more. He was anxious to see his stretch of the Pacific Coast develop into a resort akin to

New York's Manhattan Beach. The sandy expanse was already a popular destination for horseback riders, and small residences gradually began to pockmark the otherwise barren landscape. To capitalize on the community he envisioned springing forth from the dunes, in the 1860s Brooks purchased 52 blocks of surrounding land. At the time the acreage was more than sandbanks, but these blocks, he was certain, would be cleared as the vacationers' borough emerged. It turned out to be an incredibly poor business decision for the renowned real estate specialist. The resort failed to materialize due, in no small part, to the frigid ocean air and interminable fog that engulfed the area for much of the year. Making matters worse, the regular stream of visitors to the Oceanside House began to ebb in the 1870s. Years passed and the area remained as isolated as ever. The situation wreaked financial havoc on Brooks. He never subscribed to the practice of paying interest to lenders and called anyone who did a fool. Unfortunately for him, a number of these fools were employed by the Savings and Loan Society, from which Brooks borrowed $40,000 to purchase his sandy tracts. With debt increasing at a rate of one-and-one-quarter percent per month it was not long before arrears amounted to $90,000. The bank finally foreclosed when Brooks' debt peaked at $350,000. By this time Brooks was a pillar of San Francisco society, a celebrated and—more to the point—wealthy lawyer who had passed up several judgeships to prolong the excitement of arguing clients' cases before the bench. He covered his debt by transferring the titles of several other properties to his creditors. Brooks passed away a few years later with a substantial sum still left in his estate.

It is little surprise that the Oceanside House was popularly known throughout San Francisco as Brooks' Folly. Through the 1870s and into the following decade it struggled to compete with other beach resorts that cropped up in its vicinity. Notable among these was the Cliff House at Seal Rock. Near the western edge of Golden Gate Park and serviced by convenient streetcar routes, the

Cliff House was, and remains, very popular with both tourists and city residents. The Oceanside House struggled along until 1882, three years after Brooks' death, when its doors finally closed. In the ensuing years children threw rocks through the once glorious plate glass. Bats and owls roosted in the rafters, and bandits occasionally employed the derelict as a hideout. In the early 1890s Clifton Mayne, an investment banker, purchased the dilapidated building. He spent in excess of $35,000 restoring it, reinstalling the glass, repainting the exterior, and clearing a road to it. Rather than operate a business out of the building, Mayne briefly called the place home. Within two years, Mayne sold the property and it reverted to a roadhouse. At one point Gertrude Rayfield, recently divorced from the mayor of Tucson, managed it. But she was unable to turn a profit. By the summer of 1899 the Oceanside House was again all but abandoned. When Ida Russell drove by one afternoon in the spring of 1901 it was occupied only by a reclusive caretaker and advertised for sale [147].

5

A LEISURELY STROLL
AROUND THE WORLD

1902-1903

PART 1

WHEN Ida Russell, Elise Drexler, and the strapping Louis Howe arrived at the port of Yokohama they waded through the milling throng of travelers, past the rickshaws and handcarts carrying luggage to and from the hotels, and proceeded straight to Samurai Shōkai, or Samurai & Co. It was not difficult to find. Situated in the heart of the bustling tourist district, the ostentatious emporium was unlike any other retailer in the area. A double-doored maw, its lintels painted a bright red, opened onto the sidewalk. Purple flags waved over the navy-blue roof of the three-storied boutique. Its large display windows were unique in the district, an architectural feature familiar only to those who had visited European and American retailers. Inside was a mishmash of genuine antiques (sold with certificates of authenticity), kitsch trinkets for the cost-conscious tourist, and handicraft by local artists and artisans—everything from silk wall hangings to extensive collections of silverware.

The business practices of its proprietor were equally outlandish. Not content to wait for customers to stumble into his shop, he made arrangements to regularly receive guest registers from the Grand Hotel, favored by wealthy tourists, ships' captains, and foreign diplomats. From the registers of the hotel's newest arrivals, personalized letters of introduction were drafted, delivered directly to the guest rooms, and the pleasure of their custom cordially invited. Those accepting would be conveyed to the store in a bright red coach emblazoned on each side by the Samurai Shōkai moniker. The same coach would transport patrons back to their hotel and, when they were ready to depart Japan with their souvenirs, to the port.

Nomura Yōzō—the "Kurio King"—was in the process of amassing a considerable fortune from the business. He would soon run the Grand Hotel, own a stylish restaurant in Tokyo, move his family into a sizable mansion, and command an international operation that exported valuable artworks to American collectors. Now in his mid-thirties, he had an expensive suit on his barrel chest, a neatly cropped mustache on his lip, and three curious Americans on his front step.

Ida—who seemed to always act as spokesperson for the group—explained that his wife's exposition on Japanese Buddhism had impressed them considerably. She and Elise traveled to Japan with the express purpose of furthering their education in the subject. Yōzō, gregarious by nature, was enthusiastic and invited the troupe to stay with him and his family as his personal guests. They did not linger in Yokohama for long, however. Within days Yōzō was escorting his visitors across the country. They started in Tokyo, only an hour by train from Yokohama. They proceeded to Osaka, where Yōzō had lived when, at the age of fourteen, he had left home to take a course of intensive English lessons. They were then off to Nara and Kyoto, in the latter of which the teenaged Yōzō had worked in a hotel, refining his English by guiding tourists to the city's many historical sites. In reprising his role as tour conductor, Yōzō helped secure introductions for Ida and Elise to the foremost priests and prelates of each city.

Yōzō proved himself to be no ordinary dragoman. Not satisfied with making introductions and traipsing through Japan's ancient religious sites with his enthusiastic charges, he also undertook to personally instruct them in Buddhist philosophy. It soon became clear, however, that the weeks-long temple tour served only to whet Ida Russell's interest in Japanese religion. She was by no means ready to bring her exploration of Buddhism to a close. "We feel now that our minds are very peaceful with our exposure to Buddhism," Ida confided to Yōzō upon their return to Yokohama. "The feeling we have now acquired was not available to us through Christianity." She was particularly enamoured with what he said of the Zen sect and its emphasis on meditation. Ida may have sensed that her host, who continued to practice Zen, was not among its most accomplished practitioners. It was a point that the businessman freely conceded. And that led her to her next request. "We would like to learn even more about Buddhism," she said to the merchant. "So please introduce us to a good teacher" [148]. Yōzō's thoughts naturally bent in one direction. "There's a place nearby, in Kamakura, where they have a program open to both monks and laypersons alike," Yōzō said. "Then you must take us there directly," was Ida's reply [149].

The account of Ida Russell's first days in Japan is based on the recollections of Nomura Yōzō. There is an alternate version that has her arriving at the port of Yokohama and asking her guide where she might practice *zazen*. Happening to know Engakuji, the hireling took her there directly without her visiting any of the historic sites in advance. Her singleness of mind is said to have much impressed the abbot of the monastery [150]. Regardless of the exact details, prior to conveying the American party to Kamakura Yōzō privately approached Sōen with Ida's request. The monk, who may have encountered nosy tourists before, was cautious: "We cannot be sure how strong their will is. They may only be curious. But they seem to be drawn to me so send them over" [151].

Train tracks had recently been laid to connect Kamakura to Yokohama and Tokyo. They passed directly in front of the ancient gates of Engakuji, making it more convenient to visit the once isolated district but introducing dangers unforeseen by the railway companies. Sōen once assigned one of his students the *kōan* "Stop the sailing boat on the far-away sea," but modernized it to "Stop the train running outside the temple gate." The intent was to break the student from dualistic thinking through realization that there is no distinction between mobility and immobility. However, the neophyte took the words literally, assumed a position on the tracks as the train approached, and barely escaped with his life [152].

On the train for less than an hour, Ida passed by the picturesque homes of Kamakura's 10,000 residents. On some white rice paper covered their walls as it had for centuries; thatched roofs occasionally bloomed with lavender irises. Misguided monks presumably stayed clear of the tracks. The small party entered the unimposing outer gate and ascended a succession of stone steps. These led to a second, inner gate. Unlike the first, this portal was magnificent, two stories high, four centuries old, and crowned with the sweeping gables favored by the Sung dynasty architects who designed it [153]. Passing beneath the massive structure, Yōzō led the party to the abbot's residence. "Inside the Abbot's quarters were busy," another visitor, not long before Ida, said of his visit to the same room. "A great table was placed in the center of the hall, something rather unusual for a reception room in a temple, around which the Abbot and his attendants were seated upon chairs, interviewing the visitors. They gave the impression of quietly bustling. The usual atmosphere of a busy day at a Zen temple" [154].

Yōzō ushered Ida in. Here she encountered a man in his early forties, slightly smaller than her in stature. His head, smooth and cleanly shaven, formed a semi-circular dome. His mouth was also contoured into something of a semi-circle, with the ends tending to drop down slightly on either side. The result was a somber frown that Sōen wore to most formal occasions. His eyes could blaze as if on fire, and timid students recalled he could use them to burn holes through anyone daring to meet his gaze. "I have never yet had such an impression of inwardness, coupled with equal martial energy," recalled one visitor. "This delicately built monk is thoroughly military in appearance" [155].

After the appropriate introductions, Ida told Sōen that she had been raised in a wealthy family that provided for all her needs. This was accomplished by an immersion into the hectic, competitive workaday world of American business. What she lacked, what she desired most of all, was peace of mind. "In short," Sōen observed, "Mrs. Russell was a person weary from the mad pursuit of those caught up in the struggle to survive, and was seeking a place where our hearts could find refuge. … It was no doubt in this frame of mind that our travellers [*sic*] set out on their spiritual journey. And she told me that, thus motivated, they started to sit in meditation" [156].

Sōen listened with mounting interest. He was clearly impressed, particularly with his guests' practice of meditation and that they were a band of Americans who throughout the 1890s sat in silence together. "Since the value of seated meditation (*zazen*) has been inculcated in us from the time we were children, we tend to take it for granted. But for those who had never received a word of instruction, we must recognize how remarkable it was that they arrived at these matters all by themselves" [157]. Yet nothing could have prepared the abbot for his caller's astonishing request. "Give us permission to practice alongside the other monks." They wanted, Ida continued, to experience the true spirit of Zen Buddhism and the practice of Zen meditation, which they felt could best be gained by living a monastic life [158].

Ida's unorthodox entreaty to immerse herself in Zen Buddhism by taking up residence at Engakuji reminded Sōen of the American enthusiasm for Buddhism that he had encountered in Chicago nine years earlier. Since then he had corresponded regularly with Paul Carus but otherwise had little direct contact with Americans. Ida's desire to practice Zen under his tutelage rekindled the abbot's interest in contributing to the expansion of Buddhism— and more specifically Zen Buddhism—in the West [159].

Her request, however, presented certain difficulties. It was not uncommon for laity to reside at Kamakura's Zen monasteries for certain periods of time. Since Kōsen's day, Engakuji welcomed lay Buddhists who, like Daisetz Suzuki, wanted to temporarily live and practice Zen alongside its monks. A special dormitory, the *Koji-rin* (literally, "layman's grove"), was used to house and train laity in the intricacies of Zen practice. There were also hermitages scattered about the monastery grounds where visitors could live for days, weeks, or even months at a time. But Engakuji had never been host to Western practitioners—much less female Western practitioners [160]. The differences in language, etiquette, and social customs would be formidable obstacles to Sōen's ability to teach and Ida and Elise's capacity to learn.

Weighing these matters, Sōen refused the request. He reasoned that Ida and her companions, clearly of an urban and affluent background, were accustomed to a comparatively comfortable lifestyle. The austerity of monastic life was certain to overwhelm them. "To be a monk you have to dig potatoes, sweep and scrub floors, cut firewood, even haul manure at times," he later recorded, rationalizing his refusal. "Just seeing the chores awaiting them, and thinking it beneath their dignity to perform them, they might reach the wrong conclusion that the Zen life had nothing to offer them" [161].

The lieutenant of Belmont Hall, the captain of the Oceanside House community, was not used to taking no for an answer. Ida entreated the Zen master to reconsider. He would not. "But the more I refused, the more they implored me for permission until I had no choice but to grant their wish," Sōen recalled. Though giving in, Sōen resolved to not spare his curious new disciples from anything. They would be allowed to study alongside his other students as they requested. But they would also work alongside them. They would not be exempt from the meanest of duties, Sōen explained to them, "from here to the furthest corner of the outhouse." Once embroiled in the drudgery of day-to-day monastic life, the abbot was certain his guests' resolve would break and they would soon be returning to their comfortable lives in America [162].

PART 2

With Sōen's permission to remain at Engakuji, Ida Russell, along with Elise Drexler and Louis Howe, became the first Americans to live at a Zen monastery and receive instruction directly from a Zen master. In the days that ensued, they had ample opportunity to explore their new home. The monastery precinct was long and narrow, filling a small valley that sloped gently upward as it penetrated the hillside. Stone steps led from one pagoda-filled tier to another. Caves—some used for private meditation when mosquitoes were not too distracting, others containing the remains of honored eremites of bygone eras—lined the craggy rock face along the cloister's perimeter. About forty single-storied structures were scattered about the 500 acres. Shrines, temples, hermitages, and free-standing belfries were interspersed with countless fir and cypress trees. Groves of bamboo, thick and towering, provided little relief from the muggy summer heat. Cicadas, whose screeching filled the air, found brief homes in among the small patches of plum, banana, and palm trees. Like the surrounding village, structures in the monastery compound were crowned with rustically thatched roofs. Ancient pine and cedar blanketed surrounding hills.

The largest buildings on the grounds were the administrative offices, a dormitory for monks in training, and the memorial temple of the Hōjō clan that had founded Engakuji six centuries earlier. A belfry perched atop a steep hillside. Climbing the ancient steep steps leading up the promontory, Ida had a bird's eye view of neighbouring monasteries. The center of life for the monks was the meditation hall, or *zendō*, called the Hall of the Eye of Right Dharma, a reference to meditation's ability to open the practitioner's inner eye to wisdom. The hall measured 36 feet by 65 feet and could hold fifty or more monks. Outside the entrance hung a wooden plaque with the somber admonishment:

> BIRTH & DEATH IS A GRAVE EVENT:
> ALAS, HOW TRANSIENT LIFE IS!
> BEGRUDGE NOT A MINUTE OF IT.
> TIME WAITS FOR NOBODY.

At various times of the day a monk would strike this plaque with a mallet to call the community—and its American guests—to meals, lectures, and devotional ceremonies, as well as to communicate the beginning and end of the meditation period. Inside the hall, along the two longer walls, ran *tatami*-covered platforms eight feet wide and three feet high. Each monk had an assigned space on the platform, in which he would sit in meditation each day. In the center of the room, between the two platforms, was enshrined a statue of the Bodhisattva Mañjuśrī, a representation of wisdom [163].

During their stay at Engakuji, Ida and Elise's home was Shōden-an, the "Lodge of the True Transmission" [164]. It was one of seventeen hermitages on the grounds, by no means the largest or most elaborate but in some ways more isolated than the rest. This is not to say that it was far from the other structures, for no building was very far removed from its neighbours. But Shōden-an was nestled against the western rock face of the valley, at the end of a cul-de-sac in the paths that crisscrossed the grounds. Its main connection to the monastery grounds was a rising walkway that arced around a mossy pond on the periphery of which turtles basked in the afternoon sun. A number of shallow caves were carved into the rock walls surrounding the hermitage, one of which was a tunnel to the compound that contained the monastery's kitchen, meditation hall, and a few shrines filled with ancient statuary. The relative isolation of Shōden-an was ideal for providing the Western women with a degree of privacy from the monastery's otherwise masculine population.

Located about two-thirds along the length of the canyon, on the western side, Shōden-an regularly housed laity on retreat. During such stays it was customary for a junior-level monk to also live in the structure, cooking and otherwise caring for its inhabitants while they sat in meditation. In this case, the attendant was Uemura Sōkō. His command of English and interest in foreigners made him their ideal companion and guide. Sōkō explained to Ida and Elise the rules of the monastery, the daily schedule, their personal responsibilities. He would lead them to the *zendō* for meditation and translate at their meetings with Sōen.

Electricity was still years away from enlightening Engakuji, so when Ida's party rose and retired darkness was absolute. Their days began at 3:30 in the morning. Upon rising Ida and her companions either meditated alone in their hermitage or made a short but precarious trek—in the dark and across slippery stepping stones—to the meditation hall. "I understand that your customs and sense of decor may make it difficult for you to follow suit, but this is what you must do," Sōen advised them. "While sitting, you must bow down reverently, like this. When the morning talk is being given, you too must sit at attention, like this. When we are reciting sūtras, you must feel as if you too are reciting the text along with us. I had them do just as we were doing. They were most grateful for my instructions, and did their best to follow them" [165].

By the time Ida and Elise arrived at the meditation hall in the morning, the monks would have already gathered, sitting along the wall facing their comrades on the opposite side. A witness at the time reported, "The method by which [Sōen] teaches meditation is hard. The pupils sit in a large, empty room in the attitude of Buddha; the abbot walks up and down between them, stick in hand, and if someone goes to sleep he kicks him; if anyone gets tired he is not allowed to rest before the lesson is at an end, but only to go the round a few times in silence with his hands folded and held up above his head" [166]. Sōen was surprised to discover that his American visitors' style of meditation was not entirely dissimilar to that of his own monks. He would not go so far as to say it was indistinguishable, but there were noticeable similarities that impressed the Zen master [167].

Following the day's first pre-dawn meditation session, Ida and the others joined the monks in breakfast [168]. It was the day's first meal consisting of rice gruel served at 5:00. There was also the main meal, served at 10:00 in the morning and consisting of little more than rice mixed with barley, miso soup, and pickled vegetables. In principle, only two meals a day were allowed at the monastery, though an evening meal of leftovers was provided to those needing "medicinal food." When assembling for meals, monks recited religious verses that Ida and Elise may have been taught. Otherwise, meals were eaten in silence. Monks brought to the refectory their own wooden bowls, one of their few personal possessions. When complete, supper was concluded with a recitation of vows to practice good, destroy evil, study religion, and work for the enlightenment of all sentient beings. A hand bell then rang, dismissing the monks who silently filed out of the dining area.

All monks attended regular lectures at Engakuji. A wooden block was struck, announcing the commencement of the abbot's speech. Monks gathered in the meditation hall, donned a surplice, and solemnly entered into the lecture hall. Among them were Ida in a full-length white gown buttoned tight around the neck and adorned with subtle frills and Elise in a more somber black that better matched the monks' dark robes. When the community assembled, Sōen entered and offered three sticks of incense—one to the Buddha, one to the founder of the monastery, and another to Kōsen. He then sat in a chair at the head of his community and began the discourse.

The abbot's formal lectures could be quite complicated, filled with subtle nuances and technical terminology. Even with Sōkō translating, much of the speech would have been lost on the American neophytes receiving their first formal introduction to Zen Buddhism. To make up for what they might miss in his general lessons Sōen privately tutored his special guests. They used as their text the *Sūtra of Perfect Enlightenment*, the *Engakukyō*, after which Engakuji was named [169]. The choice was doubly relevant in that this particular sūtra detailed the practice of meditation and was written by one of the first Buddhists to begin spreading the religion east of its Indian homeland.

Sōen also knew how to meet students at a variety of levels, and for individuals new to Zen he was full of practical advice: "Free yourself from all incoming complications and hold your mind against them like a great iron wall," he advised students new to the practice of meditation. "No matter what sort of contending thoughts arise in you, ignore them and they will perish and disappear of themselves. And just as soon as your thought expands and unites with the universe, then you free yourself from your stubborn ego. … This is not the true realization, but you are walking near the palace" [170].

Days at Engakuji ended at about 9:00 at night, at which time the novices gathered in the meditation hall to chant. They then bowed three times before a statue, unrolled their futons and slept in single rows within the hall. The cushions on which they sat in meditation doubled as pillows at night. Ida and her companions made their way to Shōden-an, carrying lanterns to make out their way in the otherwise impenetrable darkness.

True to his word, Sōen treated his American guests in much the same way as his other students. He bestowed on each of them a religious name. Ida was Keikaku. Composed of one of the same Chinese characters used to spell out Engakuji, it translates as "Given Perfect Enlightenment." Elise was Keimyō, "Received Bright Enlightenment," while Louis Howe was dubbed Sōgen, the name of Engakuji's ancient founder [171]. They not only shared the rigorous schedule and meager diet of other students, they also involved themselves in the daily chores necessary to maintaining the monastery. As Sōen promised, much of the work was menial. Like the other monks, Ida and Elise had to mend and wash their own clothes. They drew water and shared in cleaning the bath house and lavatory. They may have swept up the dry leaves raining down from the treetops as the seasons changed. At the end of the day, they would collect the leaves and other refuse, bringing them to the kitchen to be used as fuel. Sōen was surprised that the drudgery did not cause his refined guests to recoil from their monastic existence in the slightest. "None of them ever showed the slightest sign of weariness, and they went about their chores with a smile on their faces, as if they were taking a leisurely stroll around the world" [172].

PART 3

Besides being one of the first three Westerners known to take up life at a Zen monastery and practice meditation under the direction of a Zen master, Ida Russell is remembered as attending *nyūshitsu dokusan*, the private interview with the Zen master at which *kōans* are assigned [173]. It was the first time any Westerner engaged in a practice so characteristic of Rinzai Zen.

During this time, both popular and academic interest in Buddhism tended to focus on it as a rational, philosophical religion, a so-called "religion of science." For this reason, ever since the Parliament of Religions, Sōen consistently described Buddhism to foreigners as free from mythology and superstition, compatible with the dawning age of Western science.

However, *kōans* are in one sense non-rational. As noted, they are intended to suddenly break the mind away from dualistic thinking. By assigning *kōans* to foreigners, Sōen was experimenting with new ways of introducing Buddhism to the West.

That a Westerner would be interested in *kōan* practice was remarkable enough for the religious press to make special note of it [174]. Ida may not have precisely understood the fuss. While the actual content of the *kōan* may have been lost on her, its description as something the Zen practitioner should always keep in mind, particularly during meditation, would have had a familiar ring.

The style of meditation Ida had long practiced in the United States involved a topic on which to focus the mind during sitting. She would have equated musing over divine goodness, a subject she once recommended as a topic for meditation [175], as similar to contemplating the sound of one hand or whether a dog has Buddha-nature. It may not have gotten her far in correctly responding to the *kōan*, but it at least gave her a frame of reference. Unfortunately, exactly which *kōans* were the subjects of her meditation has gone unrecorded.

The experience of *dokusan*, for its part, would also not have been entirely unfamiliar. At Belmont Hall, Josephine Holmes communicated much of her teachings in "private lessons." In them she would assess the spiritual state of each follower before giving them the spiritual advice she felt they most needed. Also like *dokusan*, Josephine's students were not to discuss with others their experience in the private lessons [176]. According to one account, Josephine Holmes never actually volunteered information to her students, but required them draw it out from her [177]. Given that Zen masters tended not to volunteer advice in *dokusan*, but rather required students to solicit instruction from them, one wonders whether the Belmonters had stumbled across a description of *nyūshitsu dokusan* and were using it as a textbook.

Senzaki Nyogen, for his part, was free from the private interviews he so dreaded. He left Engakuji sometime the previous year, returning to his native prefecture of Aomori to the northeast. He left with Sōen's blessing, but not his *inka*, the certificate that confirmed a Zen practitioner had achieved enlightenment and was authorized to teach Zen. Sōen did not even seem prepared to recognize Nyogen as even loosely associated with Engakuji or Rinzai Zen. The abbot recommended him to others as a non-sectarian priest "with no connections with cathedral or headquarters" of any particular branch of Buddhism.

If Nyogen failed to grasp the subtleties of Zen, Sōen freely recognized other qualities in the 25-year-old bonze, including his humility and dedication. "He keeps no property as his own, refuses to hold a position in the priesthood, and hides himself from noisy fame and glory. He has, however, the four vows—greater than worldly ambition, Dharma treasures higher than any position, and loving kindness wealthier than church properties" [178].

Sōen also supported Senzaki's new endeavor. Upon his return north, Nyogen founded a kindergarten along the lines detailed in the Fröbel books he had been reading. He called it a "Mentorgarten," which he described as a place where children's independent activities are encouraged rather than formal instruction given. Each morning he would burn incense and sit down in meditation for half an hour. "I did not, however, recount colourful religious stories for the children; I only guided and watched over them, helping them to learn about nature while they were playing. … As for their manners, I just tried to train them to be in a harmonious relationship with their parents" [179].

Nyogen's desire to look after small children may not have stemmed entirely from perusing the pages of German philosophers. His own childhood had been less than ideal. Nyogen, whose given name was Aizō, was the son of Kudō Heijirō, a ship's carpenter, and his wife Rin, the adopted daughter of an Aomori innkeeper. She died suddenly when her son was four. He would retain no memory of her. He may also have had no memory of his father who deposited the boy with relatives and seems to have taken no active role in his upbringing.

One of these relatives was Aizō's grandmother, who loathed the unwanted child and received Aizō's dislike in return. She would sometimes tell him he was an orphan of partly Russian or Chinese extraction, carried to her by a Kamchatka fisherman. Perhaps she said this to psychologically disassociate herself from her unwelcome charge. Throughout his life Senzaki would feed speculation that he had Chinese or Russian blood [180].

Aizō also spent some of his childhood with his grandfather, a priest of a Pure Land Buddhist temple [181]. The education he received at the temple could be exceedingly strict, though it allowed him to master Chinese at an early age [182]. The little that is known of his ensuing years are characterized by doubt, frustration, and fear. He attended a public school for a while, where he encountered the autobiography of Benjamin Franklin.

"I imitated his method for spiritual growth: Every night I would reflect on what I did during the day, and I was surprised by how many times I did the wrong thing. My days were without any peace. I lost my self-confidence." When at the age of 16 he expressed an interest in entering religious life, his grandfather, on his deathbed, asked that he reconsider. But "I thought about how I had been supported by the offerings of others while living at my grandfather's temple. I thought if I didn't return to society what I received I would be terribly punished" [183].

It was perhaps a desire to exorcise some of his personal demons that led Senzaki Nyogen from Engakuji back to the land of his troubled childhood where he might make the childhood of others a bit less miserable. Shaku Sōen referred him to a wealthy man in Tokyo who might be able to provide financial assistance for the venture [184]. At about the time Ida Russell and Elise Drexler were firmly ensconced into life at Engakuji, Nyogen was running two kindergartens, each with ten to twenty children romping about.

PART 4

Weeks passed at Engakuji, and then months. Ida, Elise, and Louis remained, watching Kamakura's abundant greenery ignite with the colours of autumn. Branches then grew bare as winter began to set in. Still, Ida and her party would emerge from Shōden-an each morning to meditate in the *zendō* and tend to their chores.

Nomura Yōzō and Michi, unable to leave their business and family for an extended period and therefore not at Engakuji on a daily basis, were astounded when they learned of the Americans' resolution [185]. Uemura Sōkō initially considered himself little more than a babysitter to his callow foreign charges. But, looking after Ida and Elise for months longer than he had anticipated, he had ample opportunity to witness the enthusiastic way they threw themselves into their new surroundings.

Ida's voracious hunger for information about all aspects of Buddhist life and Elise's kind and gentle manners to senior monks much impressed him [186]. Before their tenure at Engakuji ended Sōkō had "unconditional respect" for these first Western practitioners of Zen [187]. He noted that when new monks first arrived at the monastery they would spend much time complaining bitterly about the severe living conditions. Not so with Ida and Elise. They never seemed to tire, never seemed to complain. Admiration went both ways. Of all Sōen's students whom Ida met it was the earnest young Sōkō who earned her greatest respect [188].

Sōen was perhaps the most impressed of all. Sometime during Ida's stay the relationship between the Zen master and his American guests transformed from that of teacher to student to one of mutual friendship. "We all started applying ourselves assiduously to help one another," Sōen would later recall. "We opened our hearts to one another, and could talk about anything frankly" [189]. Ida, for instance, revealed her frustration with the lack of opportunities available for women in America to lead an active, productive life in society [190], somewhat strange words from the woman who extolled the virtues of tranquility and meditation.

That Ida Russell and Shaku Sōen got along so well together is not entirely surprising. Despite their very different backgrounds, the two shared much in common. At 43, Sōen was only two years younger than Ida [191]. He was involved in religious life much longer than Ida, having become a monk at the age of twelve. It was the idea of his older brother, who wanted to join a monastery himself but inherited responsibility to oversee the family estate. He sent Sōen, whose given name was Ichinosé Tsunejirō, in his stead [192].

By the time Sōen met Ida, both were leaders of their respective religious communities in which they guided the spiritual development of those in their charge. Both enjoyed travel. While away from home they did not simply sightsee but applied themselves industriously to the study of religion. Ida was intensely curious about different religious traditions in the same way Sōen interested himself in different Buddhist sects. Not only did he explore the Buddhist traditions of Southeast Asia, as a young monk he studied at a Tendai monastery. There he applied himself so seriously that his mentors invited him to abandon Zen for the Tendai sect. Both valued meditation, a vegetarian diet, and a regulated daily schedule.

Sōen arranged for a tour of Japan's temples, apparently Ida's second since she had already ventured out with Nomura Yōzō. In late August and early September, Sōkō escorted Ida, Elise and Louis to Nikko, Nagoya, and Kyoto. En route, Ida shocked her fellow train passengers by publicly rebuking those smoking in the first-class car despite the existence of a smoking room [193]. Examining Ida's copy of Murray's *Handbook for Travellers in Japan*, Sōkō told her that the explanations of the temple sites and their histories were very misleading. Ida lamented that in America books presenting Japanese Buddhism were similarly imprecise [194]. When the party arrived at Kyoto, they visited Konkai Kōmyōji, a temple of the Jōdo sect where Ida and Elise found peacefulness pervading the grounds. When the huge bell rang, with its deep, sonorous tone, Sōkō observed that "the minds and souls of the two women seemed to have been stolen away by the atmosphere of the place" [195].

Alexander Russell arrived in Japan in early October 1902. At this point, his wife and her friends had been living at Engakuji for several months. As Nomura Yōzō recalled it, after an extended period without any communiqués from Japan Alexander set sail for Japan to discover what had become of his wife. In fact, the reunion was carefully planned out in advance. When Alexander arrived in Yokohama, he was accompanied by Jean MacCallum, Elise Drexler's 17-year-old niece. Like Louis Howe, Jean shared in her aunt's religious interests, as well as assisted with her personal and business matters.

Gathering at Yōzō's home, Ida and Elise extolled the virtues of Zen meditation and monastic life. They eventually persuaded a doubtful Alexander to join them at Engakuji. Alexander, though perhaps a periodic inmate of Belmont Hall, did not share the intensity of his wife's spiritual interests. He joined the Theosophical Society with her, though he may have viewed this as similar to his affiliations with the Odd Fellows, Order of the Mystic Shrine, and Freemasons where he attained the 32nd degree in the Scottish Rite. These secret society memberships may reflect at least a certain level of interest in esotericism, though they were just as likely manifestations of his highly sociable nature. Alexander's active temperament proved an insurmountable obstacle. Unable to sit still through the long sessions, he abandoned Zen meditation after a single day. There is nothing to suggest that he ever resumed the practice [196].

Details like this, however, were lost on the press. The religious journals still followed Sōen's words and deeds rather closely, and the presence of foreigners at his monastery did not escape notice.

> This July the multimillionaire Mr. Russell, who owns a famous rubber company in San Francisco brought to Japan his wife (a graduate of an American woman's university), Mr. Howe (a medical doctor), Mrs. Drexler, and Miss MacCallum. Mr. and Mrs. Russell believe Buddhism and have practiced *zazen* for more than ten years. They meditate together with 70 or 80 other Americans. They were impressed with the fact that the Big Vehicle (Mahayana Buddhism) prevails in Japan. Soon after they came to Japan they went to Engakuji in Kamakura to visit Shaku Sōen and study Zen. Mr. and Mrs. Russell completely abandoned meat and practiced *sanzen* all day long. [197]

There is little about the brief article that the reporter managed to get right in regards to Alexander, from his position at Bowers Rubber (where he was a salesman) and characterization as a millionaire to the date of his arrival and degree of his involvement in daily life at Engakuji. The implication that the Russells became vegetarians only after their arrival to Japan was of course also inaccurate. The reporter had entertained other obvious misunderstandings about the Russells, which Sōen himself may have shared.

While the statement that they "believe Buddhism" may have been accurate at a certain level, it omitted that Ida propounded a number of religious beliefs and was more apt to quote the Bible than the Tripitaka. Sōen may not have known—or chose not to see—that this curious American seeker prided herself on gleaning wisdom from a wide range of religions, only one of which was Buddhism. If Sōen shared in the belief that the Russells "meditate"—rather than meditated—with dozens of other

Americans, he likely overestimated Ida's sway in these post-Belmont Hall years.

Barley gruel, predawn devotions, and latrine duty may not have been high on Alexander's list of priorities for what he considered a Japanese vacation, but he was open to other, less ascetic possibilities. December found him in the town of Atami, a winter resort renowned for its hot spring baths. Ida and Elise joined him, as did Sōen and Sōkō, the lattermost still serving as translator. Long soaks in snow-rimmed pools of steaming spring water alternated with religious instruction that continued even through this holiday. Sōen lectured on the Buddhist sūtras. Ida, in turn, discoursed on her interpretations of Biblical themes that increasingly piqued Sōkō's interest [198].

Elise and her niece returned to California later in December. They shared a steamer with Swami Trigunatita, who was on his way to take charge of the Vedanta Society's operations in San Francisco [199]. Given the eclecticism of the Russell community it is conceivable, though there is no evidence to confirm it, that they were students of his and returned to help in the guru's plans to establish a Hindu presence in the city. Ida, Alexander, and Louis Howe returned to Kamakura following the excursion to Atami. They remained in Japan until March 1903. Just before their departure the monks of Engakuji held a farewell party for Ida, who had resided with them for nearly nine months. At the fête, she donated ¥700 to the monastery [200].

Ida took a practical view of her accomplishments at Engakuji. She readily recognized she had not achieved the enlightenment sought by students of Zen Buddhism. Nonetheless she felt that she had learned quite a lot about the sect and its practices. Before departing she said to her teacher, "This has been a most wonderful experience for us. It is a shame we cannot share it with others, so some day, when your circumstances allow, you must come visit our country" [201]. Sōen was touched. In response to this once strange foreigner who now numbered among his friends, Sōen composed a poem. The abbot recited it in Japanese; Sōkō repeated it for them in English:

> One of these days
> I will try
> to propagate the truth of Buddhism
> in the West.

[202]

6

Rush to the Front & Enter the Skirmish

1904

Part 1

As Ida Russell was preparing to leave Kamakura in early 1903, Daisetz Suzuki was preparing to leave LaSalle, at least temporarily. For the past six years he had lived in Illinois, worked for Open Court Publishing, studied under Paul Carus. The translation of the *Dao De Jing*, Carus' initial motive for hiring him, was completed within a year. After its publication Carus did not seem to know exactly what to do with his newest editorial assistant. Daisetz's responsibilities at Open Court Publishing were diverse. When authors submitted articles on Buddhism, it was often Daisetz's job to edit and otherwise improve them. On occasion he translated Chinese works into English for publication either in the journal or for a book. He reviewed books on Japanese culture and religion, on occasion even prepared the odd article, such as "The Breadth of Buddhism" in which he proposed that both Buddhism and Christianity share a common spiritual source, that they "spring out of the depth of the human heart which is everywhere the same" [203]. This article was quickly followed up by a book that borrowed less from common Theosophical ideas and better presented Japanese Buddhism: *The Awakening of Faith in the Mahayana*. But more often than not, Daisetz's responsibilities at Open Court Publishing involved the less glamorous—"slavish" is the word he used—duties of proofreading and typesetting. He boarded with one of Carus' other employees, for whom he sometimes split wood, worked in the garden, cooked, and shopped for groceries. Unlike Ida performing such menial tasks at Engakuji, Daisetz was unhappy with the "common person's work" [204]. Perhaps this was because—again unlike Ida—he could not, at a whim, slip off to an exotic new city or pamper himself at a luxurious hotel as Ida did throughout her stay at Engakuji [205].

Throughout this time, the propagation of Buddhism in America was on his mind. When Harvard University's Department of Ethics invited Sōen as a guest lecturer, Daisetz was excited at the missionary prospects of the post. "This is an opportunity to reignite the light of Buddhism over Americans," he wrote to his teacher. "I am not sure I will be able to effectively assist you, but I want to share your hardships in propagating [Buddhism]" [206]. To Daisetz's disappointment, Sōen declined the lectureship.

Then in the summer of 1903 Daisetz was asked to deliver a series of lectures on Buddhism in San Francisco. The invitation came from the Pure Land sect's Buddhist Mission. Despite being backed by one of the wealthiest of Japan's religious organizations, the Buddhist Mission was underfunded and had received orders to cut expenses wherever possible. It was perhaps to quickly raise money that they sent for Daisetz. They most likely heard of his missionary zeal from Dr. John Fryer of the University of California, Berkeley. The professor of Chinese Studies and Buddhist sympathizer chanced to meet Suzuki while both were visiting Yale earlier that year. They needed him to depart immediately. Though the Mission could not pay for his train ticket, he was promised a share of the proceeds raised from his lectures. Daisetz dashed off a quick note to Carus, requesting a leave of absence, an advance on his salary, and an understanding that the excursion could benefit Open Court business. "If you permit me to go West, this will afford me a very good opportunity to get acquainted with the Buddhist movement in California and to secure a good sale of my forthcoming book among them" [207].

Daisetz would spend more than two months in California with the Pure Land Buddhists, embroiled in what he called "our missionary work" [208]. He was received by the Dharma Sangha of Buddha, a group of Caucasians associated with the Buddhist Mission's otherwise Japanese-speaking immigrant membership. They were sometimes at odds with the Pure Land priests, whose limited English and naïveté sometimes let others take advantage of them. Daisetz was not overly impressed with the group, finding it to include "a number of cranks and quacks" [209]. It was probably an accurate assessment. Among its thirty or so members was Anna Fay, "Spiritual lecturer," and Eliza Stoddard, a professional medium [210]. Yet Daisetz seemed to think there was hope to disseminate a sound knowledge of Buddhism among them.

Daisetz delivered a series of well-advertised lectures, where he was billed as "Prof. T. Zuzuki of the Imperial University of Japan," rather than as a copy editor from the breadbasket [211]. Given at both the Buddhist Mission and the Theosophical Society, they seem to have attracted moderate attendance, though Suzuki's income was less than he had hoped. A regular paycheck compelled Daisetz to return to LaSalle in early October. However, a foundation had been laid for the Pure Land sect to play a crucial role in a later missionary endeavor Daisetz did not yet know of.

PART 2

There is a certain amount of irony that at about the same time Ida Russell invited Shaku Sōen to teach Zen in San Francisco, both her closest associate and his most trusted disciple overseas were in the same city and probably unaware of each other's existence.

Elise Drexler, having departed Japan at the end of 1902, remained in San Francisco until October, the same month Daisetz returned to LaSalle. Elise, with her niece Jean still in tow, was then off to meet Ida in Germany. When they finally left Engakuji, rather than return home, the Russells traveled throughout Asia. It was no plain sightseeing tour. Ida wanted to make a detailed survey of all religions in the world. She went to China to investigate Confucianism and to India to observe the Hindus, probably stopping in at the Theosophical Society's headquarters in Adyar to visit with Colonel Olcott. She also trekked through Siam and may have visited Ceylon and Burma. In Java she toured the Buddhist temple of Borobudur [212]. "I have traveled widely in the Orient and studied all religions, taking what I think best from each," Ida would later state [213].

She and Alexander, still accompanied by Elise's nephew Louis, continued on to Europe so Ida could investigate the various branches of Christianity in the Old World. The round-the-world pilgrimage ended in June 1904. After two years away, Ida was able to again sit in meditation with her seaside community, sharing with them her acquired knowledge of the world's religions and most likely dictating letters to Japan to ask the abbot of Engakuji when he might continue her instruction in Zen.

PART 3

Shaku Sōen's thoughts were also on a community of religionists across the Pacific Ocean. Ida and her associates' fascination with Buddhism and, more particularly, Zen Buddhism, had rekindled his interest in contributing to the eastward spread of Buddhism by propagating it in America [214]. With Ida meandering back to San Francisco, Sōen knew he had a band of American sympathizers who were not just curious about Zen. They were eager to incorporate its tenets into their daily lives, just as they had during their months-long stay at Engakuji. Not since the World's Parliament of Religions had he had such an opportunity to introduce Buddhism to the West. His initial plans were to follow

Ida to San Francisco several months after her departure from Engakuji. "*Rōshi* [the teacher] is sometimes sick, but it is not serious," Uemura Sōkō reported to Daisetz just before his 1903 missionary excursion to San Francisco. "He seems to have made up his mind to go to America this winter, but he keeps his plans deep in his mind and hides them from people. Even I, going to *Rōshi's* room twice a day, don't have the chance to ask him if he will go to America" [215].

This lack of communication was apparently short-lived. In time an understanding developed between master and student. Working together, the two would propagate Buddhism in America and perhaps Europe. Sōen counted on Sōkō to accompany him. His linguistic ability (which not only included English but also German) had allowed him to develop an easy rapport with Ida's party. Equal boons were his degree in Philosophy and increasingly firm grasp of Buddhist theology, which had allowed him to easily convey his master's thoughts to his American guests. Of all his disciples, only Sōkō possessed the combination of skills that would allow Sōen to attempt the propagation of Zen in the West [216]. Sōkō was to be appointed Sōen's attendant monk while abroad. It was a position that would keep the two in close contact with one another on a daily basis. The younger monk would not just arrange for his master's daily needs, he would introduce him to audiences and make brief addresses before giving the floor to the featured speaker. It was expected that Sōkō, with his fluency in English and desire to travel widely, would remain in America for an extended period. To help prepare the young man for his public duties, Sōen arranged for a tour of the Zen temples in Kyushu under Engakuji's jurisdiction. The younger monk would hone his speaking skills by addressing audiences at the smallest of them [217].

Sōkō also began making a careful study of the Bible. To effectively communicate religious ideas to Americans, he knew he would need to better understand their very different religious mindset. Once he could converse in language Americans recognized as religious, it would be a simple matter to explain Buddhism in terms not so foreign to them. The Bible, however, proved to be a rather confusing document. Its quaint fables and moralistic proverbs were very different from the abstract philosophy and psychology he recognized as religion. Sōkō sometimes despaired of making sense of the prophets and patriarchs, psalmists and apostles. Whenever he felt like giving up, Sōkō would recall Ida Russell's stay at Engakuji and the scripture lessons she gave to the assembled monks. Fortified by the knowledge that Ida saw so much in the Christian scriptures, Sōkō's resolve to persevere in his biblical studies strengthened [218].

As the abbot of a prominent religious institution, Sōen knew it would be difficult to disentangle himself from the administrative responsibilities that occupied so much of his day. Besides, times were quickly changing in Japan. National events would prevent him from immediately responding to Ida's invitation to teach Zen in America. Rather than setting out for a house of tranquility in the west, he would soon head for bloody battles being pitched in the east.

In the months following Ida Russell's departure from Engakuji, relations between Japan and Russia became increasingly strained. Even if Ida retained her Belmont Hall habit of isolating herself from the buzzing distractions of newspapers, she would have heard much about the pending conflict between the two empires while on her extended European travels. Over the past several years Russia had been actively expanding into Manchuria and other parts of East Asia. By 1898, it had established a naval base on the Liaotung Peninsula, situated uncomfortably close to Korea and other mainland territories occupied by Japan. Russia's incursion was a slap in the face. Japan had won the peninsula upon the conclusion of the Sino-Japanese War only to have it taken away by the diplomatic wrangling of America, Great Britain, and Russia. Russia steadily increased its military presence in Manchuria and China in the years following the Boxer Rebellion of 1900. Japan, which also had its eye on Chinese territory, begrudged each and every inroad Russia made into Asia. Diplomats agreed that Russia would evacuate its troops from Manchuria and return the territory to Chinese control. Russia never bothered to make good on the agreements. This fueled the frustrations of Japan, which was busily building a dozen armored cruisers and battleships for its fully modernized navy.

Sōen had long relished invoking militaristic imagery in his public addresses. "Zen-monks are the generals of Zen," he said on the day he was installed as abbot of Engakuji. "Open the firing-line and each of you show your banner. Do not spare your body or life. Whoever wants to prove his own attainment, rush out to the front and enter into the skirmish" [219]. It was pure metaphor, of course, meant to inspire the dedication of his fellow monks to their religious and meditative practices.

Ironically, at the World's Parliament of Religions in Chicago Sōen was portrayed as possessing a pacifistic streak. "And what is gained by war?" he was recorded as saying at one of the special-interest sessions. "Nothing; it only means the oppression of the weak by the strong; it simply means the fighting among brothers and the shedding of human blood. We are not born to fight one another. We are born to enlighten our wisdom and cultivate our virtues according to the guidance of truth" [220]. In fact his words were generally misunderstood in Chicago. The Japanese version of the address reads quite differently. In it he was not calling for nations, but different religious bodies, to avoid conflict. He proposed that religious groups around the world follow the example of international law, to recognize their differences by setting up a common belief that they could share. When his speech was translated for the Parliament's official proceedings, the address was presented instead as a call for arbitration as the best way to resolve international disputes [221].

Leo Tolstoy evidently had a copy of the Parliament papers in hand when he addressed a letter to Engakuji. The Russian count asked the abbot to sign an appeal for their countries to end hostilities with one another. Tolstoy, a renowned pacifist, would arrange for the petition, bearing both of their signatures, to be delivered to the Japanese and Russian governments. As head of a sizable Zen subsect, as well as one of Japan's more prominent religious figures, Sōen found Tolstoy's request problematic. Not to support the war would have been highly suspect in the jingoistic clime, while to proclaim opposition would have amounted to treason. Voices of opposition did, in fact, arise from within the Buddhist establishment. The government was quick to locate these radical clerics, imprison them, and in some cases impose capital punishment [222]. It was Sōen's responsibility to support his government and to rally popular support for its causes. So while the Buddha of pious legend allowed armies to march against and destroy his family and motherland, Sōen was in the paradoxical position of advocating a military action that would ultimately claim more than 200,000 souls [223].

This is not to say that Sōen was in any way coerced into supporting the government's military action. Traveling in Southeast Asia opened his eyes to the threat colonialism posed to Asian nations. While in Ceylon, he noted the way its people suffered under the British. "Ceylonese people are living like they were people of another land and paying rent for their own ground," he had written to Kōsen. "They have no freedom to establish any kind of manufacturing or other enterprises and must use only imported materials from England. Even to the eye of a stranger like myself, they are slaves, drudging hard to supply the English people who are having a good time idly. Ceylon is getting poorer year after year, while the English are increasing their wealth by the same ratio. Monks have no country, but still when one sees or hears these true facts, one must shed bitter tears secretly" [224]. Such observations certainly contributed to the Zen monk's sense of nationalism as he watched Russia, Britain, France, and Germany busily establish colonies and settlements throughout Southeast Asia. To Sōen it was clear that Japan must strengthen its standing among Western nations if it was to escape a fate similar to Ceylon's.

Whether out of an obligation to support his government, an authentic sense of national pride, or a combination of the two, by the time hostilities between Japan and Russia reached a head Sōen had attached a just war theory to his theological musings. The abbot considered war despicable in a general sense, something that should be avoided whenever possible. It caused a misery that starts at the field of battle and spreads to the most remote areas of the embattled nations as news of the loss of sons, fathers, husbands, and friends reaches home. However, he concluded that war was a necessary evil in a generally unenlightened world. The war with Russia was particularly crucial to the future of Japan. "Now that the relations between Japan and Russia have changed from diplomatic negotiations to military actions, we have apparently crossed the crucial juncture," he wrote to a colleague. "The nation's future for 100 years depends entirely on this venture" [225].

Sōen came to the opinion that so long as ignorance—and the evil thoughts and actions that result from it—exists in the world, war would be an unavoidable reality. Moreover, Sōen contended that Buddhists, who regularly combatted ignorance in a spiritual and ethical sense, must fearlessly take up arms and lay down their lives if necessary to oppose the spread of ignorance through the actions of unenlightened individuals and nations. "War is an evil and a great one, indeed. But war against evils must be unflinchingly prosecuted till we attain the final aim." In persecuting the wicked, Sōen's ideal Buddhist warrior must not feel hatred toward his enemies. He must dispassionately dispatch their lives, freeing them from the corporeal existences they use to propagate evil. In this way, the world would be free of their wicked actions and their spirits would be able to speed on to new incarnations with new opportunities for enlightenment. The ideal warrior must feel the compassion of Buddha and recognize that the deadly force meted out ultimately advances the world to enlightenment. "The hand that is raised to strike and the eye that is fixed to take aim, do not belong to the individual, but are instruments utilized by a principle higher than transient existence," Sōen wrote. The corpses littering the front line are not so many pounds of decaying flesh, so many multitudes of unrealized dreams: "these sacrifices … are an inevitable step toward the final realization of enlightenment." In Sōen's idealistic fantasy, the Japanese army was a host of such transcendental warriors who sought only "the subjugation of evils hostile to civilization, peace, and enlightenment" [226].

Given these views, Sōen found it impossible to sign Tolstoy's petition. Not content to simply lay out his position in a personal letter, Sōen used the opportunity to publicly proclaim his wartime theology and support for the conflict with Russia. In an open letter to Tolstoy, Sōen wrote, "Even though the Buddha forbade the taking of life, he also taught that until all sentient beings are united together through the exercise of infinite compassion, there will never be peace. Therefore as a means of bringing into harmony those things which are incompatible, killing and war are necessary" [227].

Shortly after Japan's formal declaration of war, Sōen traveled to Hiroshima. It was the port from which soldiers departed for the Asian mainland. Here he preached his militaristic sentiments to troops about to join their comrades on the front. Not content to simply inspire soldiers at home, Sōen joined the Japanese army. Replacing his straw sandals and priestly robes with high black boots and a brown uniform, he was assigned chaplain of the First Army in the summer of 1904. Stationed in Manchuria with the troops, Sōen sought to instill courage into the soldiers before they thrust themselves before the bayonets, bullets, and bombs of their Russian adversaries. The abbot insisted that those who did not return from battle would not have forfeited their lives in vain. They would remain alive in the hearts and minds of those that they left behind. Their spirits, as temporal manifestations of "the great spirit," would transmigrate into new physical shells on their long journey to enlightenment. In this way, they would never really be absent from the world and their loved ones. Sōen was also responsible for caring for the wounded, comforting the dying "writhing in their last agony," and conducting funeral rites for the dead [228].

Early in his term of service, the First Army engaged in a perilous assault on Nanshan Hill. The strategically important prominence was on a narrow isthmus that served as the sole land route to Port Arthur on the Liaotung Peninsula. It was the center of Japanese and Russian hostilities. Winning this territory meant controlling Russia's main route of supply and reinforcements to the port. The Japanese forces outnumbered the Russians, but the enemy possessed considerably more firepower and was deeply entrenched on and around the promontory. The battle commenced at 2:30 in the morning with a three-hour artillery duel, the loudest and most vicious of the war up to that point. At dawn, Japanese troops made a brazen frontal charge on the hill. Sōen watched as the Japanese infantry charged over land mines, entangled themselves in thickets of barbed wire, and were mowed down by rows of machine guns. "Guns roar, bombs burst, but we do not see whence they come, and their knell only offsets the solemnity of these peaceful surroundings. But when I look through a powerful field-glass, I behold the hillsides strewn with dead and wounded, and the soldiers rush onward over these wretches, while the enemies on the hill are madly scrambling, stumbling, and falling. I shudder at the sight," Sōen later recalled [229]. Within the first fifteen minutes of the battle two entire divisions of Japanese forces ceased to exist. Wave upon wave of soldiers rushed up the hill until finally, after hand-to-hand combat with bayonets, the Japanese took the hill. More than 4,200 soldiers, approximately fifteen percent of the Japanese force, were killed or wounded that day, a heavy price for a single strategic position [230].

Though he had temporarily exchanged the serenity of Engakuji for the chaos of the battlefield, Sōen had not forgotten his plans to travel abroad in more peaceful conditions. "After the war we have to see Europe and America," he wrote to a colleague with whom he was discussing the need to visit foreign nations before being overly critical of them. "Saying things about these countries without knowing them is arrogant" [231].

In the weeks following the battle of Nanshan Hill, Sōen's health began to deteriorate. Ulcers and hemorrhoids plagued him during his service in Manchuria, and he suffered from painful bouts of rheumatism [232]. A photograph from the period shows the First Army chaplain, seated in a chair and elevating his left leg with a crutch that he evidently also used to assist in walking. His condition did not improve when he returned to Japan in mid-July and he was soon discharged from service.

It was an exhausted and ailing abbot who returned to his followers at Engakuji. Sōen's brief role in the war was over. Unknown to him at the time, the continuing conflict would have disastrous consequences for his plans for spreading Buddhism to America.

Rather than immersing himself once again in the taxing yet mundane administrative duties that awaited him, Sōen's attention remained overseas. It was not the frenzied battlefields of Manchuria that occupied him, however, but a house of serenity on the far side of the Pacific Ocean. Immediately upon his return to Kamakura Sōen began preparing in earnest for his second trip to America. Ida had written him several times, repeating the invitation for him to visit America [233]. It was agreed he would reside at the Russell mansion for an unspecified amount of time. There he would continue her and Elise's instruction in Zen spirituality, as well as teach other members of the household. Ida was in fact eager to continue her education in Buddhism. Inspired by her stay in Japan, she was making modifications to her property that she was certain the Zen master would appreciate.

Sōen announced his intent to resign as abbot of Engakuji in January 1905. After returning from Manchuria he had also been elected abbot of a neighbouring monastery, Kenchōji. He resigned his post at that institution at the same time. It was not until May that his tenure formally ended and he moved to Tōkeiji, a neighbouring monastery separated from Engakuji by the railroad tracks that passed through Kamakura. For the first time in more than a dozen years, Sōen was again a plain monk with no responsibilities within his sect's intricate hierarchy. He now had the freedom to renew his friendship with the Russells and fulfill his dream of propagating Buddhism in America. Still, the situation was delicate. There was public distress over the pending voyage of the famed Zen master. One magazine raised the alarm, reporting that Sōen planned to live overseas for ten or twenty years [234]. Sōen determined that a quiet departure was best, as he explained to a friend in New York: "I will sneak out before people notice" [235].

7

WE HAVE MUCH TO LEARN

1905

PART 1

WHEN Sōen embarked on his second journey to America it was clear that the famous and esteemed abbot would be doing no sneaking out. Not only was the mayor of Yokohama present to see him off, but eighty of his followers had gathered at the dock, braving wet weather that was brewing into a summer squall. As the *Manchuria*, one of the largest intercontinental cruisers ever built up to then, pulled out into the Pacific, heavy winds and high waves buffeted its 13,000-ton bulk. Conditions on board were initially stormy as well when Sōen was removed from his private suite, purchased by Nomura Yōzō and other wealthy followers, and required to share a room with another Japanese passenger who was regularly drunk. Within a few days the weather cleared and the Pacific was worthy of its name for the remainder of the voyage. Sōen, for his part, found it fairly easy to avoid his annoying cabin mate for much of the two-week crossing, passing pleasant hours in the company of the senators, diplomats, and Japanese noblemen in the ship's music hall.

Among Sōen's new acquaintances was the aristocratic Count Mutsu Hirokichi, former consul in San Francisco now on his way to a new diplomatic assignment in London. For the past three generations Count Mutsu's family had been formal members of the Zen sect. He had never been educated in the religion of his forefathers, though he held decided opinions about Buddhist priests' contribution to society. "The majority of them are about as useful as corpses," he said frankly to Sōen who dressed in his priestly robes each of his sixteen days aboard the *Manchuria*. Mutsu criticized the Buddhist priesthood in general, but particularly that of the wealthy Pure Land sect, as being more focused on lining its pockets than looking to the welfare of common people. The comments may have stung Sōen. On his last transpacific voyage, when returning from the Parliament of Religions twelve years earlier, he was criticized for not attending to the spiritual needs of a commoner on board. The man was dying and, when summoned by Western passengers whose religious sensibilities dictated a priest should be present, Sōen declined to visit the stranger's deathbed. This was allegedly because he was of the lower classes and therefore not worth the important prelate's time [236]. Warming to his subject, Count Mutsu opined that Buddhist priests should live a simple lifestyle and profess a simple doctrine meaningful to the general populace. Sōen, turning the tables, pointed out that falling short of one's ideals was not particular to practitioners of Buddhism. Calling to mind Americans' prejudice against Asians, which had recently resulted in segregating Japanese children from California's public schools, he chastised Christians for not practicing the charity at the heart of their religion. They might give a mite to the proverbial widow, but at the same time blame all sorts of social ills on Asian immigrants and foreign religions. "I will propagate the Buddha's compassion to the [American] people," he proclaimed to the nobleman, "telling them how Buddhists have deep compassion for the Christian countries" [237]. Mutsu conceded that if Buddhism could offer doctrines leading to a pure lifestyle it might yet hold a relevant place in modern society. He also commended Sōen's plans to spread Buddhism abroad: "If there is a suitable teacher, the propagation of Buddhism in Europe and America should not be exceedingly difficult."

Sōen's defense had not only smoothed out his relationship with the count, it also made an impression on the other travelers.

Before long he was presiding over dinner lectures for the first-class passengers. During the day he descended into steerage where a hundred or more Japanese immigrants would crowd into cramped quarters to listen to him speak. His thoughts were never far from his role in Buddhism's continued path to the east. In his poetry at this time Sōen likened his journey to those of the ancient Buddhist pilgrim Sudhana and Bodhidharma, the Zen sect founder who traveled east from his native India to introduce seated meditation to China:

> Like this boat on the Spring Ocean
> A monk comes or goes by the karma-relation.
> The horizon seems to be extending endlessly.
> The current, however, takes us to the New World.
>
> Yesterday, the whales swam around us.
> Today, the clouds shut off the sight of old Japan.
> Following the course of Bodhi-Dharma,
> From the west to the east I go.
>
> Then, turning to the south, I may visit
> India and Ceylon again, making a pilgrimage like Sudhana.
> Before long, our boat will enter the Golden Gate
> And the sea-gulls, perhaps,
>   may guide me to the destination.

[238]

Sōen had not intended to further Bodhidharma's efforts alone. Uemura Sōkō was supposed to be at his side on this pilgrimage, helping to introduce Zen to lands east of Japan. He had instead gone west to places long ago explored by Buddhist pilgrims but in turmoil nonetheless. Seven months earlier, in November 1904, the Imperial army recalled Sōkō to active duty. The war with Russia still raged. Previous military experience made Sōkō a valuable commodity in an army comprised largely of unseasoned conscripts. Priestly robes were replaced with an officer's uniform, the pilgrim's staff with a pistol.

Sōen's own tour of duty left him with numerous strings to pull. He tugged at them all, without success, in hopes of having Sōkō discharged and returned to Engakuji. In the end, all Sōen could secure was the promise of a high-ranking officer to personally watch over his pupil. This officer promised to keep Sōkō from harm. Despite such assurances, Sōen could not have been reassured when he learned his protégé was stationed in Manchuria where he commanded a troop of commandos near the front line. The assignment could hardly be more dangerous. As he steamed past the Sandwich Islands toward Honolulu and on to San Francisco Sōen was understandably anxious for this prize student and future collaborator in the propagation of Zen abroad.

In Sōkō's place, Sakurai Kō would attend to Sōen's personal needs in America. A 21-year-old layman lacking any kind of monastic training, Sakurai was somewhat conversational in English [239]. However, he was neither fluent nor educated enough to translate the complicated religious lectures that would be central to Sōen's mission. For this vital role, Sōen would need someone else. Prior to his departure, the Zen master fired off a missive to Illinois. Daisetz Suzuki quickly arranged for time off from Open Court and promised to join his teacher at the Russell residence.

There was another unexpected change in Sōen's travel plans. Senzaki Nyogen also planned to rendezvous with his erstwhile teacher in San Francisco. When Nyogen opened his two Mentorgartens, Sōen acknowledged them as having been founded "with no other assets than his [Senzaki's] accumulated knowledge of Buddhism and modern thought" [240]. More tangible assets would have helped. By 1905 both schools were in serious financial difficulty and close to closing their doors. Alerted to Sōen's imminent departure for America and perhaps inspired by letters he received from Daisetz describing the beauty of the mountains and fields of the American West, Nyogen conceived a plan. For two or three years he would remove his priestly robes and labor in America. He would send his profits back to Aomori to put his struggling institutions back on solid financial ground [241]. Writing to Sōen for permission, the careworn schoolmaster said he was willing to perform any kind of work necessary. He felt assured his labors would be watched over by compassionate buddhas and bodhisattvas, particularly Dainichi Nyorai venerated by the esoteric Shingon sect Nyogen once studied: "If I work at making beds, then the beds I make will have the pure fragrance of Bosatsu. If I become a cook, the meat will shine with light. If I work at washing dishes or shining shoes, that is also acceptable. Whatever I choose as my job, Nyorai will protect me" [242].

Nyorai failed to ward off illness, however. An eye infection prevented Nyogen from traveling with Sōen as planned. After he recovered, he was to undertake the journey on his own.

PART 2

The dock was crowded on June 27 as the hundreds of passengers aboard the *Manchuria* disembarked. It was not long before Sōen made out the familiar features of Alexander Russell and Dr. Louis Howe waiting to meet him. With them were several members of the Buddhist Mission. Though not of the same sect as Sōen, the Pure Land priests were eager to greet the famous Zen monk who shared their ambition to introduce Buddhism in America. With their help Sōen and Sakurai completed the paperwork and medical examinations at the immigration office. It would take a day or two for Sōen's luggage to be offloaded from the ship, so the troupe proceeded to Alexander's horse cart. He wove a path around freight vans that were drawn along the docks by lumbering workhorses. In order to reach his remote estate,

Alexander navigated his vehicle across town, bisecting the peninsula from the port facing the San Francisco Bay to his mansion on the Pacific. The most expedient route was to drive the horses a few blocks north to Market Street, before turning sharply left on the great commercial thoroughfare. It was a Tuesday afternoon and the street would have been crowded. Four streetcars—some cable, others electric—could simultaneously occupy the wide street, clanging noisily and sometimes spooking horses that shared the wide boulevard. Flower merchants peddled violets and roses along the concrete sidewalks, shrill calls from newsboys announced the day's headlines, and pedestrians paused at public fountains for a sip of water. The first several blocks, starting at Montgomery Street and continuing to Jones, would have greatly impressed Sōen. From an architectural standpoint, they were among the most attractive buildings on Market Street. The carriage rolled past the massive facade of the Palace Hotel, which occupied an entire city block. Then there was the curiously triangular base of the Crocker Building and the domed monolith of the Claus Spreckels Building, a skyscraper that towered an impressive fifteen stories above the street.

After passing City Hall, the carriage clip-clopped due west, past the green rolling hills of a few cemeteries and then along the southern boundary of Golden Gate Park. To his right, Sōen may have glimpsed a cycling club riding along tree-lined paths, or even one or two female motorists, among the first of their sex to be granted permits to drive in the park. By contrast, much of the land to the left was a wasteland. Since the days of Benjamin Sherman Brooks, the Sunset District had only seen a modest amount of urban development. Here and there a few houses could be made out in the sandy expanse. A network of planks over the sand served as sidewalks to some of these residences, and a couple of dairies operated in the district. But for all intents and purposes the city's suburbs ended at the park's easternmost extremity and miles of barren sand dunes dominated the area south of the park.

Brine replaced the pungent scent of cow manure as the carriage reached the end of the park and turned south on Ocean Boulevard, running parallel to the Pacific coastline. The vehicle first passed a little resort area filled with restaurants, saloons, and other businesses catering to those seeking a day by the seaside. Alexander might have cast a disapproving sideways glance at "Carville." An odd community, its houses were built from the horse-drawn streetcars, now obsolete and abandoned, that had been deposited along the coast and converted into the humblest of domiciles. Carville provided a patchwork of residences for high-spirited Bohemians, the vacationing middle-class, and impoverished families who could afford nothing better. The populace of this little community regarded the Russell mansion as a spooky place, the home of "mystics, mahatmas, occultists" [243]. Alexander, in turn, considered Carville an eyesore that drove down property values. Driving past the quirky neighbourhood, he may already have been devising a way to eradicate it—a feat he would accomplish some eight years later [244].

After passing the last streetcar-turned-domicile, Sōen caught his first glimpse of the Russells' remote estate. From a distance, he would have been struck by its cloistered appearance. A towering fence enclosed the entire four-acre lot. The few dwellings nearby were of the humblest kind—mere shacks in some cases—and separated from the Russell estate by a sea of sand. The carriage entered the perimeter and came to a halt before the mansion. Few of the old roadhouse's features remained after the extensive renovations Ida introduced after purchasing the building five years earlier. Ninety-degree right angles still gave the structure a boxy appearance. The exterior walls were painted in a light brown and pierced with numerous windows. These not only drew sunlight into the interior, they also let guests survey their peaceful surroundings. But the long, colonnaded porch, where drunken miners once argued over their poker winnings, had been removed, providing the four spacious bedrooms in the front of the house with unrestricted ocean views.

The main doors opened to a parlor adorned with much of the art that Ida collected on her travels through Asia and Europe. Adjacent to this was the mansion's centerpiece, a spacious hall that was often the center of activities. This hall was a new element to the house's design, carved out by completely gutting the interior of the mansion. Walls and floors had been removed to create the great open space that rose from the downstairs floor to the ceiling of the second story just below the roof. A massive brick fireplace dominated one end of the hall. Wide enough to hold logs six feet in length, it easily kept the fog-induced chill at bay. Fumed oak dining tables could each accommodate eight high-backed chairs.

Though Sōen would not have found the hall exactly home-like, he would have recognized a definite Asian aspect to it: teak armchairs from China, folding screens from Japan, and curtains imported from India filled the room. From the ground level of the hall, velour portières filled doorways leading to the drawing room, reception room, nursery, gymnasium, and hothouse. A balcony, reached by a grand staircase that touched down in the parlor, crowned the hall and led to a labyrinth of galleries and bedrooms on the second story. A library contained histories of China, the sayings of Confucius, translations of Buddhist sūtras, Ida's Sanskrit dictionary, and transcripts of lectures on Buddhism recently delivered by the renowned scholars F. Max Müller and Thomas Rhys Davids. Also on the shelves were *The Buddhism of Tibet* by L. A. Waddell, *The Land of the Lamas* by D. W. Le Lacheur, *The Mikado's Empire* by William Griffis, a collection of poems composed by the Japanese emperor, and a children's book of Japanese fairy tales. Western religion was represented by commentaries on the Hebrew scriptures, travelogues of the Holy Land, and a book about "Bible mysteries."

Throughout the mansion, rooms were filled with works of art that the Russells had collected on their travels. Ida is remembered as having purchased hundreds of original artworks while in Japan alone [245]. There were also Chinese vases that decorated niches and ornate iron lanterns brightened otherwise dark corners. Potted palms, rubber trees, and Japanese paintings on long silk panels enlivened various rooms. Athenian rugs were spread over well-waxed hardwood floors. Velvet carpets covered the stairs [246]. There were large paintings in various European styles, basketwork from South America, Persian rugs, plaster imitations of ancient Greek and Roman sculptures, and Ida's growing collection of Buddhist statuary. Yet the artwork did not crowd the living space. "Unlike some homes housing such things, there is not the least suggestion of a museum, for everything seems to serve a definite use," a society page editor would later croon. "There is a feeling of restraint and poise, a fine balance…. One feels conscious of the majesty which art can convey" [247].

Some of the faces of the large and rather unusual household were already familiar to Sōen. Ida was of course present. Her commanding presence tended to dominate social occasions like this. At this time she tended to arrange her hair in a psyche knot and, as in Los Angeles and Japan, dressed expensively [248]. Alexander was also at hand, as affable as ever. Elise Drexler and Jean MacCallum, who periodically stayed at the mansion with her aunt, emerged from the house. "They greeted me as if I were a member of the family returning from a long trip," Sōen said, pleased [249]. The old friends reminisced about their days in Japan so exuberantly that he "forgot for a moment that I was in a foreign country" [250]. Sōen introduced his old friends to his attendant, Sakurai. His presence seems to have been unexpected since, in a letter to Engakuji, Sōen expressed relief that the valet was "fortunately accepted at the Russells' and they treat him very well" [251].

Sōen also encountered numerous new faces on his first day at the mansion. There were the Crossleys with their daughter, Katherine. Bertha Christopherson from Ida's Gough Street community still ran the household. Mary Crittenden and Georgia Woolsey, Grace Crossley's two sisters, kept rooms. Also present were Mary C. Russell, of no relation to Ida and Alexander, a Mrs. Cody and Miss Gall of whom nothing is known, and Eugene Wells, Alexander's nephew from the East Coast. The domestic staff, which numbered about ten, included Japanese houseboys and Japanese gardeners. The cook, Makakichi Gunji, whom Ida called "my faithful Japanese servant" [252], was particularly skilled as a baker. Hired help also included at least one chauffeur, an automobile mechanic, and a handful of stable boys. Periodically Elizabeth Conner, Ida's aged mother who now lived much of the time inland with a nurse, would visit, as would Dr. Louis Howe. Having inhabited the Russell mansion until earlier in the year, he now lived downtown where he attended medical school at the University of California. Though he had already received medical certification before his trip to Japan, it was from one of the numerous homeopathic or "eclectic" colleges that awarded degrees in nontraditional forms of medicine. With the qualifications for practicing physicians becoming more stringent after the turn of the century, Howe would receive his new M.D. degree three years later.

After introductions, Sōen was led to a room that Ida had specially prepared for him. It was redesigned in Japanese fashion, complete with *tatami* mat floor and Japanese furnishings. Sōen spent his first few days recuperating from his long journey and exploring the mansion, which he initially took for a seasonal beachfront residence. "The resort house is seven miles from the pier. It has a spectacular panorama and is surrounded by a vast forest," he recorded in his diary, probably referring to the nearby Sutro Forest and still heavily wooded peninsula to the south. "The waves that wash off the beaches of Japan immediately come here and strike the hand rail of the back porch. It is all very quiet and serene" [253].

PART 3

Ida was eager to resume her lessons in Zen Buddhism under her Japanese mentor, but without Daisetz Suzuki Sōen was only able to communicate with his hosts at an elementary level. For this he apparently relied on his imperfect English skills and assistance from Sakurai and Reverend Hori Kentoku of the Buddhist Mission, who visited him daily. Shortly after Sōen's arrival Daisetz sent a telegraph saying he would arrive within a couple days [254].

As he bided his time, Sōen had ample opportunity to get to know the rather unusual household in which he found himself, as well as attend to the mundane tasks of settling into a new home. He went downtown to alert the consulate of his arrival, visited Count Mutsu at the Occidental Hotel, shopped for boots, a bowler hat, and 30 postcards. When Sōen's luggage arrived from the dock he distributed the gifts that he had brought for his hosts. Among these was a silk kimono for Katherine Crossley, and for the Russells an antique tea set, once possessed by the Emperor's sister who had entered a Buddhist convent [255].

Ida, Elise, and Dr. Howe showed off their city to Sōen, taking him on tours of Golden Gate Park, downtown San Francisco, the Presidio army hospital, and the Cliff House restaurant. On one sunny morning, when the fog that generally blanketed the coast withdrew, Alexander drove with Sōen to the Sausalito Ferry and, purchasing a pair of $1.40 tickets, enjoyed a day trip to the peak of scenic Mount Tamalpais. From time to time, Alexander broke out his stereopticon, treating mansion residents to a show of slides he had taken in China, India, and Japan, including the mountains of Kamakura.

Ida was exceedingly proud to play hostess to Sōen. She believed Asians in general to be more spiritually advanced than Westerners, who would require decades—perhaps even centuries—to attain comparable levels of spiritual achievement. "The Hindu esoteric is backed up by generations of ancestors as highly developed as himself, and his whole life is devoted to meditation and to his own unfoldment," she would say. "The nervous fretful people of this country will not be conditioned to reach this stage for some time to come" [256]. Particular to Sōen, she recognized and respected his position within the Japanese religious establishment. When speaking to him directly, or when speaking of him to those in the mansion, Ida addressed Sōen as *Rōshi*, the proper way for a Japanese student to address her teacher. When referring to him in conversations with others outside the mansion, he was "his Reverence." On more formal occasions she would introduce her guest more grandiosely as "the Right Reverend Soyen Shaku, Lord Abbot of Kamakura and head of eight hundred Buddhist monasteries of Japan" [257].

Considering the length of time Ida lived in Kamakura and how well she knew Sōen, it is surprising that the titles she bestowed on him were not more accurate. The English titles "right reverend" and "abbot" followed a standing tradition practiced by other Buddhists in America who adopted Western and traditionally Christian terminology to describe their organization and its members. In addition to leading Engakuji, Sōen had also been appointed abbot of two other monasteries in Kamakura: Kenchōji, when senility claimed its previous abbot, and Tōkeiji, which had recently been converted from a nunnery. Engakuji and Kenchōji were head temples that presided over nearly one thousand subsidiary temples (*matsuji*) spread throughout central Japan [258]. It must have been from this number that Ida derived her 800 monasteries. However, before leaving the country Sōen resigned from all of these posts and could no longer be described as an "abbot" of any institution. Sōen had either failed to inform his hostess of his present standing as a plain monk (*unsui*) or Ida chose not to recognize her guest's humbled position. Ida's description of Sōen as "Lord Abbot of Kamakura" was pure whimsy on her part. Kamakura was home to dozens of temples, only a few of which were of the Zen sect, yet fewer of the Rinzai subsect of which Sōen was a member, and fewer still of the Engakuji branch. No single monk, regardless of his standing or sect, could lay claim to a position of spiritual leadership over the entire city [259].

Three days after his arrival Sōen was introduced to the daily religious life at the mansion, his initiation taking the form of his first dinner within the community. Sixteen people took seats around the large tables in the two-story hall. Before food was served there was a moment of silent prayer. The meal was simple and of course vegetarian. If there was conversation it was brief for dishes were cleared in thirty minutes. There was then another silent period of prayer and everyone retired to their individual rooms, presumably for private reflection.

The vegetarianism of the Russell household pleased Sōen, who had long advocated that Japanese monks should maintain a meatless diet despite the relaxed dietary practices adopted by some monasteries. When in Ceylon as a young man he tried to avoid the custom of his fellow *bhikkus* who ate meat when it was offered to them. "If you do not hear the killed victim's suffering voice, or do not know that the killing was made especially for you, then the meat is clean," was an argument that left Sōen unconvinced. He hoped that such sophistry would not reach the ears of Japanese monks looking for an excuse to add meat to their diets [260].

Sōen was less strict with other monastic prohibitions. For much of his adult life he had kept a pipe, and from the age of 17 enjoyed saké while in Japan, whiskey when traveling abroad. "I have been drinking and smoking for thirty years and am almost addicted," he confessed in his diary [261]. Sōen had learned about Ida's opposition to both tobacco and alcohol before embarking for America, probably having heard her or Elise expound on the topic during their stay at Engakuji. Determined to halt vices he had long permitted himself, Sōen swore off both alcohol and tobacco while en route to America. During the voyage nicotine withdrawal may have taken the form of an inability to concentrate, which he again confided in his diary: "Since I boarded I prohibited myself from smoking and drinking and have tried to absorb myself in deep thought. However, the evil spirit of drowsiness attacks me" [262].

Besides mealtime prayer, religious practices at the Russell household were identical to many of those practiced at Belmont Hall. They included group prayer and meditation at specified times, regular instruction on spiritual topics, and restrictions against wanton travel, particularly on religious and national holidays. Employees, even the horses, refrained from work on these days. A traditional monastery bell, which Ida purchased while in Japan, hung near the hall and was rung to gather the community to prayer [263].

"The daily life of the family is thoroughly religious," wrote Sōen to a Japanese colleague a few weeks after his arrival. "Three times a day they practice Zen meditation, sing hymns ringing a hand bell, and have simple meals with the accompaniment of Western music. The whole family, even the servants, abstain from meat, wine, and smoking" [264].

Ida may not have been aware just how impressed Sōen was with her community. Buddhist priests in Japan had relaxed monastic rules to such an extent that few lived a lifestyle similar to that at the Russell mansion. "Their life is very clean and pure," he wrote in the same letter. "This kind of spiritually harmonious life cannot be seen in well-established temples in Japan. In this regard we have much to learn from them" [265]. This is an aspect of Sōen's relationship with the Russells that is rarely commented on. While residing with Ida and her household, he did not just instruct them in Zen Buddhism. He learned from them as well. Ida's idealistic lifestyle challenged him, caused him to reassess his way of living, and introduce changes to his own religious practices. For years after returning to Japan Sōen continued to refrain from alcohol and tobacco.

Ida recognized the monastic quality of life at her mansion. It was probably for this reason that she called her home the House of Silent Light [266]. The name was likely a reference to Jakkō-in, an ancient nunnery in Kyoto that would have been on her itinerary three years earlier. During Sōen's stay, Ida presented him with a large woodblock, asking that he paint on it the Chinese characters that spell out *jakkō*, the same characters used in the name of the convent. Perhaps Ida was inspired by the woman-led association operating within Japan's largely male-dominated Buddhist establishment. Or she may have felt the term *jakkō*—"silent light," that is, the light of quiescence, the light of nirvāna—encapsulated the search of tranquility that occupied so much of her adult life. She hung the calligraphy over a Japanese-style peaked gate at the entrance to her estate [267].

If Sōen found Ida's community similar to a Buddhist monastery, he would also have detected elements not at all reminiscent of Engakuji. The mansion's second-story chapel, he would have noticed, was decidedly Christian in decor. Rows of pews faced an altar traditional enough in appearance for it to be later acquired by San Francisco's Roman Catholic archdiocese [268]. The centerpiece above it was a painting called "Portrait of Christ" by Heinrich Hofmann. Ida and Elise had met the famed realist in his Dresden studio several months after their departure from Japan. Hofmann explained to the women that he endeavored to limn "that expression of countenance in which the soul and thought reveal themselves." The German master only reluctantly sold it to the American collectors "because he had caught the expression of the 'peace that passeth understanding,' and found perpetual comfort therefrom" [269]. Also in the chapel were copies of Guido Reni's Renaissance masterpieces "Aurora" and "Crucifixion," as well as two other Hofmann originals: "Christ and the Rich Young Man" and an interpretation of the resurrected Christ.

In the latter, Hofmann has Jesus robed entirely in white, his left hand slightly raised in the posture of benediction. Unusual among Hofmann's works, which tends to place Jesus in biblical scenes and interacting with various figures from the Gospels, in this painting Jesus stands alone, making direct eye contact with viewers. The canvas meant much to Hofmann. He painted it solely for himself, rather than public display. "I wanted to hang it over my bed," the artist confided to Elise and Ida. "And when I went to rest at night it should look at me, seriously examining me and asking, 'Have you lived this day in my spirit and according to my commandments?'" However, Hofmann's friends admired the composition so much that they convinced him to place it in his studio so that others could enjoy it. When the American ladies convinced the artist to part with it, he was distraught. "For many years, I was accustomed to see my Lord looking at me. So I feel some holy influence has gone from my room, and the only thought consoling me is that my work has gone to another who will love and cherish it" [270].

That Ida held a position of leadership over other residents of the mansion had long been clear to Sōen. It was her custom to lecture on religious topics every Sunday. The audience of these lectures not only included those in the household, but also as many as twenty visitors who trekked out to the remote district [271]. Ida's allocutions seem to have made quite an impression since Mary Crittenden, Mary Russell, Grace Crossley, and others committed her sometimes pithy, sometimes verbose aphorisms to memory. "Cultivate the art of happiness," was one. Others: "Let us love so well [that] our work shall be sweeter for our love; and still our love be sweeter for our work." "Realize your opportunities, your blessings, your privileges; and in this recognition, grow in dignity, sweetness, in nobility, in purity, in honor." "Be what you can, and thus gladden those who stand near to guide, to watch over, to protect, to bless." "To do the right we see to-day; to aspire for the power to see clearer, to do better in the tomorrow: let this be the aspiration of our lives, forever and ever. Amen" [272].

Meditation was both a private and public affair. Ida would meditate alone in her room before dawn. On weekend mornings at 11:00, the temple bell would sound to call the residents together. They quietly filed into the chapel and took seats in the rows of church pews. There, facing the Hofmann Christ and its "peace that passeth understanding" they would meditate together for an hour. The urban noise that drove the community to distraction while living at Gough Street was no longer a factor at the House of Silent Light. In some ways the residence was even more remote than Sōen's monastery. Here there were not only no nearby train tracks, there was no convenient public transportation whatsoever. On Sunday afternoons, a fair number of cars would drive down Ocean Boulevard, but on other days the din of motors was not to be heard [273]. The "neighbourhood" surrounding the mansion was parceled into blocks that existed only on the maps of real estate agents and city developers. Except for Ocean Boulevard, which ran from north to south along the coast, few other streets were evident. With the exception of a handful of resort houses, the few structures rising from the barren area tended to be small, almost shanties. Exploring the district, Sōen would only occasionally come across a small business, such as "Shorty" Roberts' Sea Breeze saloon due north of the mansion and once famous for its bear baitings and barbecues [274].

While Ida might not be distracted from meditation by her few neighbours in the sparsely populated district, sometimes the bustle typical of maintaining a sizable manor house could overwhelm her. On such occasions she would retire to the garden. Protected by the fourteen-foot fence was a traditional Japanese garden, "laid out with that wonderful art of the Japanese landscape architect that makes every little vista a view miles long, and combines all the forms and colours of tree and shrub, grassy bank and gray rock into one beautifully harmonious whole" [275]. Stone pagodas mingled with bonsai conifers, while small bridges arched over a running stream. A giant red *torii* dominated the area. There was also an outdoor chapel. While in this sanctuary Ida would neither receive visitors nor respond to the telephone [276].

PART 4

In the diary he kept throughout his travels abroad, Sōen consistently referred to the residents of the Russell mansion as a family. This is certainly the way that Ida preferred people to think of her house. She always bristled at the word "commune." In all likelihood many of the residents considered each other as family, regardless of whether or not blood relationships existed among them. Like a family they picnicked and vacationed together. They took weekend strolls along the beach together, ran errands downtown together, and piled into buggies to see P. T. Barnum's circus when it came to town. Like a family, some members regularly commuted to work despite the distance of the mansion from the city center. Elise Drexler, for instance, maintained offices at the Claus Spreckels Building. From this fashionable address she managed her late husband's various business interests. Sōen would have observed that Alexander, still employed at Bowers Rubber where he now managed the sales department, worked downtown on a daily basis. There were, of course, numerous family relationships among the residents—between Ida and Alexander, among the Crossleys, between Mary Crittenden and her sisters, between Elise Drexler and her niece. However, it was a shared lifestyle, as opposed to blood relations, that joined Ida's coterie together.

Nowhere was the intersection of typical family and religious community more apparent than in the mansion's nursery. Among the new faces that greeted Sōen when he arrived at the Russell estate was that of the toddler Baldwin Lee Russell. He was a friendly and intelligent child. His fair hair contrasted with Ida's brunette tresses and the dark filament receding from Alexander's forehead. Ida made sure that he was always well-dressed, and on Sundays he would wear an entirely white outfit. Sōen would sometimes amuse himself by solemnly bowing to the boy who would return the greeting in traditional Japanese fashion [277].

Sōen was either told or assumed that Baldwin was Ida and Alexander's natural son. He recorded as much in his diary and seems to have been given no reason to believe otherwise [278]. Baldwin was, in fact, a foster child, a ward of the San Francisco court system, who had been placed in the Russells' care at their request just a few months after their return from Europe. The child was already two or three years old at the time. Though neither a biological nor adopted son, Baldwin was identified closely with his foster parents' families. From Alexander he received the Russell surname, while his forename came from Ida's lineage, Baldwin being Elizabeth Conner's maiden name. Naming a child after a maternal relative was a Russell family tradition. Alexander also received his Christian name from his grandmother, Eleanor Alexander [279]. If details of Baldwin's presence at the Russell mansion ended here, everything would be straightforward. Alexander and Ida had been married twenty-two years in 1904 when the boy arrived. They had no children of their own. Ida, now in her late forties, was no longer able to bear children of her own. Foster parentage would have been a natural way to fill the void nature had placed in their lives. But like so much at the Russell house, immediate impressions were very often misleading and the easiest explanations of life there often proved erroneous [280].

Elise Drexler also played a very active role in rearing Baldwin. The boy and, as they arrived over the next several years, his six brothers and sisters would come to know her as "Aunt Lee," an abbreviated form of Elise easier for children to pronounce. Elise's familial bond to Baldwin was formally reflected in his middle name. Lee had been a traditional middle name in Elise's family for the past four generations. It was a salutation to Elizabeth Lee who, with her husband Arthur Owen, was among the first of Elise's ancestors to immigrate to Prince Edward Island from England at the turn of the nineteenth century. Elizabeth Owen bestowed her maiden name onto her firstborn son, who in turn passed it on to his daughter, Elise's mother. Elise's parents halted the tradition, but the childless Mrs. Drexler revived it when Baldwin was taken in [281].

Elise was responsible for considerably more than simply playing the role of auntie to young Baldwin and his future siblings. Not simply the latent maternal instincts of two childless women nearing middle age or a simple act of charity, Ida and Elise's actions were regularly described in terms of a social experiment. Both women had long been interested and active in child welfare issues. Besides her work with children at the Woman's Christian Temperance Union, Ida had previously served as corresponding secretary for the Pioneer Kindergarten Society. With the kindergarten movement still in its infancy, the organization was something of a novelty in San Francisco. It was established by "a number of public spirited citizens in kindergartens as a means of preventing the spread of crime" [282]. Perhaps Ida's experience at the kindergarten started her incubating her own opinions on the education and upbringing of children from the less fortunate social classes. Elise shared these opinions. As administratrix of the sizable Drexler estate, Elise distributed large sums of money to the Protestant Orphan Asylum, the Catholic Orphan Asylum, the Beulah Orphan Asylum of Alameda, and the Young Men's Christian Association [283].

At some point—perhaps before they purchased the mansion or in the early years of their life there—Ida and Elise conceived of a plan. The mansion would become home to a number of children. Some might be illegitimate, others abandoned by their natural parents or otherwise given up due to an inability to care for them. Children taken in would be raised in a gentrified environment. They would be surrounded by art and music, educated by private tutors. There are also indications that Baldwin and his siblings were gradually introduced to the practice of meditation as they grew older [284].

The two women's project was well known to San Franciscans of the time. "It was their belief that environment mattered more than heredity," one journal recalled many years later. "Whatever they [the children] lacked in heritage their foster mothers proceeded to offset by the atmosphere in which the children were surrounded" [285]. In other accounts, Ida's role in the experiment was completely eclipsed by Elise: "Mrs. Drexel [*sic*] took the old Ocean House [*sic*] near the Ingleside beach for an experiment in practical philanthropy. She had a theory that the right kind of environment would make real men and women of any human material" [286]. Louis Howe also played a role in the experiment. Howe's medical practice involved, at least in part, delivering the children of unwed mothers. Alexander's East Coast relatives specifically remembered Howe as the one who brought seven illegitimate children to the Russell home [287]. It is entirely possible that Baldwin was among the waifs introduced to the Russells through Dr. Howe's ministrations.

The presence of the foster children in the mansion can perhaps be described as a manifestation of sympathy, that third tenet in Ida's triumvirate of guiding principles. "Instead of saying we are part of the Universal Spirit ... it is better to manifest a heart of compassion and charity," she said to Sōen while still at Engakuji [288]. Taking in a band of unwanted children and raising them as her own in an environment of wealth and privilege, culture and holiness was most likely, to Ida, nothing more than the outward expression of an enlightened mind.

Ida and Elise's "experiment in practical philanthropy" was by no means unique. The women may have taken as their model the Theosophical Society's Point Loma colony of Southern California. The Theosophical Society, of which Ida was a member, was an unrestrained critic of the public education system which it described as infusing children's plastic minds with cold materialism and a religiosity filled with gross superstitions. "The whole [public education] system in vogue seems to be carefully calculated to crush out all originality, stunt the growth of the inner nature, and deprive the soul of its natural means of action," Ida may have read in the literature in the Society's library. "The Theosophists' only remedy against these adverse conditions is to take the education of their children largely into their own hands, supplementing by home-instruction the work of the schoolmaster" [289]. The Point Loma commune was home to 37 children by 1900, nineteen of whom were orphans of no blood relation to the colonists. These children were educated in the colony's Raja Yoga School and supervised by unmarried instructors who invoked the doctrines of reincarnation and karma to justify their lack of hands-on experience with child rearing. (Since they had been wives and mothers in previous lives they were fully qualified to take a maternal role in their current incarnations.) The Raja Yoga School, which was also described as an "experiment" [290], steadily increased in enrollment. In 1901 more than 100 were enrolled and by 1907 the institution had reached capacity with 300 students enrolled and more on a lengthy waiting list [291].

The word "experiment," used repeatedly in reference to Ida and Elise's taking in of foster children, carries with it a decidedly clinical ring. Contemporary accounts of the venture leave the impression that Baldwin and the others were little more than subjects of study. This impression is both unfortunate and inaccurate. There can be no doubting that Ida Russell had authentic maternal feelings for the children she would nurture for the rest of her life. Elise Drexler, for her part, remained close to a number of the Russell wards long after the "experiment" ended. The Russell children, for their part, considered Ida and Alexander their parents throughout their lives, long after their elders had passed away.

PART 5

When Daisetz Suzuki telegrammed shortly after Sōen arrived at Oceanside House, he said he would be delayed by a day or two. In fact, it would be three full weeks before he arrived. With his lecture schedule at the mansion on hold, Sōen spent some of his time away from the secluded estate. He met with representatives at the Buddhist Mission and reviewed the collections of the Hopkins Art Building. He had a dentist tend to a nagging toothache. On two separate occasions he bought tickets for the ferry that crossed the bay, once to tour the University of California's Berkeley campus and again to cultivate the society of a wealthy Japanese grocer in Oakland. Even with these diversions Sōen found himself with a considerable amount of time on his hands. A diary entry at this time reads, pathetically, "I erased the day by reading books" [292]. Daisetz finally arrived on July 14, the day after Sōen hiked Mount Tamalpais. Despite not having seen each other for nearly a decade the tie between master and student remained strong. Sōen introduced the 35-year-old Suzuki as "my disciple & friend" [293], while Daisetz held Sōen in utmost respect. The two launched into their work almost immediately.

Sōen delivered his inaugural lecture at the Russell mansion on the evening of July 17. It was a synopsis of Buddhism, perhaps intended to refresh the memories of those who had studied under him in Japan and provide an introduction to those less familiar with the religion. His exact words went unrecorded so it is impossible to determine exactly what was said. However, Daisetz took notes of Sōen's addresses throughout his stay in America. They were not word-for-word transcriptions, but intended to reflect the substance of his speeches. They later would be published by Open Court Publishing, under the title *Sermons of a Buddhist Abbot*. In that collection there are two essays that can be described as synopses of Buddhism. Since Daisetz specified one as having been delivered at a later date, it is likely that at least portions of Sōen's first lecture at the Russell mansion, his first speech on Zen in America, is in the chapter entitled "Buddhist Faith." In it Sōen presents Buddhism as being based on three fundamental principles: all phenomena partake of a single essence, this single essence has allowed itself to be diversified into separate and distinct phenomena, and all phenomena are constantly acting and being acted upon by one another. To illustrate the point, Sōen conjured up a metaphor of the moon popular in Zen circles:

> The moon is one and serenely shines in the sky, but she will cast her shadow, wherever the conditions are mature, in ever so many different places. Do we not see her image wherever there is the least trace of water? It may be filthy, or it may be clean; it may consist of only a few drops, or it may be a vast expanse, such as the ocean; but they all reflect one and the same moon as best suited to their inherent nature. The shadows are as many as different bodies of water, but we cannot say that one shadow is different from another. However small the moon may appear when there is only one drop of water, she is essentially the same as the one in the boundless sheet of water, where its heavenly serenity inspires awe and reverence. So many, and yet one in all; so diverse, and yet essentially the same ... [294]

To recognize the oneness of apparently diverse phenomena, Sōen recommended two of the three principles on which Ida Russell based her religious practice: serenity and purity. "The most practical way to solve these problems is not through mere intellection. We must first acquire mental tranquility, we must be purified spiritually, we must be freed from all disturbing passions, prejudices, and superstitions" [295]. The homily seems to have been well received. It was agreed Sōen would address the community every other evening at eight o'clock.

For his second lecture Sōen took for his topic "The Standard of Good and Evil," in which he presented morality in terms of two sets of "Buddhist Ten Commandments"—ten "Thou shalt nots," followed by ten "Thou shalts." In this oration, Sōen identified ignorance as the root of all evil. In each living creature, there exists "the indwelling reason of the universe" [296], which enlightenment will allow the Buddhist to recognize. Other introductory lectures that Sōen may have delivered early in his stay covered the practice of meditation and the concept of God. Having laid this foundation, Sōen embarked on a series of lectures on the *Sūtra in Forty-Two Chapters*. It was said to be the first Buddhist manuscript carried from India to China in the middle of the first century. The fact that it provided the textual foundation for Buddhism's early migration made it ideal, Sōen felt, in his own effort to continue its eastward journey. For the next month and a half he would discourse on this topic, with the exception of one evening when Ida induced him to make an impromptu speech on the patriarchs of Buddhism.

Following his first lecture, Sōen invited members of the household to participate in *dokusan*, the private interviews that Zen monks were allowed to have each day with the master. Whenever they wished, Sōen said, anyone in the mansion was free to meet with him privately to receive private instruction. Nearly private, that is. Daisetz would presumably be present to translate. As noted, three years earlier Ida had become the first American to attend *dokusan*. Now she was the first to participate in these most characteristic of Rinzai Zen practices in America.

Between July and September Sōen delivered more than twenty lectures at the House of Silent Light. Each was followed by a question-and-answer session. About twenty people attended, the group consisting of mansion denizens and probably a number of outsiders. Japanese visitors, probably from the Buddhist Mission, were occasionally present [297]. Conspicuously absent was Alexander Russell. Since Sōen arrived, Alexander seemed quite willing to interact socially with his Japanese guests. He took them on excursions to the countryside, on drives in his roadster, or for a bird's-eye view of the city from the top floors of San Francisco's tallest buildings. Sociable by nature, Alexander politely greeted those who arrived for Ida's weekly lectures. But before the sermon commenced he discreetly disappeared to another, more private part of the mansion [298]. As evidenced by his disinterest in living as a Japanese monk or residing regularly at Belmont Hall, Alexander's religious zeal did not match that of his wife. There is no indication that he attended any of Sōen's discourses.

It was not only the denizens of the Russell mansion who drew on Sōen's time in the first several weeks of his California sojourn. The Buddhist Mission, which had so eagerly welcomed Daisetz Suzuki as a guest lecturer two years earlier, was all the more pleased to receive an orator of Sōen's celebrity. The Pure Land priests were alerted to his visit in advance, evidenced by their presence at the dock when he first arrived. They went out of their way to help him settle into his new environs, visiting him on a daily basis in those first awkward weeks before Suzuki's arrival, introducing him to prominent members of the Japanese community, providing him a place downtown to rest, eat or spend the night when trekking out to the Russell mansion was inconvenient. By now they had a well-established network of temples in San Francisco, San Jose, Sacramento, Oakland, Fresno, Portland, and Seattle, and a second facility being constructed in Los Angeles. Sōen was invited to speak at a number of these locations, where he was treated as a guest of considerable honor. He responded warmly, accepting every opportunity to address gatherings of Pure Land Buddhists.

On its surface, the Zen priest's willingness to involve himself so closely with this other sect is puzzling. Sōen's long-term goal in America was to popularize Zen, just as the Buddhist Mission was popularizing its own branch of the religion. The two were technically rivals in Japan and now promised to also contend for the attention of adherents in America. Sōen, however, had long advocated cooperation among Buddhist sects, recommending that they overcome their centuries-old rivalries and join forces in joint missionary efforts. While in Ceylon in the late 1880s Sōen wrote a book on South Asian Buddhism in which he advocated that members of Mahāyāna and Theravāda traditions join forces to proselytize Buddhism in Western nations [299]. He seemed particularly prepared to work with the Pure Land Buddhists, not because their form of Buddhism bore a close resemblance to his Zen sect but because it was so different. Sōen pointed out that the devotional nature of Pure Land Buddhism, which promised a paradisiacal afterlife to those who simply had faith in Amitâbha Buddha, was completely dissimilar to the intellectual approach of Zen, which offered adherents enlightenment through their own efforts. "The gap which seems to divide them so widely is only superficial," he noted. "The former [Pure Land Buddhism] may be properly called religious, while the latter [Zen] contains more philosophical elements. Nevertheless both of them aim at the recognition of truth and deliverance from sin" [300].

On a practical level, Sōen may have felt that by popularizing Buddhism through the Buddhist Mission he was in fact tilling a soil in which the seeds of Zen in America might one day sprout. By speaking to Pure Land audiences he probably also recognized that the Buddhist Mission network could put him in contact with Japanese across California, helping him build relationships that might later be beneficial to the establishment of a permanent Zen foothold in the state. Uemura Sōkō, when he arrived to continue these labors, might be able to call on those Sōen met for their assistance. As it turned out, Shaku Sōen was almost entirely dependent on the Buddhist Mission to provide him with public speaking venues. Were it not for the Pure Land temples, he would have had few, if any, opportunities to address West Coast audiences beyond the Russell parlor.

A day before Sōen's first address to Ida's intimate gathering, he stood before an audience of 1,200 at Golden Gate Hall. Reverend Hori had rented it in order to introduce his community to the well-known prelate. A couple weeks later, at the same time Sōen was beginning to introduce Ida and her community to the *Sūtra in Forty-Two Chapters*, he was with Reverend Hori in Oakland speaking to an audience of 600. Sacramento was next on the itinerary. Despite his impression of the Japanese neighbourhood as a "pathetic and filthy place," another 600 immigrant laborers braved the searing summer heat to hear Sōen speak. Two hundred more turned out the next day for an account of his battlefield experiences and a memorial service for the Japanese war dead [301].

With such a warm reception it is little surprise that Sōen soon received a letter from Southern California inviting him to speak before the Mission's growing Japanese community there. He accepted immediately. On September 16 Sōen boarded a Southern Pacific sleeper car about to pass over the 400 miles of track between Oakland and Los Angeles. As he watched the golden-brown hills pass by his window, Sōen may have reflected on the progress he had made since arriving in America. Nearly three months had passed. He had delivered 21 lectures at the Russell mansion. Ida had received private instruction in formal *dokusan* sessions nine or ten times. Before long Uemura Sōkō would arrive to help establish a permanent Zen presence in America. Perhaps Daisetz Suzuki would assist him and they might present some friendly rivalry to the Buddhist Mission.

Shaku Sōen had no way of knowing that, as the train clattered south, his busiest days at the Russell mansion were now behind him. Upon his return from Los Angeles he would remain at the House of Silent Light for another six months. However, he would encounter more silence and less enlightenment, at least when it came to Buddhist instruction there.

8

I Feel Somehow Uneasy

1905-1906

Part 1

DESPITE a pleasant ride south Sōen was not feeling at all well when he detrained in Los Angeles. Since arriving in California persistent toothaches had troubled him. Medicine did not alleviate the pain, so a Japanese dentist extracted a tooth—just hours prior to his first "Synopsis of Buddhism" sermon before the Russells. Perhaps the doctor removed the wrong tooth because two weeks later, while Sōen was in Sacramento, he was again in so much pain that a dentist was required to make an emergency visit to his hotel to pull another.

Sōen's dental problems seem to have been resolved because there were no more extractions during his stay in America. However, at the end of August Sōen was bedridden with what seems to have been a stomach flu. His evening lecture was postponed a day while he recovered. Still not feeling well when his lessons resumed it soon became apparent that the virus was gamely roving from one resident of the close-knit community to another. When it finally reached Ida lectures were canceled indefinitely. When Sōen detrained in Los Angeles five days later he was still suffering from severe stomach cramps and dysentery [302].

The local Pure Land priest, Izumida Junjō, seemed to know a thing or two about promotion and possessed the publicist's flair for exaggeration. At the same time Sōen and Daisetz were checking into the Westminster Hotel the *Los Angeles Herald* was running a classified advertisement alerting locals to their arrival.

> Grand treat for American believers and students of the higher life. The Very Reverend Soyen Shaku, widely known throughout the civilized world as the foremost authority of the teachings of Buddha, will lecture on Buddhism for the instruction and benefit of those desirous of becoming acquainted with the sublime philosophy of Buddha, assisted by the Rev. Prof. Suzuki, A.M., of Harvard, [*sic*] ... Silver collection to defray expenses. A large audience is respectfully requested to attend and hear this learned divine and gifted orator of the Orient. [303]

A respectable amount of silver must have been collected that evening since a thousand people crowded into Turner Hall to hear Buddhism's foremost authority. The agenda included five speakers whose addresses were interspersed with "a fine programme of oriental music" performed by a French pianist. The first was "Swami Mazziniananda," a local medium who sometimes styled himself as a Buddhist teacher from the Himalayas. He would chant in "Hindoostani," a gibberish he called his native tongue, which may have been at least partially true since its nonsensical syllables were produced with a distinct Cockney accent [304]. The evening continued with homilies delivered by Daisetz and representatives of the Buddhist Mission. Sōen was allotted the place of honor and spoke last, taking for his topic "The Essence of Buddhism."

As at other Buddhist Mission gatherings, the vast majority of the Los Angeles audience was made up of Japanese immigrants. But even in this remote outpost, Sōen noted that as many as one hundred Caucasians were present at his lecture. Some may have attended out of mere curiosity, but many had an established interest in Buddhism. A year earlier three Caucasian Americans in

Los Angeles formally converted to Buddhism and, by the time of Sōen's visit, about fifty Buddhists attended services at the Pure Land Mission [305]. Given Sōen's intent to "propagate the Buddha's compassion to the [American] people," as he told Count Mutsu, one would expect him to be pleased when after his address three Angelenos voiced their desire to convert to Buddhism. This was a singular experience for the Zen monk. There is no evidence that Sōen ever converted any other Westerner to Buddhism [306].

Sōen stayed in Southern California for nearly a week, speaking at both the Buddhist Mission and the Vedanta Society. He also devoted several days to seeing the sights. Sōen was an enthusiastic tourist and welcomed the chance to stroll along Venice Beach, scrutinize the Ocean Park pier, and explore the amusement park in Santa Monica. His diary entries give a flavor of how much he enjoyed outings like this:

September 19
11 A.M. Went to Buddhist Mission. I wrote calligraphy on [their] request.

After lunch, Uchida, Suzuki, and I took a car to Mount Lowe. Arrived at 2 P.M. Changed to a "steel car" and went up incline track 3,000 feet. Our bodies almost touched the white clouds and I felt that I could touch the sky. The scenery is very different than it is from the ground, so I cannot describe it easily. Just beautiful.

Returned from Mount Lowe at 4:30. Went back to the city to rest.

8 P.M. Invited to Japanese club. Forty people attended. Talked and laughed at dinner. Their manners, etiquette, and hospitality are very good.

10 P.M. Returned to hotel. Took shower. Went to bed.

[307]

PART 2

Upon his return to San Francisco on September 21, Sōen found Ida had still not regained her health. Despite his sojourn in a sunnier clime, Sōen was still not feeling well either. Plagued with diarrhea he spent his first day back at the mansion in bed. Despite nausea, on one occasion he spoke to the Dharma Sangha of Buddha, the Caucasian group associated with the San Francisco Buddhist Mission [308]. He agreed to deliver a weekly sermon to the Russells' Japanese servants. He also accepted an invitation to later spend five days in Fresno, where five or six thousand Japanese immigrants worked as seasonal agricultural laborers. About 200 of these attended each of his three lectures. Yet the Russell community's further education in Zen was still on hold, mainly because Ida remained ill. It seems that if she was not able to attend the lessons, no one else in her community would either.

After three weeks without her condition improving, Ida— along with Elise Drexler and Clarence Crossley—fled the sick house for Santa Barbara. Alexander Russell would join them a little later. They would remain for nearly a month. During Ida's absence, residents of the mansion continued to meditate together on Sunday mornings at 11 o'clock. Sōen exchanged letters regularly with his convalescing hostess. But without the regular lectures to the mansion residents, Sōen and Suzuki faced long days at the isolated residence. Sōen spent hours walking the beach or gadding about the sand dunes behind the mansion, sometimes alone, sometimes with Daisetz. After this constitutional, the afternoon might consist of little more than reading or responding to mail. When the Russells finally returned to the mansion Sōen was still not asked to resume his talks to the community. In fact, though he would remain at the mansion for six months after his return from Los Angeles, Sōen never actually resumed his regular lecture schedule. Nor did Ida ever restart her practice of *dokusan*.

With Ida's return, religious life in the mansion continued as usual, with the Sabbath rest observed and the day spent in quiet meditation. Occasionally, Sōen was asked to give a spontaneous speech after dinner. But these talks were no longer the regular events scheduled earlier in the year and many days would often pass between them. The Zen master seems to have begun questioning why he remained in this suddenly awkward environment. "Our hostess is still sick and we do not know how long we are going to stay here," Daisetz reported to his employer. "I feel somehow uneasy" [309]. With little to do at the mansion, Sōen and Daisetz discussed leaving California before the end of the year, but quickly decided against it, not because he felt a sense of purpose in remaining in the Russell house but because he was aware of harsher winter conditions elsewhere. "The Reverend Shaku is afraid of coming East at this time of the year, for this is the best season in California," Suzuki explained to Carus. "Except for occasional rainfalls, [the] temperature is so mild that flowers keep blooming and birds singing" [310].

Daisetz had other reasons to feel uneasy while at the Russell house. On the one hand, he truly appreciated the time he could spend with the teacher on whom he doted. He also reveled in the role of propagating Buddhism at his side. Much later, after many years stood between him and the tedium of day-to-day life at the mansion, Daisetz looked back on his time in San Francisco with reverie, saying, "Those several months were the happiest times in my life in North America" [311]. On the other hand, he had the distinct feeling that his hosts did not fully appreciate him. This may have stemmed from the fact that his translations of his master's lectures were never literal. Often Sōen used Buddhist terminology that Daisetz felt would be impossible for his audience to comprehend without a more thorough background in Zen philosophy. So Daisetz often modified the content in an effort to make it more understandable. Whether or not the community realized that they were not getting a word-for-word translation of the famous Zen master's discourse, someone was clearly frustrated by Daisetz's intermediary role. It may have been Ida, who had gotten along so well with Uemura Sōkō and found the less-educated, socially awkward Daisetz a poor substitute. Or perhaps it was Elise, who during her temple tours in Japan tried repeatedly to communicate directly with a senior monk, bypassing Sōkō and another translator that accompanied them [312]. One or more people in the mansion complained that it was not worthwhile to attend the lectures because the teachings did not come directly from Sōen [313].

Regardless of its source, the reproach was taken quite seriously. Early in his stay, having delivered only a handful of lectures at the mansion, the Zen master was attending English lessons for two hours every morning. His goal was to deliver a lecture in English by the new year. The language instruction was usually the responsibility of Mary Russell, though on occasion Ida conducted it herself. Sōen was an eager learner throughout his life, once commenting, "One can only make true studies after he is over forty. Any studies made in a man's twenties or thirties are, I think, just introductory steps to learning" [314]. During his tenure with the Russells he faithfully attended the lessons, "using the spare time I once spent smoking and drinking to learn English." However, Sōen was no linguist and he found it difficult to revive foreign language skills not actively fostered since his years at Keiō University. "I neglected learning English for more than 20 years, so it is now difficult to communicate in English in everyday conversation," he wrote to an associate in Japan. "I am taking English lessons every day from Miss Russell, but I will turn 47 this year, and my memory seems to be getting worse" [315].

If it was Ida who did not entirely approve of Daisetz's ability as a translator of Japanese and interpreter of Zen, Suzuki did not harbor the highest opinions of her either. This was not particularly obvious in the regular missives Daisetz sent back to Paul Carus, to whom he described Ida as devoted to Buddhism [316]. His correspondence to Japan was more candid. "The owner of the house I heard is a vice president at a rubber company. His wife controls everything in the household. She behaves like a queen. … People are impressed with the wife's beliefs and follow her. More than ten people live with the wife. They hit gongs and make rules and practice something like *zazen*" [317]. Years earlier Sōen, recognizing that Ida's style of meditation differed from that of Zen orthodoxy, spoke of her attainments approvingly. Daisetz did not seem ready to make any such concession.

Daisetz also noted that Ida tended to monopolize Sōen's time. This was particularly plain in her attitude toward *dokusan*. Exerting her position of authority over others in the mansion, she would not permit anyone else to receive private instruction from Sōen. The Theosophist in her seems to have interpreted the experience as a transmission of esoteric knowledge, a secret teaching that was to be communicated only to the spiritually advanced. It was her ambition, Daisetz noted, to be the only one who could say that she studied directly under him. This behavior did little to endear Ida to Daisetz, who characterized her actions as selfish, egocentric, and narrow-minded [318].

Daisetz had long struggled with his feelings toward women in America. Though particularly close to his mother, Daisetz was often ill at ease around the opposite sex. It was hardly surprising: Japan's male-dominated society and tradition of arranged marriage did not necessarily promote the development of social skills leading to meaningful interaction between the sexes. When he arrived in America, where men and women regularly intermingled, Suzuki found himself a clumsy conversationalist. Unable to buoy his palaver with talk on academic matters, unskilled and uninterested in small talk, Suzuki soon found he had little to say to American women who, as a group, he considered gossipy, arrogant, and unsophisticated. "Even educated women are, after all, just women," he complained in a letter to Sōen. "It is rare to see a respectable woman, especially here (in America)" [319]. To avoid uncomfortable situations Suzuki would, at least early in his stay, sequester himself in his room, reading or practicing meditation [320].

Sōen faced tensions between two important students on whom he depended, one for communication, the other for assistance in remaining in the United States and perhaps establishing Zen there. A change was needed. The plan had always been for Uemura Sōkō to assist him in America. Unlike Daisetz, whose critical nature seemed to alienate him from the chatelaine of the House of Silent Light, Sōkō respected Ida's religious pursuits and in return earned her trust and esteem. It was becoming increasingly clear that Sōkō's presence would be critical to the introduction of Zen in America.

Sadly, Sōen would never again see his talented protégé.

PART 3

In the fall of 1905 the war with Russia had ended with a Japanese victory. Japanese throughout California were elated and celebrations ensued in the immigrant enclaves of San Francisco, Sacramento, Fresno, and Los Angeles. The victory, however, was bittersweet, for the terms of the peace treaty, brokered by America and various European powers, deprived Japan of war reparations. The Japanese people, who had never anticipated footing the bill for the war themselves, were incensed. Without reparations from Russia, Japan's economy was soon to be thrown into recession. It was not long before celebratory parades were replaced by riots on the streets of Tokyo. Such an outcome was a blow to Sōen, who had publicly endorsed the war and only a year earlier portrayed it as an idealistic battle between ignorance and enlightenment. In Japan, he wrote, "the people are in the flush of victory, declaring that Japan has now advanced to be a first-class power in the world; they are thus puffed up and are drunk with toasts; they are not aware of the high responsibilities resting on their shoulders, such as the heavy taxes which are to be levied on them after the war, but are enraptured, and are taking a dangerously optimistic view. There are many such people. I cannot help worrying about the situation" [321].

Throughout the fall, Sōen regularly corresponded with colleagues in both monastic and military circles. He inquired about Sōkō, whom Daisetz knew was to replace him. Requesting an extension to remain away from his duties at Open Court, Daisetz wrote Carus: "The war is over, and before long [Sōen 's] secretary who is serving in the Manchurian army as a commissioned officer will be discharged from his duty and will be able to come over to this side of the ocean. Until then I think I have to stay with his Reverence. I wonder if you will let me stay so long" [322].

However, in the fall, Sōen began receiving conflicting reports about Sōkō's safety. The first was waiting for him at the mansion when he returned from Fresno. Opening the envelope, Sōen found a letter warning him that Japanese newspapers would soon report that in one of the final battles of the war Russian forces obliterated the division under Sōkō's command. Sōen's correspondent instructed him not to take this report at face value, for Sōkō's fate was far from certain and his division had most likely only been captured. Sōen was distraught. As casualties were tallied, the price Japan had paid for its first significant international military victory was becoming clear. More than 85,000 Japanese soldiers perished in battle. For every five that fought, one did not return. Self-consciously, Sōen acknowledged to friends that a Zen master of his standing should be more detached from the potential doom of one individual. However, Sōkō was very dear to Sōen— and many of his plans for spreading Zen in the West hinged on this talented young monk. "If he is still alive it is a very auspicious thing for us and our religion," he wrote in a letter to Engakuji. Unable to simply wait, Sōen secretly dashed off letters to his high-placed contacts within the army [323].

Weeks passed, the ink on the armistice document had long since dried, and still there was no definite word about Sōkō. It was not until early the next year that Sōen learned the truth. A Japanese officer, who knew of Sōen's concern for Sōkō, was passing through San Francisco and visited the Japanese consulate. He notified the officials there that the military listed Sōkō as permanently missing and presumed dead. On January 14, the consul located Sakurai, who was now living downtown rather than at the Russell mansion. The faithful follower was dispatched to inform his master of the news. It pained Daisetz, who was present when Sakurai arrived, to witness Sōen's anguish. "I still cannot forget *Rōshi's* depression when he heard the news. After a while he murmured, 'I should not have treated him so harshly' " [324]. But Sōen refrained from lamenting his loss in public. "Tens of thousands of families lost their loved ones. My affection for Sōkō is small by comparison," he tried to convince himself through his diary, "so I should not write more about it" [325].

Many years later, additional details about Sōkō's fate came to light. Long after the war Sōkō's commanding officer remained troubled about the unsolved fate of his lieutenant. He had personally assured Sōen of the young monk's safety and felt personally responsible for his death. The officer made several trips to Hōten-shō (Fengtian xing), the part of Manchuria where Sōkō was stationed at the time of his capture by a division of the Cossack cavalry. There he met a merchant who had formerly made a business of selling provisions to the Russian troops and claimed to have been present at Sōkō's death. According to this old man, the Cossacks kept Sōkō under constant guard and, as the commanding officer of the subjugated force, treated him well. But when he was offered food and drink, he refused both. Turning to the southeast, toward Japan, Sōkō sat upon the ground, folding his legs beneath him. He entered into a deep state of meditation. Over the following days Sōkō continued to meditate—and to refuse the nourishment his captors offered. Feeling disgraced by leading his troops into captivity, Uemura Sōkō starved himself to death. His commanding officer found the approximate location of Sōkō's final days, gathered some soil from the spot, and returned with it to Japan. The earth was interred in a stone memorial that still stands just outside of Sōen's hermitage on the grounds of Tōkeiji [326].

PART 4

Sōen's immediate plans to establish a permanent Zen presence in America were thrown into disarray by the untimely death of his prize student. His possession of both philosophical and linguistic knowledge made him unique in Sōen's circle. "Only Sōkō had these two capabilities that could allow his master to attempt the undertaking in North America," noted the soldier's obituary, which Sōen himself may have penned [327].

The mission was important to him, however, and Sōen was determined that the loss of Sōkō would not completely cripple it. Letters were dashed off to Kamakura and Tokyo as Sōen devised an alternate plan. As is so often the case in the realization of grand plans, however, careful preparation was not to prove as effective as pure serendipity. Some of the most effective proponents of his campaign to spread Zen Buddhism in America were right under his nose in 1905. He had no way of knowing this at the time, or indeed throughout his life. This oversight was entirely understandable since one of these helpers seemed barely able to meet his own daily needs, much less champion Sōen's grand plans for spinning the wheel of Dharma further east.

When Senzaki Nyogen arrived in America he was eager to immediately begin earning the money his struggling Mentor-gartens so needed. He seems to have anticipated working at O. Kai & Company, a dealer in Japanese art goods, for this is the address he gave to Seattle customs officials asking his destination [328]. This may have been arranged by Nomura Yōzō, who had begun actively exporting Japanese art to the United States at this time.

Such plans were quickly abandoned. Upon his arrival in San Francisco Nyogen reported to his former teacher who seems to have pulled a few strings of his own. One of the Russells' domestics resigned shortly after Sōen's arrival. It was probably at the Zen master's suggestion that Nyogen joined the ranks of the mansion's Japanese servants. As Sōen and Suzuki prepared for lectures, planned their travel to Buddhist Mission communities, and generally strategized about how best to establish a permanent Zen presence in America, they observed the ordained priest polishing Ida's furnishings, toiling in the garden, and performing odd jobs about the property.

Strangely, Sōen never seems to have divulged to the Russells that their newest domestic was in fact a Buddhist priest and had been under his tutelage for five years. Perhaps Sōen did not believe the Russells would be willing to play host to his growing entourage of assistants. More likely, Sōen was respecting Nyogen's own desire to establish himself in the secular world. If this were the case, then it was equally strange that Sōen also neglected informing his hostess of Nyogen's considerable experience in the care and education of children. It was an interest that paralleled her own work in private kindergartens and the care of foster children. Ida, who could be quite liberal with her money when used in causes she deemed worthwhile, might have been instrumental in providing the Aomori Mentorgartens with the funding they so desperately needed. She might also have been interested in seeing similar types of institutions founded in America, perhaps under Nyogen's experienced guidance. Instead, the experienced educator busied himself with broom, mop, and dust rag.

Nyogen's days at the mansion proved short-lived. After only a week and a half in the employ of the Russells, Bertha Christoffersen handed him a five-dollar gold piece and showed him the door. "Today Senzaki Nyogen left the Russell mansion because the workload was too much for him," Sōen recorded in his diary. What actually occurred is a bit of a mystery. There was certainly more to Nyogen's departure than is recorded in his teacher's terse remark. Nyogen later recalled that his English was inadequate to follow the housekeeper's instructions. He may also have been somewhat ill at the time, not quite recovered from the infirmity that delayed his arrival in San Francisco, and not up to the challenge of performing his ten hours of daily manual labor [329]. "That evening So-yen Shaku accompanied me on my way to a Japanese Hotel," Nyogen recalled.

> "We were walking through Golden Gate Park when he said, 'This may be better for you instead of being pampered as my attendant monk. Just face the great city and see whether it conquers you or you conquer it.' We were in the middle of the road, but he set down my suitcase he had been carrying, said, 'Goodbye,' and walked swiftly away. I bowed to him but could not see him. Was it my tears or the evening fog? I do not know…. I have never seen him since." [330]

It is a pitiful scene, a poignant tale, one oft-repeated in one form or another. Nyogen recounted it nearly fifty years after the fact. Certainly elements of it are true, such as his short-lived experience as a domestic for the Russells, verified by Sōen's diary, and the difficulties presented by his limited English skills. There are, however, a number of problems with his account of this "last" meeting between master and student. At no time, whether before or after Sōen's arrival in America, was Senzaki Nyogen considered the Zen master's attendant. Sakurai Kō fulfilled this function throughout Sōen's stay. Nyogen's identification of himself as filling this role was pure fantasy on his part. As noted, Nyogen himself clearly stated that he came solely to earn funds for his schools, not to run errands for Sōen or assist in his missionary endeavors. Further, there was little about Nyogen's first laborious days in America that could lead Sōen to describe his student as in any way pampered. Finally, Nyogen's claim that he never again saw his master after his brusque farewell in Golden Gate Park is untrue. The Zen master's diary records repeated meetings between the two men for Sōen's entire stay in San Francisco. On some occasions the two met in the city, at other times Nyogen trekked out to the Russell mansion. When the Zen master was preparing to leave the city, Nyogen helped pack his bags [331].

It is difficult to believe that Sōen, no matter how harshly he could treat his students, would actually abandon one of them in a foreign land with no clear means of support or way to return home. It is more likely that the pair had long discussions about Nyogen's immediate plans and in these talks it was decided that the younger monk would simply continue his original goal of raising money for his kindergartens, only outside the Russell mansion. Nyogen quickly found work as a houseboy for a more forbearing housekeeper than Bertha [332]. It may not have been an entirely stable position since the abbot reported back to colleagues in Japan: "Senzaki is struggling with his life as usual" [333].

PART 5

As fall turned to winter, Ida and Elise treated Sōen to an afternoon performance of *The Merchant of Venice* at the Grand Opera House. Alexander continued to amuse the family with stereopticon presentations of Java, Italy, and other exotic locales he and Ida had visited on their round-the-world pilgrimage. Mansion residents celebrated Baldwin Russell's birthday. The hall was specially decorated for the occasion and a raffle was held. Mary Crittenden, a music instructor before joining the Russell community, played a few tunes on the upright piano, as did Jean MacCallum and Ida. Thanksgiving was a few days later. Ida explained the history of the holiday and its traditions to a somewhat bewildered Sōen. Among the Thanksgiving customs peculiar to the Russell mansion was an hour of communal meditation.

Through the winter, at 11:00 every Sunday morning, Ida and the others would convene in the chapel for meditation. By late December the Zen master trekked into the city every Tuesday to deliver a lecture on religious topics at the consul's mansion. "Since I came to the United States six months have passed very quickly. The time has disappeared like a dream," he wrote to Japan at the end of December [334]. But talks by Sōen at the mansion remained precious few and far between. Between September 11 and December 31 he addressed Ida's community only once, a spontaneous speech at Ida's request. He would address the household three more times before he left in the spring.

As the year drew to a close, the House of Silent Light received three new guests. Alexander's sister-in-law Mary arrived in San Francisco on November 9. A year earlier, in December 1904, Mary had given birth to a daughter, her eighth child. The girl was named Ida, after Ida Russell whose intelligent conversation, high-minded religiosity, and good taste in fashion endeared her to her in-laws. Ida's namesake only survived a few months of life. Weakened and despondent from the tragedy, Mary Russell (like Charlotte Farnsworth at Belmont Hall and Grace Crossley at Gough Street) turned to Ida for consolation, rest, and a change of surroundings [335]. With Mary were two of her daughters, 22-year-old Mabel and ten-year-old Janet. Janet was fascinated with "Aunt Ida's 'menage' " of Japanese guests, Chinese interpreter (as she mistook Daisetz), and Scandinavian and German servants [336]. Mabel was more impressed with Ida's out-of-the-ordinary religious beliefs. Years later, when her mother had passed away, Mabel sought solace in religion [337]. Inspired by her unorthodox aunt, Mabel turned—not to Buddhism—but to Christian Science, which she studied under Bliss Knapp, himself a student of Christian Science founder Mary Baker Eddy [338].

Christmas was a grand affair at the Russell mansion. For some reason the holiday was formally celebrated on Saturday, December 23. Perhaps this was to accommodate visitors making the long drive from the city. Or it may have been that Ida wanted her community to observe the holy day privately, in a more solemn manner. Whatever the case, after dinner the parlor doors, which had remained firmly shut for the preceding few days, were opened to reveal a giant Christmas tree inside. It reached from floor to ceiling, which was two stories up. The branches were decorated with silver, gold, and mottled ribbons. Hundreds of candles burned in the branches. Thirty-seven guests entered with a certain degree of pomp. They were instructed to march into the parlor in pairs, holding hands. Each couple circled the parlor twice, then sat down in chairs designated for them. "Mr. and Mrs. Russell handed out gifts as if they were happy gods descending from the sky," commented a charmed Sōen. Earlier in the week Ida instructed that each gift given at the ceremony must be accompanied by a poem personally composed by the giver. Sōen distributed forty fine silk handkerchiefs which he had ordered specially from Japan and emblazoned with a geometrical pattern he himself designed. The distribution of gifts was followed by a tea party in the mansion's greenhouse adjacent to the nursery. The evening concluded with group meditation.

Christmas Day was considerably less ceremonious. Mansion residents meditated for an hour in the morning. In the afternoon, Ida asked Sōen to give an extemporaneous lecture on Kannon Bosatsu, the bodhisattva of compassion. Kannon is typically figured as a woman, leading western scholars of the day to draw analogies between her and Mary, the mother of Jesus. Ida may have had similar thoughts when she asked Sōen to take up the topic that particular day. A week later, on New Year's Day, Sōen rose early to privately recite prayers for the Emperor. Just before midday he gave a brief address "in my limited English" at Ida's request. It was the culmination of months of language lessons. The talk, on a poem by Ikkyū, would be his first and only address in English. It was very brief and followed by a longer discourse in Japanese which Daisetz translated. Ida followed up Sōen's talk with a speech of her own, taking for herself the more privileged position of final speaker.

Sōen would remain in San Francisco for another three and a half months. As he diligently continued his English lessons each morning, he planned out the next stages of his journey. He would meet Paul Carus in LaSalle, travel to New York with the Buddhist Mission's Hori Kentoku, and reside in London with Count Mutsu. A tour of Europe, a pilgrimage to India, and a reunion with his friends in Ceylon were also on the itinerary. Funding the expedition proved problematic at first. When Sōen arrived in San Francisco the previous summer he had brought only fifty dollars with him, the minimum immigrants were required to have on hand to prove they could support themselves. This might have been supplemented by collections taken during his Buddhist Mission lectures and funds sent from Japan, but throughout his stay in California money proved consistently scarce.

Sōen's financial constraints were obvious when he requested that the monks of Engakuji mail his army uniform to San Francisco. The erstwhile Army chaplain probably planned to wear it at one of his public lectures in which he recounted his wartime experiences. When the package arrived, it was detained at the customs office and a tariff was placed on it. Unable to afford the tax, Soyen never claimed it [339]. Daisetz could not help his master in a pecuniary way. Despite his regular employment at Open Court his salary was not large enough to tuck away any savings. Since leaving LaSalle, Daisetz was no longer on the Open Court payroll, despite the fact that he occasionally spent time scouring San Francisco shops for artwork suitable for publishing in the magazine and translating Japanese texts for publication. When required to accompany Sōen to official gatherings at the Japanese consulate, Daisetz found he needed to add a Prince Albert frock coat to his wardrobe. On more than one occasion Ida hinted at assisting Daisetz with some cash, a pledge she never fulfilled. Though he complained to friends that he could not trust Carus, a notorious penny-pincher, to provide an advance on his salary [340], the slight proved unjustified. His request resulted in two $50 checks being quickly dispatched [341].

When planning his travels to the East Coast Sōen again wrote to Engakuji, requesting that his followers take up a collection for this journey—¥4,000 or ¥5,000 would suffice. Shortly after sending the missive, however, Ida heard of Sōen's predicament and presented him with a gift of $1,500, approximately ¥5,000, for his travels. Sōen penned a letter to Engakuji to tell his fellow monks, still scrambling to gather funds, that the "god of blessing" had smiled and he needed no additional money to complete his travels [342].

Sōen's detailed diary entries show that he and the American student for whom he traveled across an ocean to teach, were living largely separate lives in the final months of his San Francisco sojourn. Ida took her entire community for an extended stay at a far-off hot spring resort. Sōen remained behind, busying himself with planning out his upcoming journey and embarking on one last lecture tour for the Buddhist Mission. Traveling south he visited rural San Jose, whose mountains and fields reminded him of Japan and conveyed a twinge of homesickness. He returned to San Francisco, addressed the Dharma Sangha of Buddha one last time, and presided over another commemoration of the Japanese war dead. On her return from the sulfur baths, Ida still did not attend the private *dokusan* sessions with Sōen. He formally addressed the Russell community only twice, both lectures identified as wrapping up his discourse on the *Sūtra in Forty-Two Chapters*. From details like this, one gets the impression that Ida Russell's enthusiasm for Zen was on the wane or that her friendship with Sōen had become strained. However, this period was punctuated by events that clearly indicate Ida's continued interest in Buddhism and Sōen's deep appreciation for his hostess.

As Sōen descended from his rooms the day after his final talk on the *Sūtra in Forty-Two Chapters*, Ida excitedly told him about an exhibit advertised in the local papers. Theodore Wores, an artist of considerable local repute, was publicly showing his rendition of the Daibutsu, the giant bronze statue of Amitâbha Buddha so near to Sōen's home in Kamakura. Wores had completed the painting, which he called "Light of Asia," years earlier while living in Japan. He was extremely proud of the piece, but rarely displayed it. When he did, it was at the Bohemian Club and other private venues. But when George Kellogg Claxton requested to display the painting at his gallery on Post Street, the artist had little grounds to object. Over the years, the gallery owner regularly displayed Wores' work, exhibitions that provided valuable public exposure and regularly led to the sale of paintings and well-paid portraiture contracts. Besides, Claxton only wanted to exhibit the painting. It was understood that the artist had no intention of selling. Claxton would explain this to his habitués, quickly drawing their attention to other works in his collection.

Ida and Sōen made their way to the Claxton Gallery, located in a neighbourhood she knew well [343]. Up and down Post Street were innumerable bazaars that specialized in Japanese prints and embroidery, Persian rugs, and Oriental brasswork. Ida may have omitted telling Sōen that the gallery was only two blocks from her mother's boarding house, the humble abode where she grew up.

At the gallery, Sōen and Ida encountered the elaborate setting Claxton assembled for the painting. The walls of the display room were painted an impenetrable black, creating a dark, mysterious environment. Japanese prints and gold embroidery hung from the walls, while ebony settees and small Japanese tables were tastefully arranged along the walls. The air was thick with incense. "Light of Asia" dominated one wall. Though not exactly enormous—approximately three feet on either side—it was by far the largest work Wores ever produced. The composition was formal, with the image of the serenely seated Buddha centered within the frame, eyes partially open but downcast, hands resting on his lap in formal meditation posture. The lips, which on the original statue form a scowl of concentration, are in Wores' rendition raised at the edges in a sublime smile. Though Wores' portrayal of the statue itself is generally faithful to the original, the surroundings in which it is located are completely imaginative. A watery bed of lotus flowers replaces the temple court, crowded with tourists and pilgrims, in which the statue actually stands. A thin layer of mist, almost transparent in places, covers the flowers but is well below the head of the Buddha. The intent, the literature at the gallery explained, was to show that the Buddha rose above the mist of human ignorance, that he could dissipate this metaphorical haze for the betterment of humanity. The effect was impressively realistic: when light hit the painting in the right way the mist looked as if it could flow out from the canvas [344].

Sōen gazed at the image for a while in silence. It soon became clear to Ida that he was impressed by the work. In his diary that evening, Sōen would write, "It has a very sacred tone that is attractive to people." Discussing it with Ida he was more munificent: "The man who painted this, he knows the Mind of Buddha; no one could paint this who did not" [345]. Ida needed to hear no more. She inquired about its price. Claxton said it was not for sale. Three years earlier, when Sōen initially denied her request to live at Engakuji, Ida did not truckle. The present situation was no different. She requested to speak with the artist himself. Wores, Claxton said, was unavailable. He was in Southern California working on the portrait of a local socialite. Ida left the gallery with Theodore Wores' Los Angeles address. That same day she penned a letter on stationery that belied her Buddhist interests. In the upper lefthand corner was an imprint of the Buddhist "Dharma wheel" with the word "ONWARD" written in block letters within the hub. Relating Sōen's opinion, she hoped Wores "will feel the depth of such approval." She concluded the missive with her direct, carefully-phrased appeal: "I cannot tell you what happiness and stimulus the possession of your picture would give me. May I purchase it from you? Trusting I may have a favorable reply, I am, Gratefully Yours, Ida Evelyn Russell" [346].

Wores, receiving the letter in his Los Angeles studio, was evidently taken off guard. Despite the praise of this woman's eminent guest, he still had no desire to sell. But to dismiss the request offhand would be both improper and impolite. Wores addressed a letter to Ida, stating that the painting was quite dear to him and parting with it would be difficult. If she insisted on purchasing it, the price was $5,000. The sum was outrageous. It was nearly the annual salary of San Francisco's mayor, equivalent to approximately $150,000 in today's currency. Rarely would a painting by an artist still living sell for such a price. That, of course, was Wores' intent. Such a sum would surely deflect this unwanted, unsolicited offer. Wores' shock was complete when, a few days later, he received a second letter from Ida—enclosed with a check for $5,000. With no way of backing out of the hole he had dug for himself, the artist hastily arranged a trip to San Francisco. Among the things he needed to do to close the deal was add his signature to "Light of Asia." Because he never intended to sell the painting, he had never bothered to sign it.

On March 10, 1906, two days before Sōen departed for Chicago, the House of Silent Light held a dual celebration in honor of Ida's birthday—her forty-ninth—and the conclusion of Sōen's stay. A vegetarian cornucopia descended upon the parlor, and all members of the household ate their fill at the dinner party. At some point in the midst of the revelry, Sōen allowed Ida to wear his most prized surplice (*kesa*), one that was woven with gold. It was a flattering gesture by the monk, who would not allow so sacred a garment to be worn by just anyone. But Sōen felt the honor was well deserved. He viewed his friendship with Ida as no mere happenstance. Rather, he noted in his diary, the bond that they shared had been decided before birth. It was the product of good karma that they each had acquired in previous existences. Because of their acquaintance, which spanned multiple lifetimes, Sōen felt justified in letting Ida don this symbol of office and enlightenment [347].

9

Strange Women in a Strange Land

1906

Part 1

I T is curious, given the amount of time Shaku Sōen spent in California, that he did not do more to personally prepare for the establishment of a Zen temple or center in America. It was certainly the hope of those in Sōen's circle in Japan that during his stay in California he would successfully plant the seed of Buddhism in America [348]. He clearly wanted to bring such an establishment into being, as his plans for Sōkō revealed. As his train sped across the snow-clad Rocky Mountains and toward a still bitterly cold Chicago, he had already directed others to take the place of his unfortunate disciple. In the summer, not just one priest but an entire Buddhist community would arrive in California, ready to continue Americans' introduction to Zen.

However, during Sōen's stay in San Francisco he seemed to take no particular interest in preparing their way. This is curious. Ever since he witnessed Ida Russell and Elise Drexler's enthusiasm for learning about Buddhism and practicing meditation, Sōen strongly desired to see Zen propagated throughout America [349]. Upon resigning from his official posts at Engakuji and Kenchōji, he clearly stated his intent to propagate Zen in the West [350]. Writing to an associate from the battlefields of Manchuria, Sōen suggested that the purpose of his journey to America was to "save Americans" by teaching them about Buddhism [351]. With Daisetz's assistance—his fluency in English, his missionary zeal, his contacts among local Theosophists from

165

his 1903 lectures—Sōen could have begun identifying groups most likely to find Zen an appealing philosophy, individuals most capable of supporting the efforts of his followers. Such groups and individuals would not have been difficult to find in San Francisco's avant-garde religious atmosphere.

In the fall and winter of 1905, Swami Abhedananda of the Vedanta Society was instructing his fifty or so followers in Raja Yoga and the "science of breathing." The community of Christian Science renegades at the Home of Truth also continued to sit in meditation, having been introduced to the practice when the famous Hindu, Swami Vivekananda, had resided with them several years earlier. A few years earlier Stanford University received Anagarika Dharmapala, whom Sōen knew from both the Parliament of Religions and his years in Ceylon, as a guest lecturer on Buddhism [352]. The University of California, Berkeley, had a Chinese department interested in Mahayana Buddhism. The Second Unitarian Church also fostered an active interest in the religion, giving an overview of the Buddhist Tripitaka as part of a "Bibles of the World" sermon series. And the Theosophical Society remained as fascinated with Buddhism as ever. A variety of classes at the time detailed the concepts of *dharma*, karma, and reincarnation, as well as introduced members to the life of Siddhârtha, the historical Buddha. In these assemblies Sōen would have found appreciative audiences, interested in everything from a general overview of the little-known Zen sect to instruction in the mechanics of meditation. Daisetz, who had addressed the Theosophical Society not long before, could have helped arrange for a lecture series. Ida, for her part, might have opened doors for him at Stanford University. She was a friend of its president, David Starr Jordan, whose liberal religious leanings were well known [353]. There was also the Japanese consul, who could have arranged for public addresses throughout the city. As Sōen traveled east, this is precisely what his diplomatic counterparts in Washington D.C. were doing. For reasons of his own, however, Sōen did not take up these most promising of podiums. Nor did he seek out other forums from which he might pique San Franciscans' interest in Zen.

Instead, Sōen largely restricted his public addresses in California to Buddhist Mission audiences, besides occasionally lecturing privately to small groups at the Japanese consulate. At these events he tended to present a Buddhism that was not particular to any one sect, but one with which all Buddhists could identify. Only with the inhabitants of the Russell mansion did Sōen discuss Zen doctrines and religious practices in more or less detail. When his talks to Ida's community became fewer and farther between, Sōen seemed to while away days at a time when he could have been developing the organizational framework that would be needed for the spread of Zen in America. Yet, during lulls between lectures, Sōen seemed to feel no pressure to make contact with others in California who might help establish Zen. Shaku Sōen—in his letters, reminiscences, and diary entries— never fully explains his relaxed attitude toward laying the foundations of Zen in what would later be described as his second missionary journey to America. This leaves us to guess at his motive, or rather his apparent lack of motivation.

First, during his stay in America Sōen did not think of himself so much as a missionary, but rather as someone both retired and on vacation. When he arrived in California, he identified himself to immigration officials as a tourist [354]. And when addressing the large audience in Los Angeles he explained his presence in America as a social call, a vacation during which he hoped to renew his friendship with his "old American sympathizers" and at the same time regain his health which had been broken during the war [355]. "I am not here on a proselytizing visit, but have been ordered here for a brief stay to benefit by the climate. My health has been much affected by the rigors of the northern atmosphere" [356]. This was further borne out in his visit to Chicago. In a week and a half filled with philosophical conversations with Paul Carus and his elderly, but highly astute father-in-law, Edward C. Hegeler, Sōen made time to not only visit the city's main tourist attractions and the remnants of the Columbian Exposition buildings, he also scheduled tours of the Carus in-laws' zinc factory, a local cannery, and the First National Bank [357]. As a retiree (*kanjin*) [358] and rubberneck tourist only temporarily in America, Sōen does not seem to have considered it his role to begin formally organizing an American Zen establishment.

Sōen was also keenly aware that whoever popularized Zen in America would need to be fluent in English. For the better part of nine months he tried to rejuvenate his long dormant English skills, attending the daily lessons of the dedicated Miss Russell. However, he recognized that he had made limited progress in mastering the language. The fact that only his abbreviated January 1 address was in English is evidence that he was simply not comfortable communicating his thoughts on religious practice in the language. Both he and Daisetz knew he needed at least two or three years in America to improve his language skills to the degree necessary to effectively communicate his ideas in English, and five or six years to be proficient enough to deliver a speech [359]. This linguistic handicap was most likely another factor in his decision not to try personally to popularize Zen beyond the walls of the Russell mansion.

Sōen might also have considered his work lecturing at the Buddhist Mission as indirectly benefiting the spread of Zen in America. Through his association with the Pure Land sect Sōen was able to come into contact with hundreds, perhaps thousands of people in America seeking spiritual counsel of one sort or another. This included not only the laborers and agricultural workers who attended his Buddhist Mission lectures *en masse* but also the more educated, more moneyed members of the Japanese immigrant community. While in San Francisco he traveled east to Oakland to meet the wealthiest Japanese man in California, then north to Santa Rosa to cultivate the friendship of Nagasawa

Kanaye, a prosperous agriculturalist whose vineyards were inherited from the curious religious commune to which he once belonged [360]. Sōen may have viewed his duty as one of reconnaissance, determining whether or not conditions were right for the establishment of a permanent Zen presence in America. Once he had decided that the time was ripe, he may have considered his portion of the work complete. It would be the responsibility of others—primarily Uemura Sōkō—to establish a center for Zen in America and attract membership to it. In short, Sōen did not see it as his role to be an evangelist on the streets of America. That would be the work of others who followed him. It was his job to assess the situation and direct ongoing efforts.

Sōen may also have wanted to avoid personally offending the priests of the Buddhist Mission. The friendship of the Pure Land sect representatives had been a constant comfort during his stay in California, their network of temples a way to reach audiences vaster than he could ever have attracted on his own. This continued even after his departure from the West Coast. A few days after Sōen's arrival in Illinois Hori Kentoku arrived from Boston. Shortly after Sōen's arrival in California, Hori had enrolled at Harvard where he was now a divinity student. Hori escorted Sōen to New York where he arranged speaking engagements at the Theosophical Society and Vedanta Society. After the Buddhist Mission's hard work in arranging his public speeches, Sōen may have considered it bad form to begin setting up his own shop, so to speak, competing in however friendly a manner with the Pure Land priests' own religious organization.

Finally, Sōen may have anticipated Ida Russell playing an active role in spreading his sect in the United States, considering it more effective to spiritually nourish one clearly capable woman than a multitude of ham-handed American disciples who may or may not retain their interest in Zen over time. He communicated this very sentiment to the inhabitants of the Russell mansion in one of his lectures on the *Sūtra in Forty-Two Chapters*: "The Buddha said: 'It is better to feed one good man than to feed one hundred bad men. It is better to feed one who observes the five precepts than to feed one thousand good men'" [361]. If this was Sōen's strategy, it would have been his priority in San Francisco to continue Ida's instruction in Zen. When he left, Sōen would then leave it to others—perhaps assisted by Ida and her friends—to carry the banner forward.

PART 2

When Sōen, Daisetz, and Reverend Hori left LaSalle they continued by rail to Niagara Falls, "where we were met by a miserable cold rainfall" [362]. They detrained for twelve hours, enough time to take in both the American and Canadian perspectives of the cataract, snap a few photos of themselves, and provide Sōen with the inspiration to compose a poem:

> Crushing the rocks, scattering the fragments,
> Cold fog shuts off the sky.
> From the top of the Thirty-third Heaven
> Water pours down washing away human delusions.

[363]

The trio continued south to New York City. They remained only three days—touring Central Park, the Brooklyn Bridge, Grant's Tomb, and Columbia University—before continuing on to Washington D.C. Though Daisetz informed Carus, "We have not yet any definite programme to follow while there" [364], the statement was not entirely accurate. The Japanese Legation had been alerted to Sōen's impending visit several weeks earlier, probably by the consulate in San Francisco. The office promised to do everything in its power to make the priest's visit worthwhile, a vow they fulfilled admirably. While still in LaSalle, Sōen received a letter from the Legation telling him that the National Geographic Society was prepared to convene a special session to hear him speak.

When Sōen, Daisetz, and Hori arrived in Washington, the Zen master was not feeling at all well. The same waters that washed away delusions at Niagara left him with a lingering cold. The condition worsened when he discovered that the bags of medicine, which he took with him everywhere, had ripped shortly after this arrival in the capital. The various pills mixed freely with each other, leaving Sōen to guess at their identities. As a result, "he took the wrong medicine which loosed [sic] his bowels too freely and he did not discover the error until [after] he took a second dose," Daisetz candidly related to Carus. "He is still weak but will try to deliver a lecture at George Washington University this afternoon" [365]. Despite his infirmity, Sōen addressed every audience that expressed an interest in Buddhism. The day after he arrived in the capital, Sōen spoke on "The Fundamental Principles of Buddhism" to a hastily convened midweek audience of National Geographic Society members [366]. Despite its unusual timing, Sōen's lecture attracted five hundred people.

That same day the Legation had some remarkable news. It had succeeded in scheduling a meeting between him and President Theodore Roosevelt.

Considering that Sōen and Daisetz were without "any definite programme" when they arrived, an interview with the president was a coup de maître on the part of the Japanese Legation. It is not entirely surprising that Roosevelt should have agreed to meet with the Asian itinerant. On a political level, Japan's victory over Russia marked its debut as a world power, so receiving visiting dignitaries from the country was a matter of course. Moreover, tensions were presently high between Tokyo and Washington. Japan remained not only affronted by the peace treaty that Roosevelt helped broker, with its lack of reparations, but they also opposed the San Francisco School Board's decision to segregate

Japanese children from public schools. Roosevelt himself had been trying to resolve the latter of these issues, to the point of sending militia into California to forcibly reintegrate the schools. However, his efforts had not yet met with much success. The president may have reasoned that meeting with one of Japan's better known religious leaders might help smooth some of these wrinkles in international relations. On a more personal level, the cosmopolitan president had long fostered an interest in Japanese culture, particularly in its more martial manifestations. He took an active interest in judo, having first encountered it at a public demonstration that left him with a dislocated shoulder. When the president recovered he arranged for a Japanese jiu-jitsu master to give him and his sons private instruction in the White House [367].

The day after addressing the National Geographic Society, Sōen was at the White House. Daisetz and Hori also attended, as did a functionary from the Legation who acted as chargé d'affaires. Also present was Dr. William Sturgis Bigelow, the head of the Department of Chinese and Japanese Art at the Boston Museum of Fine Arts and a close personal friend of the president. He was also an acquaintance of Sōen's, the two having met at Nomura Yōzō's home years earlier [368]. While overseas the doctor became an authority on Japanese art. He also practiced Shingon and Tendai Buddhism for seven years, formally converting before his return to the United States [369]. Roosevelt complimented the former army chaplain on Japan's martial spirit, saying it must derive from the samurai. Sōen agreed and noted that the samurai spirit was unique to Japan. Turning to Bigelow, the president asked whether the samurai spirit derived from Buddhism. Before the scholar could respond, Sōen explained that it in fact stemmed from the fusion of Buddhism, Daoism, and Confucianism that is peculiar to Japanese spirituality. Bigelow had previously presented Roosevelt with a synopsis of Japanese Buddhism. "However, I have the impression that Buddhist countries have not fully helped women develop their intellectual abilities," he said to Sōen. "What are your thoughts on this?"

"Although Buddhism may appear to traditionally disregard women," Sōen responded, "in fact it merely acknowledges that women's physical strength is dissimilar to that of men." Sōen was also quick to note that the Japanese government was presently attending to the issue and actively promoting the education of women. "However, viewing women as less important than men is a common tendency in Asian culture. I acknowledge your criticism and deeply apologize."

Sensing that he had created an awkward moment, Roosevelt said that every country has its positive and negative characteristics. In the United States, for example, the economic difference between the upper and lower classes is very great, which sometimes causes a disruption in the peace. "That your country does not have this problem is quite impressive." Sōen said he did not entirely agree that there were no class tensions in Japan, but that problems resulting from it were in fact rare.

Changing subjects, Roosevelt declared it was his firm belief that world peace would eventually be realized. "It is indeed inevitable," Sōen agreed, speculating that scientific knowledge and religion seemed equally able to bring this about. The president beamed. "Religion and science are both ladders toward world peace, aren't they?" he asked rhetorically. A few concluding remarks wrapped up the brief meeting. According to Roosevelt's appointment book, the half-hour time slot was also reserved for the reception of two congressmen, one senator, and a delegation of four hundred school teachers from Pennsylvania and Massachusetts [370].

While on the East Coast, Sōen encountered numerous individuals with not only a general interest in Buddhism but also an inquisitiveness about Zen in particular. Among these was Anna Hanes of Brooklyn, with whom Sōen had been corresponding since before he left San Francisco. A pious Theosophist, she had heard about the acclaimed Zen master, probably from Amakuki

Sessan, a Zen friend of Sōen's who hosted his stay in New York. Her nearly seventy years dulled neither her curiosity nor sense of adventure. After hearing Sōen speak, Miss Hanes told him that she craved to move to Japan and, like Ida Russell, take up residency at Engakuji. Later, after Sōen had returned to Kamakura, Miss Hanes sold her house and purchased a cross-continental train ticket to San Francisco. Just before boarding the steamer for Japan, however, she fell ill and was not allowed to depart. Returning East, she corresponded with Sōen for the rest of her life [371].

Another American keenly interested in Zen was Beatrice Erskine Lane. She read Sir Edwin Arnold's *Light of Asia* at an early age and translations of Buddhist sūtras while attending Radcliffe College, where she studied Sociology and Philosophy. Like Ida Russell and Elise Drexler, Beatrice Lane's interest in Asian religion freely mingled with an active concern for social issues. She inherited this trait from her mother, a socialist, suffragist, opponent of child labor, and animal rights activist [372]. Beatrice was in the audience when Sōen presented a synopsis of Mahayana Buddhism at a Vedanta Society commemoration of the historical Buddha's birth [373]. Deeply impressed by Sōen's exposition, Beatrice asked to study Zen under him. This was impossible since Sōen would shortly leave America, so he recommended that Daisetz instruct her.

Sōen briefly visited Boston for a meeting with the chancellor of Harvard University. Returning to New York, he remained until the end of April when he boarded the German steamer *Kaiser Wilhelm II*, which would carry him on the next step of his trek around the world. As he departed he ruminated on Beatrice Lane and Anna Hanes, Ida Russell and her largely female community on the other side of the continent, weaving them into his poetry.

> At the Eastern end of America
> Strange women in a strange land
> Also attained the fruits of meditation.

Facing the setting sun at the seaside
My wish flies on to England and France.

[374]

PART 3

As Sōen steamed east Daisetz returned west. It was not a
journey he particularly looked forward to. When he arrived in San
Francisco nine months earlier he had anticipated staying for more
than a year, perhaps longer if Sōen so desired. He entertained
hopes of accompanying his master to Europe and perhaps back
home to Japan [375]. Generally speaking, he was frustrated with
his life at LaSalle. Part of the problem was that Daisetz had lost
much of his erstwhile respect for his employer. Suzuki, whom
Sōen once described as "greatly inspired by [Carus'] sound faith,"
had modified his opinion of the German-born publisher. Though
he respected Carus as a scholar and an intellectual, he did not
evaluate his character very highly [376]. He also criticized his
employer as possessing a superficial understanding of Buddhism,
influenced too heavily by scholarship of the Theravada traditions
prevalent in the day [377]. Suzuki was careful to conceal his feelings
while in LaSalle, and there is little indication that Carus was aware
of his employee's low estimation of him.

Even if Carus' comprehension of Buddhism was not to
Daisetz's satisfaction, the publisher was sympathetic to the
religion and could easily play a role in its propagation in America.
In a letter to Sōen, Daisetz likened Carus and other Buddhist
sympathizers in America to the wire running between a plunger
and a load of dynamite. People like Carus would not directly cause
Buddhism to explode into the Western world, but the blast would
not be possible without them [378].

Daisetz plodded away at Open Court, in part because he had
no better prospects in Japan but also because he hoped his

association with Carus' high-brow publication would eventually springboard him into American academia. At one point, shortly after the turn of the century, he was optimistic that the University of Chicago would hire him to teach Chinese literature on either a temporary or permanent basis. Daisetz spent weeks in the city, taking leave from his responsibilities at Open Court, waiting for confirmation of his appointment. The post, however, never materialized [379]. Over the ensuing years, Daisetz canvassed East Coast universities for a lectureship, bringing with him letters of introduction and recommendation from Carus. Columbia, which had organized a Chinese Studies program, planned to open a course in Buddhism. Daisetz seems to have been the primary candidate for the position of lecturer, but for some reason the job fell through [380]. Despite Open Court's rich network of academic contributors, Daisetz apparently had no one with weight enough to pull the appropriate strings for him.

For the past year or so, Daisetz had been half-heartedly contemplating a career in the diplomatic service. At 35 years old he was a little old to be taking the requisite examinations and, besides, it was not a vocation to which he felt particularly called. He had no particular ambition toward becoming an ambassador. Instead he would settle for a clerk's position, so long as it would pay well and afford him enough free time for scholarly pursuits centered around his study of Buddhism. Friends in Japan opposed his line of thought. Daisetz was of too scholarly a bent, they argued, to pass his days copying documents in some far-off consulate [381]. The situation left him frustrated and demoralized. "Farmers, craftsmen, and businessmen—only these kinds of [Japanese] people can establish themselves here," he wrote in a letter meant to dissuade a friend in Japan from coming to America to look for work. "To get a position teaching Oriental Studies in America is very difficult because only famous people can be paid" [382].

At some point in their travels along the Atlantic coast Sōen decided Daisetz would return to his labors at Open Court Publishing rather than accompany him to Europe. "I shall go back to LaSalle day after tomorrow [*sic*] and settle there in my old way," he wrote to a friend in late April. "I do not know yet how long I am going to stay there this time but will have to live there at least one more year as I have to finish my book and also to see the way of making Rōshi's lectures public if possible in this country; after that I shall be at liberty to stay or leave as I wish" [383]. When he returned to Illinois it was with a sheaf of notes written in shorthand, outlines of Sōen's many lectures. He also brought with him a framed reproduction of Theodore Wores' "Light of Asia," a memento of the Russell mansion that he would hang above his desk [384].

PART 4

Ida Russell was awake before dawn on the morning of April 18, it being her habit to rise early and meditate before beginning the day. She had not yet dressed and was in her bedroom on the mansion's second floor. At precisely 5:12, she was shaken violently from her contemplation.

The Great Earthquake devastated San Francisco. Lasting no more than forty seconds, it claimed hundreds of lives, a figure that would multiply by orders of magnitude in the chaos to follow. Thousands were injured in homes that crumbled around them. Broken gas lines, coupled by damaged electric wiring and toppled wood-burning stoves, fueled a fire that ravaged the downtown's most populous districts. Cracked water mains left the city's fire department, renowned for its efficiency, impotent before the inferno. Flames consumed more than 28,000 buildings on 500 city blocks. More than 3,000 lives were lost, while a quarter of a million people—more than half of the city's population—were rendered homeless. When the flames finally subsided and the ashes cooled,

San Franciscans found much of their city reduced to a charred wasteland. In a district once so crowded and clamorous that it drove Ida to her remote retreat, a person could now walk three miles without encountering a single standing structure. Contributing to the death and destruction were federal troops, brought into the city by Brigadier General Frederick Funston. They were under orders to shoot any civilian even suspected of looting or causing civil unrest. Mayor Eugene Schmitz, who in ensuing years would become one of Alexander Russell's political allies, approved this unconstitutional use of force in a written proclamation. In the first day of martial law, a dozen San Franciscans were executed without trial. Scores more would follow in the ensuing days.

Little remained of the San Francisco Shaku Sōen had known only three weeks before. The Victorian edifice that housed the Buddhist Mission was now mere rubble and ash. The Japanese consulate, the consul's mansion, and George Claxton's art gallery were likewise consumed in the holocaust. The Drexler mansion, which Elise had rented out since residing with the Russells, was dynamited to create a firebreak to prevent the flames from spreading west of Van Ness Avenue.

Because of its distance from the quake's epicenter, the House of Silent Light fared better than much of the rest of the city. Vibrations set the grandfather clock in the hall spinning around on its base. Baldwin's bed, with the child still in it, careered across his room. The house received a bit of structural damage, but its inhabitants were unscathed. Ida wrote Theodore Wores to reassure the artist of the safety of his favorite painting. The letter, one of the few surviving productions of Ida's pen, is worth reproducing in its entirety. It not only provides a firsthand glimpse into her household at the time of the quake, but also displays how she harmonized diverse religious traditions. Additionally, Ida indicates that "Light of Asia," which she had purchased from Wores only a month before the quake, was no simple object of art, sterilely displayed in a museum-like atmosphere. It was for her a source of inspiration.

> 2526 Ocean Boulevard, San Francisco

My dear Mr. Wores:—

I feel it is not intruding my personal affairs upon you if I attempt to let you know how the occurrences of the past few weeks have affected the home of which your divine offspring is a part; for I think it is because you are awakening to an eternal verity that your picture has been given to the West, and because I am awakening to that verity it is in my hands; not because "Mrs. Alexander Russell paid Theodore Wores $5,000 for the 'Light of Asia',"—but because Truth has found Truth. Therefore it is, that I report the preservation and safety of the picture.

In the turmoil of things thrown down and scattered about the house—many pictures being hurled to the floor—it retained its place on the wall, continuing to tell man to seek the peace that passeth understanding; the habitation not made by hands; the gold tried in the furnace; the pearl without price; the imperishable riches; the safety in self-sacrifice; the acquisition in giving;—the stillness in turmoil: just as the spirit of San Francisco was learning to know itself superior to earthquake and fire, knowing in its eternal essence it could not be shaken or destroyed; though things perished, form disappeared,—mind endured.

How interesting it is,—in our partial knowledge we say strange,—the repetition of life: the Dai-butsu was placed at Kamakura near the sea, the Eastern Pacific. The greatest earthquake Japan ever knew, accompanied by a tidal wave which occurred just about the time of the discovery of America, carried away its roof,—the temple in which it stood; it remained, continuing to teach man, and it taught you, my friend,—taught me. Its reproduction,—its great reproduction,—is placed in a home on the shores of the Western Pacific, and has also passed through the greatest disaster of the century. Interesting! … Is there more to follow?

May I tell you of that morning?

I was awake sometime before the shock,—it being my habit for years to spend the sunrise hours in meditation. I had not yet arisen. There was, as you know, no warning; the upheaval was upon us. After the shock Mr. Russell and I hurried from our room to ascertain the condition of others. All were well, no one so much as having sustained a scratch; but the rooms were in disorder and confusion, many things broken, plaster down in many places,—but I will not enter into a detailed account of all this.

By this time the morning bell rang out, it being our custom to have an early morning service. We all assembled in the hall as usual, and after a time of silent re-collection, our morning prayer was chanted:

"O God, have mercy upon us, and incline our hearts to keep Thy law. O God, have mercy upon us, and write Thy law in our hearts, we beseech Thee. Amen."

At that moment I was glad I had lived apart from the diverting, worldly life of a great city; that I had outgrown some of its necessities; that its amusements, entertainments, diversions, pleasures, I had not given up, but out-grown; they had become distasteful to me. I was glad that I had established a home where an honest effort is being made to heed the admonition of all Buddhas, of all Christs, of all Enlightened Ones, Inspired Teachers, to "abstain from all evils; promote all goodness; purify, cleanse the mind, the heart, the will."

"All earth is transient, changing, changeable: it is its nature. Virtue, Truth alone is enduring. Live for this."

So said the "Light of Asia."

I was glad I had found, that in order to follow out these admonitions, it would be necessary to establish times for meditation, for re-collection,—for prayer.

The reward that each one gained that morning was the strength and the courage and the fortitude to face—they knew not what; but all the horrors that an aroused imagination could suggest might be theirs before night; because, as you know, the shocks were continuous.

The Buddha, the Christ were justified: personal experience had proven, alas! they spoke truly. Trusting I may be assured that all is well with you, with gratitude,

Faithfully,

Ida Evelyn Russell

May tenth, Nineteen hundred and six

[385]

The quake did not treat Theodore Wores as leniently as it did the Russells. The artist was again in Los Angeles, completing the portrait work interrupted by Ida's sudden interest in his work. But the Phelan Building, where he had his studio, was reduced to rubble, and the vast majority of his paintings were destroyed with it [386]. Though Wores probably never again saw his masterpiece after having sold it to Ida, her religious interests were its only salvation.

In the aftermath of the earthquake the Russell estate became a refuge for neighbours who suddenly found themselves in dire straits. Though they were miles from the smoldering remains of downtown, many houses in the Sunset District were damaged to the point of being unsafe to live in. Moreover, broken mains left many in the western neighbourhoods without water. Ida's estate, with its well and windmill-powered pump, faced no such handicap. At the Russells' invitation, about thirty people pitched tents in the sand dunes around the mansion. The campers remained for weeks, drawing water from the well and bathing in the ocean, until water service was restored to the district [387]. Ida's sympathy for disaster victims extended beyond those in her immediate neighbourhood. Shortly after the quake, she publicly advocated low-cost housing for those displaced by the disaster [388].

Among thousands of people suddenly impoverished was a young woman who found herself unable to provide for her infant boy. The Society for the Prevention of Cruelty to Children would regularly take in children whose parents were unable or unfit to care for them. In many cases these children were placed in foster homes which ranged from those of working-class families to families quite high up the social ladder. In this case, the sixteen-month-old boy, rechristened Phillip Alexander, was placed in the permanent care of the Russells.

10

FORGETTING BOTH

1906-1910

PART 1

S ŌEN spent nearly two months in Great Britain as the
personal guest of Count Mutsu. Sightseeing and
personal appointments dominated his schedule. It seems that
without the Buddhist Mission network and Daisetz Suzuki as
translator, public lectures were by and large out of the question.
Dinners with Japanese ambassadors, consuls, and other dignitaries
punctuated days spent exploring Westminster Abbey, Kensington
Palace, the House of Commons, Oxford University, Edinburgh
Museum, and the ruins of various castles. At a brief visit to
Manchester University, Sōen met with Professor Thomas Rhys
Davids, famous for his academic work on Buddhist history and
literature.

His tour of the continent was whirlwind. France was home for
five days, Germany four, Austria two, and Italy four, before he
boarded a steamer en route to Asia via the Suez Canal. Arriving in
Ceylon in late July, Sōen was distressed to find the village where
he had resided as a young monk in the 1880s now too dangerous
to live in. After visiting his old Sinhalese teachers and hosts, Sōen
embarked on a pilgrimage to Bodhgayā, revered as the place of the
Buddha's enlightenment in India. He had wanted to visit the site
since he had first heard of it, thirty years earlier. Financial
problems prevented him from traveling there when he lived in
Ceylon as a young monk. He now had enough reserves to hire a
cart to take him there. It was pulled by a sickly horse, which the

driver whipped viciously. Feeling this was not in the spirit of Buddhist compassion that inspired his pilgrimage, Sōen paid the man to end the maltreatment. When he finally arrived at the site Sōen was ecstatic. Praying at the site, he made a vow "to save all my fellow beings, with a firm faith which shall never flinch" [389]. After a fifteen-month absence from Japan, Sōen reached Yokohama in the middle of September. Nomura Yōzō, accompanied by a throng of about thirty other followers, hired a private barge to bring the wandering monk ashore.

As Sōen was making his way to his old home in Kamakura, Shaku Sōkatsu had just arrived at his new one in California. When the death of Uemura Sōkō disrupted Sōen's immediate missionary plans, Sōkatsu volunteered to take his place. He was not just a priest, but a qualified Zen master and therefore fully qualified to instruct others. Like Sōkō, Sōkatsu was a favorite of Sōen's, so much so that at one point the Zen master legally adopted him as a son. Perhaps it was Sōkatsu's experience teaching the laity for the previous five years in the Forgetting Both Society that singled him out in Sōen's mind as the appropriate person to attempt establishing Zen in America. After all laity would comprise virtually all of the students in America. Sōkatsu was also disinclined to live in a monastery or take charge of a traditional temple, a trait that may also have flagged him for the assignment.

When Sōkatsu disembarked in Seattle in September he had with him an attendant monk, ten of his lay students, $5,000 in cash, and a plan. He would establish a branch of the Forgetting Both Society in America to complement the one that remained in Tokyo. He would then spend alternate years instructing each of the groups, in the process welcoming Americans who might want to participate [390]. The colony consisted mainly of university students, aged 15 to 24. There was also a professional school teacher and Sasaki Yeita, the sculptor whose comic monologue had so amused Shaku Sōen a few years before [391].

They told customs officials they intended to proceed to San Francisco, but perhaps viewing the ruined city, the little band of colonists proceeded to Berkeley. They would not remain on campus long. Gotō Zuigan, a philosophy student and Sōkatsu's attendant monk, discovered a newspaper advertisement for a farm being sold in nearby Hayward. Perhaps thinking of his temple among the rice paddies back home, Sōkatsu decided to purchase the ten-acre parcel [392]. It was his hope to build a self-sustaining community, which he alternately called Tomato Ranch and New Village. On clear days the colonists would work the land, on rainy days they would study Zen. Sundays they planned to cross the bay and propagate Zen among San Franciscans [393].

The bucolic idyll was soon to be disrupted. Zuigan's degree in Philosophy from the Imperial University may have put him in good stead in his priestly vocation. It was of little use in his new agricultural endeavor, however. Arriving at their property, the self-styled farmers—none of whom had any agricultural experience whatsoever—may not have immediately detected that previous owners had completely overworked the land. They proceeded to prepare the soil. "On clear days we worked hard in the fields cultivating strawberries. On rainy days we meditated," Yeita later recalled. "Our neighbours made fun of us" [394]. Months of work resulted only in a sickly crop destined to be thrown to the swine.

Sasaki Yeita suggested that they abandon the bootless enterprise. Sōkatsu would not hear of it. An argument ensued and Yeita found himself banished from New Village. Japanese neighbours suggested that the greenhorns fertilize the land and hire experienced farmers to work it. This, in addition to the unstable value of crops, did little more than eat into Sōkatsu's savings. The inexperienced farmers eventually recognized their agricultural venture as the debacle that it was. The community was forced to abandon Tomato Ranch and relocate to San Francisco. By this time two years had presumably passed since Sōkatsu's arrival in California since there were two harvests, the one that went to the pigs and another aided by paid laborers. Sōkatsu taught Zen at his downtown studio, sometimes renting a hall to address larger groups. This *dōjō* seems to have changed locations during Sōkatsu's stay in America, since it is variously recalled as having been on Post Street, Geary Street, and Sutter Street. Initially ten Japanese immigrants attended Sōkatsu's lectures [395]. At least it was a start.

PART 2

Sōen was eager to see Sōkatsu's mission in America succeed. Upon returning to Engakuji he continued to study English. At first Nomura Yōzō took time away from managing his various business concerns to tutor the priest he had accompanied to Chicago fifteen years earlier. Before long the Zen master was reading books in English for the first time. Later a Miss Shiller became Engakuji's first resident English tutor. She was a native of New York, one of the "strange women in a strange land [who] also attained the fruits of meditation" when Sōen had visited the city. She asked permission to continue her study of Zen at Engakuji and remained for three years. She intended to travel to Britain with the goal of propagating Zen Buddhism there. But, like so many of Sōen's expectations to see his Western students help spread Zen abroad, this was not to be. Shortly after leaving Engakuji, Miss Shiller died in Burma while en route to Europe [396].

By still attempting to master English, Sōen was preparing for the day when he might continue his work in America. Perhaps he anticipated speaking to the students he hoped Sōkatsu would attract to his *zendō*. "I will go to America a third time to convey Buddhism," he announced in 1907 [397]. And a year later: "I would like to go to America again if I have a good opportunity. I would like to propagate the teachings of Buddhism" [398].

However, on his return to Japan Sōen had many other matters to attend to. Uemura Sōkō, though still not officially listed among the war dead, was presumed lost. Formal funeral rites were conducted and a memorial—a large stone pagoda—was erected in Sōen's private garden at Tōkeiji. Sōen's skills expounding Buddhism to audiences of lay people, honed in his many addresses at the Russell mansion and the Pure Land sect's American missions, were in particularly high demand. A number of businessmen, politicians, and journalists in Tokyo requested that he address them on a regular basis. Sōen called this gathering the Blue Cliff Society, after one of the most essential pieces of Zen literature, the *Blue Cliff Records*, which they used as a text. Meeting three times a month and open to people of all walks of life, several hundred people attended the meetings [399].

Requests for Sōen's oratory were not restricted to Kamakura and Tokyo. In the spring of 1907 he embarked on a lecture circuit that would take him north to Echigo, south to Fukuoka, and back north to Hakodate. He would maintain an aggressive lecture schedule year after year, even after he developed chronic pharyngitis which would afflict him the rest of his life. Speaking at public schools and town halls, always to audiences of laity, the itinerant orator impressed upon them his belief that religion should permeate education, ethical conduct be infused into business endeavors [400].

While in Aomori he made it a point to stop by one of Nyogen's Mentorgartens which were apparently struggling along despite an unstable income, much like their absent headmaster. It seems Senzaki's lessons were not always as subtle as he recalled when he said he avoided talking to the children about religion, only "helping them to learn about nature." At least one student was inspired enough by the priest's talks on Zen that he sought out Sōen and requested to join him in Kamakura. The young man's father did not approve of a religious vocation. Sōen paid the family a personal visit and when the persuasive bonze left Aomori he had a new disciple. Given the religious name Zenchū, this erstwhile

Senzaki kindergartener would ultimately succeed Sōen as abbot of Tōkeiji [401].

Sōkatsu returned to Japan in 1908, either at the bidding of Shaku Sōen or the Forgetting Both Society members who had not accompanied him to America. He may have intended an extended stay since his initial plans were to reside in Japan on alternate years. However, he remained only six months. In a poem, Sōen informed his adopted son what was expected of him:

> Throughout the many roads,
>   north, south, east, and west,
> All people seek the wind of truth;
> Though America is far from this place,
> It is my earnest desire that compassion be sent
>   to ease the suffering there.
> [402]

PART 3

Shaku Sōkatsu and his followers would remain in San Francisco for another year and a half. There are few detailed or reliable records of their experiences. It is clear that he toiled hard to establish a permanent Zen presence in America, adapting his religious practices to accommodate the very different society in which he found himself. When Sōkatsu arrived he had the traditional shaved head of a Buddhist priest. This was replaced by a neatly cropped head of hair. Traditional silk robes were replaced with a smart black cassock. When vegetarian fare was not available he was willing to dig into a plate of corned beef. The tactics paid off, at least for a while. At one point about fifty people attended his classes. These included not only Japanese immigrants but also a handful of Caucasians [403]. Most of the latter, however, were apparently missionary ladies whose evangelical zeal was trained on Japan [404]. By 1910 Sōkatsu was clearly frustrated with his evangelical efforts. He returned to Japan permanently a year and a half later, taking most of his followers with him and proclaiming that America was not yet prepared to receive Zen [405].

Precisely what led to his decision is uncertain. Language was certainly an issue. Despite having studied English in his youth, Sōkatsu was in no way fluent. None of the students assisting him with his Zen seems to have been very proficient in the language either. Of the entire group, only Gotō Zuigan had a command of English sufficient enough to communicate Sōkatsu's ideas to prospective American sympathizers. It was the same problem that plagued Shaku Sōen, the inability to directly communicate his thoughts to those interested in hearing them [406]. Also, students, teachers, philosophers, and artists were not the best choices for the establishment of a self-sustaining community. Things might have turned out differently had Sōkatsu brought with him tradesmen, merchants, businessmen, and others with practical skills that could be utilized to support the colony. Instead, when Tomato Ranch failed, his followers did what came natural to serious young scholars. They enrolled in the nearest university and began attending classes. They may have increased their knowledge, but what they needed was a way to pay the bills.

Sōkatsu clearly needed help, but he seems to have had little of it. Senzaki Nyogen lived in or near San Francisco throughout Sōkatsu's years there. He might be found sitting in meditation, legs crossed, on a dew dampened lawn in Golden Gate Park. He also haunted the public library's reading room, scouring the collections for works on Buddhism, dedicating hours at a time to their study and translation. In Oakland Nyogen taught English to Japanese immigrants and Japanese to Americans. He continued to work as a houseboy when he could find employment. Increasing anti-Japanese sentiment in San Francisco, however, required him to retreat to the countryside and work the fields for at least part of 1908, returning to San Francisco as soon as possible and practical [407]. Despite his dual ordinations as a Shingon and Sōtō Zen priest, Nyogen held no official rank within the Rinzai Zen hierarchy to which Sōkatsu belonged. What is more, Sōen seems to have been uncomfortable with Nyogen's grasp of Zen, at least as he taught it, and instructed the monk not to involve himself in teaching Buddhism for a period of time. Rather than assist Sōkatsu in teaching Zen, Nyogen is remembered as attending his lectures [408].

The Buddhist Mission, which had been so helpful in arranging large audiences for Sōen to address, was also still very active in California. There is no record of their ever interacting with the Forgetting Both Society. The only direct reference to them in Zen literature at this time is a cryptic comment from Nyogen, who wrote that in 1906 "Shin-shu and Zen clash" [409]. It may have been that the Buddhist Mission was happy to capitalize on Shaku Sōen's celebrity while he was temporarily visiting the United States. But when he landed disciples to permanently establish a rival sect they were less welcoming.

Daisetz Suzuki also provided Sōkatsu with nothing in the way of support. Though he remained in LaSalle for much of Sōkatsu's stay in San Francisco, Daisetz only heard about the priest's arrival secondhand. "There is a rumor that Sōkatsu came to America, but it is only a rumor and I don't know whether or not it is true," Daisetz wrote in the fall of 1906. His letter was addressed to Sōen who was undoubtedly aware of Sōkatsu's arrival several months earlier, but failed to inform Daisetz. "I don't know where he is staying and I did not take it [the rumor] seriously until today when I received a letter from Consul Ueno saying that Sōkatsu just visited him. Why did he come to this place to begin with?" [410]. On the surface, this lack of communication between Sōen and his most trusted of lieutenants in America seems strange. Daisetz had spent the better part of a year stoutly backing his master's missionary work. He was still eager to spread Buddhism in America and, to this end, was busily translating Sōen's sermons into English. However, Daisetz and Sōkatsu had known each other for years and there had long been a rivalry between them. For a time the pair both lived at Engakuji where, as Daisetz remembered it, Sōkatsu used his position of authority to harass him. Sōkatsu was indignant at Sōen's decision to allow the penniless layman to live gratis in the monastery dormitory. Daisetz was humiliated by the treatment and seems to have never completely forgiven Sōkatsu. It is little wonder if Sōen never alerted his perplexed student of Sōkatsu's arrival or that Daisetz was loath to assist this one-time antagonist [411].

Finally, Ida Russell was an obvious potential patron for Sōkatsu's mission. Despite her conflict with Daisetz Suzuki and the limited amount of time she devoted to studying under Sōen during his stay, Ida's interest in her Japanese friends was by no means on the wane. This was evidenced by an unexpected visit to California that Nomura Michi made in April 1908. She was in San Francisco for only one day, on a round-the-globe tour with a group of fifty other Japanese travelers. A tight schedule prevented her from visiting the remote Russell estate, but a single phone call was enough to immediately bring Alexander, Ida, and Elise Drexler to the Oakland railway station where Michi was about to embark for Salt Lake City. Driving up in a limousine, they brought flowers and fruit to the friend who had introduced them to Zen six years earlier [412].

Ida is remembered as having provided some unspecified degree of support to Sōkatsu early in his stay [413]. Whatever form this support took it seems to have been limited and short-lived. The Russell household did not seem to keep close contact with Sōkatsu. Had they worked more closely together, Sōkatsu's vision of a rural Zen center might have become a reality. At the same time Sōkatsu and his followers were vainly toiling on their barren land, Elise Drexler owned thousands of fertile acres in Stockton, Colusa, Fresno, Yolo, and Tulare County. Among her holdings was an entire island reclaimed from the Sacramento-San Joaquin River delta. Its 32,000 acres were reputedly one of the best places in the state to grow asparagus [414]. Even if they did not make an actual gift of land to the struggling Zen colony, Ida and Elise could have easily put Sōkatsu in contact with the expert help he so much needed.

Part of the problem may have been rooted in Sōkatsu's own personality. He had been born into privilege, his father being a well-to-do physician of samurai rank until the Meiji government abrogated such titles. His cousin was a personal physician to the emperor. As a boy, Sōkatsu had been privately educated in Chinese, English, and mathematics. He was also trained in archery and the martial arts. Tragedy struck the precocious child when he was eleven years old and his mother lay on her deathbed. Calling her son to her side, she warned him against endeavoring to achieve success in the eyes of society. "I cannot die peacefully because I worry about you," she told him. "Become a great person so you do not disgrace our ancestors. Never make others take care of you. Be independent. I will guard you from the other world." Still clasping his hand when she expired, her final words were etched into his mind. Sōkatsu's father remarried, but also died while relatively young. The boy's stepmother, who inherited the family fortune, expelled Sōkatsu and his siblings from their own home. An uncle offered to adopt Sōkatsu into his still affluent branch of the family but Sōkatsu, remembering his mother's instructions about independence, turned him down and instead took a job as a houseboy [415]. It may have been that Sōkatsu's driving need to remain independent—the dying wish of his mother—prevented him from seeking out the help he so much needed in attempting to establish Zen in America.

11

THE HOUSE OF MYSTERY

1910

PART 1

EVEN if Sōkatsu had sought additional assistance from Ida Russell, his mission in America would probably not have fared much better than it did. Her desire to learn more about Zen led her to Japan in 1902, to become the first Western woman known to live in a Buddhist monastery, to be the first American formally instructed in Zen, to make her home the first place Zen Buddhism was taught in America.

However, Ida never viewed Buddhism with the eyes of a convert. In turning toward Zen in the early years of the twentieth century she was not turning away from any previously held religious beliefs. Since at least her years at Belmont Hall, a dozen years before Sōen instructed her household in San Francisco, Ida practiced a religion that was based on communal living, encouraged members to gather together for prayer at specified times, valued a vegetarian diet, and emphasized a Quietism that expressed itself through seated meditation not dissimilar from Zen practice. To her Zen simply reinforced and validated previously held religious practices. Buddhist meditation to her was just another means of fulfilling the Socratic decree to know oneself, something she had endeavored to accomplish through a contemplative life since at least her days in college.

Because she never considered herself a Buddhist convert Ida never possessed the convert's zeal to propagate the newfound faith. Rather, she had a set of well-formed ideas about religion—

her troika of sympathy, purity, and tranquility—that she espoused. She felt so strongly about her religious ideas that she, like Sōen and Sōkatsu, felt impelled to expound them to others. So while she may not have been hostile to Sōkatsu's preaching mission, she had one of her own that needed to be attended to.

The point that Ida Russell never solely identified herself as a Buddhist, much less a Zen Buddhist, is an important one that warrants additional comment. Her appreciation for Buddhism never negated her appreciation of Christianity or her identification of herself as a Christian. It was true that she did not belong to a formal church body or Christian denomination, but neither did many others who laid claim to a metaphysical interpretation of the Christian religion. Ida's adult life coincided with the rise of New Thought, which recognized no centralized administration or authority of religious orthodoxy. Instead, New Thought believers reveled in the diversity of their opinions, celebrated their freedom to draw inspiration from the widest possible sources. While many of the New Thought groups maintained an emphasis on Christianity, others pursued interests in Hinduism and Buddhism without considering themselves having formally left the Christian fold. To Ida's mind, Buddha, whether as a historical person or an ideal, was substantially identical to Christ.

Another reason Ida did not take a more active hand in the establishment of a permanent Zen presence in America might be attributed to the public venues Sōen and Sōkatsu needed to frequent when promoting their religion in America. There is no indication that she ever attended any of Sōen's presentations, whether at the Buddhist Mission, at the Dharma Sangha, or in the rented halls where hundreds would gather to hear him hold forth. Since her days at Belmont Hall, Ida preferred a more intimate setting, a forum of individuals whom she knew and trusted. She knew all too well from her experience in Los Angeles what could result if her ideas and religious practices were misinterpreted, her words misquoted and turned against her.

Had Ida wanted to participate more in Sōkatsu's work, she would have found that time was against her. Like the Zen priests' missions, Ida's activities at the House of Silent Light required a considerable amount of time and attention. Similar to Sōen's monks and Sōkatsu's Forgetting Both Society lay students, the people Ida Russell gathered together placed high value on her leadership. They sought her guidance to such an extent that they would exchange private life for communal living in order to maximize the amount of time they spent with her. Some stayed for a matter of weeks or months. Others remained much longer, like the Crossleys who were part of Ida's household for more than six years, leaving shortly after the Great Earthquake. Mary Crittenden, whose piano recitals Sōen enjoyed during his stay, would remain devoted to the Russell family for decades, even after Ida and Alexander passed away. Elise Drexler stayed at Ida's side for nearly 15 years. Her money allowed Ida to purchase the Oceanside House in the first place. It mostly likely also empowered her to make a number of sizable real estate transactions during this period: a lakeside retreat nestled in the northern mountains and an expansive estate in Santa Barbara that dwarfed the Oceanside House in size and elegance [416]. There was also the "experiment in practical philanthropy," the raising of children in a privileged, artistic environment that required regular direction. The amount of time Ida needed to spend managing her various projects while Sōkatsu toiled away in San Francisco would have made it impractical to take a more active hand in his endeavors.

As mentioned, Ida's approach to religion was eclectic. "I teach no isms whatever," she would say. "I have studied all the religions and have taken what seems to me to be the best from all. But I tie myself down to none" [417]. What Ida Russell took from Zen was perhaps more refined techniques in meditation than she was previously exposed to. She may also have learned the value of meditation for its own sake, rather than as a mechanism for mental healing, a means of "astral travel," or a way to master psychic powers as Spiritualists, Theosophists, and New Thought practitioners of the day tended to characterize it. It is a lesson that few others seemed to have learned, which would become painfully apparent to Ida when an uninvited visitor infiltrated the House of Silent Light.

PART 2

The *San Francisco Examiner* dispatched a small squadron of reporters to the Russell mansion in the fall of 1910 [418]. For the past few years talk about the unusual community had been increasing. The mansion's remote location combined with its ascetic residents tended to excite local imaginations. The lonely residence housed a foreign cult. A colony of religious fanatics. Hindu recluses who shunned society. Fire worshippers who prayed to the pole star and abided by some unnamed and heathen creed. They performed purification rituals in the ocean at dawn. They had abandoned society, sequestering themselves behind the imposing barricade that surrounded their property. "Mother Russell" was the cult's head priestess. Her husband was said to be superintendent of the mysterious assembly. What wild rites they conducted had become as much the subject of schoolboy banter as of barroom gossip at the Sea Breeze Café down the road from the "House of Mystery." It was a label that would remain associated with the Russell manor for the better part of a generation.

Ostensibly, the *Examiner* men were there to confirm the rumors and report the exact nature of the queer colony's beliefs. They did not bother to call ahead to schedule an interview, but instead arrived at the front gate unannounced. This was because there had apparently been a number of previous attempts "to penetrate the mystery of the place, but entrance was refused visitors to the grounds even before they could state their business. The gates were always closed. If one rang the bell a white-liveried Japanese would come from the house, descend through the garth and speak to the caller through the open-work of the high gate, telling him in impeccable English that no one was at home."

Not to be dissuaded by such tactics, the reporters found a way around this "Asiatic guardian of the outer portal," perhaps by gracelessly clambering over the high fence and into the Japanese garden. They located the doorman, compelled him to present their cards to Ida, and were ushered into an elegant, sun-drenched parlor.

Ida was at home but did not make herself immediately available to the uninvited visitors. She could not have helped remembering the outrageous intrusion of the *Los Angeles Times* reporter to Belmont Hall, now nearly twenty years in the past. Perhaps she wanted to listen in on their line of inquiry before meeting with them. Instead, "a calm-eyed, middle-aged woman"—perhaps Mary Crittenden—greeted the visitors, asking if she might convey a message. Instead one reporter, who apparently led the group, began the interview.

"This is a beautiful home you have founded for your colony," he started.

"There is no colony here," was the quick reply. "We are only a family and not a very large one at that—only nine of us in all."

"Then you spread your propaganda by means of literature?"

"We are spreading no propaganda. We are only nine of us living here under the same roof. We are seeking higher spiritual development by means of meditation and unfoldment. Mother Russell is our loving guide, and we call ourselves her disciples. Sometimes people come here for solace and consolation, but we never go into the world to preach. There is nothing for us to preach that is not known the world over. We have evolved no new ideas. We are trying principally to know ourselves—to reach a higher plane of development through constant meditation. Though we do not eschew books and learning, they, together with the interests of the outside world, are a very small part of our daily life. Absolute tranquility is essential to spiritual exaltation."

The dialog was interrupted by the sound of children playing in a distant part of the mansion. Baldwin, the toddler who used to bow solemnly before Shaku Sōen, was now about nine years old. His brother Philip was five. They had recently been joined by a sister, two-year-old Helen Hilda. She had been born in a sanitorium operated by Dr. Florence Nightingale Ward, a professor of obstetrics at Hahnemann Medical College. When the infant's mother abandoned her at the sanitorium, Dr. Ward, who would long serve as the Russell family physician, delivered her to the Russells for foster care [419]. At the mansion, governesses cared for the children on a daily basis. Rather than attending public school, they received private instruction. Tutors included Mary Crittenden, Mary Russell, and Mary Keeler, who provided lessons in English, mathematics, geography, music, and other subjects. The mansion was their playground. Basketball, hopscotch, and marbles were favorite games. They would also hold contests to see who, after a running start, could slide the furthest distance on the seat of their pants across the nursery's waxed floor. The Russell wards probably also shared in the mansion's religious instruction. They were certainly aware of, and probably took at least some part in, their foster mother's practice of meditation [420].

"We have had them all since babyhood," said the calm-eyed woman, anticipating the reporter's question. "They were adopted and brought here somewhat in the nature of an experiment. Developed under us from childhood, we hope they will be able to go much farther than we who have entered upon our development with minds already matured. Their lives at present? They are no different from that of other normally raised children. The education of the eldest is now similar to the education she [*sic*] would be receiving in the regular grammar school course."

"What position does Mr. Russell hold among you?" asked the reporter, changing topics.

"Mr. Russell is one of the disciples of his wife," came the rather startling response. At this point, Ida entered the parlor and successfully disrupted that particular line of inquiry.

"Mother Russell illuminated the room like a candle in a lantern," the reporter wrote poetically. "She is a very distinctive looking woman, and her dominant force is undeniable. She appears to radiate health and happiness and speaks of her theories and beliefs with positive conviction."

The reporter inquired about Ida's philosophy and seemed authentically disappointed to hear her describe her beliefs along the lines already set out in his previous interview.

"There is nothing new or original in what we are striving to attain or in the manner of attaining it," she explained. "It is our desire to reach a higher spiritual plane by means of meditation. A necessary condition on which our meditations are incumbent is absolute tranquility of mind. This we endeavor to obtain by living away from the rest of the world as much as possible."

"How do books and learning enter into you process of development?"

"Intellect is not essential to the development of the soul," she responded. "The greatest intellects do not as a rule reach the greatest spiritual heights. Active, nervous minds do not admit of the necessary tranquility of spirit. … In a word, we are trying to know ourselves spiritually."

At one point in the course of the interview, Ida gave the reporter a quick lesson in meditation, describing techniques that she certainly learned from Sōen. "Sit so—well forward on the spine with your hands lightly clasped in your lap, in a position of complete physical repose," she said, demonstrating. "Let the lids droop slightly until the eyes are half closed, and then center your attention for a time on some object directly within your range. Pursue this for a time until you have banished all outside thoughts, and your mind will become nearly at rest."

"To meditate on what?"

"On whatever suits your needs the most. I should advise you as a commencement, not knowing your spiritual needs, to think and meditate on the fact that there is a good and just God."

All of this must have seemed terribly mundane to the reporter. He apparently had heard of a Hindu holy man who after years of meditation claimed to have succeeded in "separating the spirit from the veil of flesh." The topic enthralled him. He wanted evidence that this local band of votaries had accomplished something similar. "Do you think it is possible to develop so that the soul is able to leave the living body and return at will, as the Hindu adepts claim is possible?"

"Most assuredly," Ida is said to have replied. "But the practices resorted to by the highly developed esoterics of India are not for this country at this time and would only result disastrously or in failure. The Hindu esoteric is backed up by generations of ancestors as highly developed as himself, and his whole life is devoted to meditation and to his own unfoldment. The nervous, fretful, untranquil people of this country will not be conditioned to reach this stage for some time to come."

The reporter was dissatisfied with the response, perhaps because he was not getting the evidence of psychic powers he hoped to uncover at what he would soon label a "confraternity of spiritual exclusives." After pursuing more neutral topics—during which Ida recommended that he simply live a simple Christ-like life—he returned to his favorite theme. "Of course you and your disciples have gone further than this," he prompted, evidently irked at Ida giving him advice that he may have once received from his Sunday school teacher. "You are able to accomplish, perhaps, a separation of the spirit from the body."

Ida must have realized the direction in which the reporter wished to take his article and that what she actually said had little bearing on his research. She would only say that she and her family had spent much time in meditation. At one point the reporter asked, "Why have you not given your teachings to the world?"

"Because the world would not receive them as I gave them," Ida is said to have responded. "They would become distorted and worse than useless. Look around you at some of the different cults and creeds preached to-day, and you can see what my teachings would become if they were given to the world." If Ida Russell needed any confirmation of her feelings on this matter, she needed to wait no longer than the publication of the *Examiner* exposé.

BUDDHA SHRINE WORSHIPED IN
HOUSE OF MYSTERY

Closely Guarded Secret of the
Famous Old Mansion on
the Ocean Beach Road
is Finally Revealed

HOME OF RELIGIOUS CULT

Mother Alexander Russell
and Colony of Devotees
Seek in Seclusion to Attain
"Perfect Serenity of the Spirit."

The article that followed this headline described the reporters' attempts to gain entry to the "strange band of votaries" and witness the "strange Hindoo rite" conducted by the "high priestess," Mother Russell. The exposé repeatedly referenced the painting that so impressed Shaku Sōen. "Theodore Wores' 'Light of Asia,' which shows the Buddha transfigured in repose over a lotus-covered pool, is in the worship room on the second floor, and this picture appears to be symbolical of what Mother Russell and her disciples are striving after—perfect serenity of the spirit."

The article dominated the front page, occupying more than half of the column space. The Hearst paper, well-known for its innovative and sometimes controversial use of illustrations, did not disappoint readers with the article. Alongside the text was a photograph of the mansion, colourfully described in the article as "of pretentious size … brown-hued, baffling, proud and impenetrable." There was also a diagram of its interior, and an illustration of several women and one man kneeling before an indistinct statuette. If there was any question as to the nature of the idol, a caption identified the Russell mansion as a "colony of Buddhist worshippers" and, to clear up any additional confusion, a line drawing of the Kamakura Daibutsu—the model for Wores' "Light of Asia"—was added to the collage.

How much of the exchange between Ida and the reporter was authentic and how much emanated from the reporter's active imagination? Many of her quotations seem to genuinely reflect her own beliefs as she described them to others. She explained her eclectic spirituality, her Theosophical tendency to glean the best teachings from different religions. She recommended meditation, equating it to Christian prayer but at the same time defining its goal—getting to know one's true self—in terms that a Buddhist could appreciate. She described life in the mansion in terms of her pursuit of tranquility, one of the three guiding religious principles that she had detailed to Shaku Sōen years earlier.

At the same time, there was a considerable amount of one-sided information—as well as outright fantasy—interwoven into the text. The reporter played up the physical isolation of the mansion and purportedly utopian existence of its inhabitants. In so doing, he chose to overlook the many ways they interacted with their fellow San Franciscans. He did not mention the temporary housing the Russells had provided to earthquake victims only four years earlier, nor did he point out Ida's campaign for low-cost housing to those rendered homeless by the disaster. He chose to present the Russells' care of children as a freakish exercise in occult training, rather than give the family credit for providing an elegant home for their wards.

In portraying the Russell community as hopelessly utopian, the *Examiner* reporter also refused to note Alexander's active involvement in civic affairs through local improvement clubs. To his wife, the Sunset District was a means of escaping the distractions of urban life and pursuing spiritual aspirations in a more placid environment. But the same capitalist spirit innate to Benjamin Brooks, who had built the Oceanside House a generation earlier, had been reincarnated in Alexander. To him the area was a promising venue for suburban development and he looked forward to the day when railroad service would be extended to the region south of Golden Gate Park. When this happened, he was certain that the sand dunes would give way to neighbourhoods of "detached houses with every modern convenience, bright sunlight, a garden, and unsurpassed view of the ocean and mountains" [421]. Alexander was also involved in business, social, and charitable causes through his membership in various Masonic institutions, the Commonwealth and Columbia clubs, Travelers' Aid of California, San Francisco Chamber of Commerce, and the Oceanside Improvement Club [422].

Instead the reporter chose to depict Ida Russell as evasive, secretive, elitist, and practicing "wild rites" for which he gave no evidence whatsoever. Outsiders portraying Alexander as one of his wife's disciples were not unprecedented. Four years earlier, in its coverage of Ida's purchase of the Wores painting, the *Examiner* described Alexander as "superintendent of the unusual colony" on the ocean beach, while Ida was depicted as "a sort of priestess" of a cult "attempting an approach to Nirvana on this earth" [423]. It would be surprising, however, if in 1910 or at any other time anyone within the mansion actually identified Alexander as "a disciple of his wife." There is nothing to indicate that he shared his wife's spiritual interests, at least to the degree she did, or that he participated in the religious activities of the mansion. Not only did he not join his wife in her monastic experience at Engakuji, he had hardly been able to remain still the one day she entreated him to attempt meditation.

The question as to why the *Examiner* chose to run the article in the first place remains an open one. There was nothing particularly newsworthy in it, certainly no revelations that warranted front-page coverage. Editors at the *San Francisco Chronicle*, the *San Francisco Call*, and the many city weeklies found no reason to pick up the story. It is possible that the *Examiner*, which by 1910 was already notorious for blurring the lines between news, entertainment, and propaganda [424], ran the article as an exercise in character assassination. Katherine Crossley, who as a child once played piano for Daisetz and with her father went boating with Sōen in Golden Gate Park, would much later speculate that Elise Drexler's relatives instigated the rumors of outlandish rituals at the House of Silent Light. Their motive, she said, was to estrange their wealthy relative from Ida and, more importantly, prevent her from dissipating her inheritance on the Russell community [425]. It is reminiscent of the *Los Angeles Times*' role in attempting to extricate Charlotte Farnsworth from Ida's influence at Belmont Hall. The *Examiner* may have been a willing participant in a very similar scheme.

The "House of Mystery" exposé may have also been printed to discredit Alexander, who the previous year ran for the San Francisco board of supervisors. Nearly twenty years had passed since his brief stint as city recorder, a term remembered as the most profitable ever. Alexander retained his interest in local politics, as well as high-placed political contacts. Both Mayor Eugene Schmitz and his crony Abe Ruef had been regular guests at the Russell mansion [426]. But by the 1909 election "Handsome Gene" and "Boss Ruef" were spent forces, the center of an ever-widening investigation into corruption at the highest levels of city government. Portrayed as "a rugged, independent republican," Alexander campaigned as a businessman who would apply commercial acumen to his political responsibilities. The *San Francisco Call*, a mouthpiece for the progressive wing of the Republican Party published editorials on their candidates—including Alexander—that amounted to little more than promotional advertisements. Despite this favorable press, Alexander failed to win his party's nomination.

Alexander was undeterred by this setback. He remained in the spotlight, in part by taking his stereopticon to public venues to deliver lectures. The magic lantern that had once entertained Shaku Sōen with images of Kamakura he now brought to the First Unitarian Church where he extolled the "industrial significance" of Holland's colonization and exploitation of the rubber-rich isle of Java [427]. By the end of 1910—the time when the *Examiner* exposé ran—Alexander was preparing for a second run for the board of supervisors. In ridiculing a Republican candidate as the stooge of his wife's unconventional religious interests, the Democrat-controlled *Examiner* may have been attempting to undermine his credibility.

If the *Examiner's* embarrassing exposé was meant to temper Alexander's political ambitions, it failed. The following year the *San Francisco Call* again promoted him as a pillar of the community, "clean, vigorous, and successful." Rather than highlight the unusual, heteroclite community in which they lived, the *Call* instead focused on the Russells' charitable concerns, making oblique references to their foster children. "Few San Franciscans have done so much in an unostentatious way in the cause of practical charity and sane philanthropy," crooned the *Call*. "For several years Russell has given most of his time to movements for the betterment of San Francisco and for clean government" [428]. Despite this support, Alexander would be frustrated once again. He failed to receive the votes of an electorate that may have still associated him with cultic practices. Tenacious to the last, Alexander in 1914 ran for—but again failed to win—a seat on the state senate [429].

Regardless of whether or not the *Examiner* was intentionally attempting to foil Alexander's political aspirations, the article was a clear slight against the characters of both Ida and Alexander. It was taken as such by a group of neighbours who objected to the Russells being portrayed as eremitic cultists. "Their home has always been open to us as visitors and we have always been welcome there," witnessed the congregation members of St. Paul's Presbyterian Church in Oceanside. "They have never failed to evidence most hearty sympathy in all our efforts for the improvement of Oceanside and in every movement for the advancement of the moral, intellectual and religious life of our community, and in the accomplishment of these ends they have always been coworkers together with us and have as well contributed generous financial support" [430].

Needless to say, Ida was also distressed by the article. She quickly composed a letter to the *Examiner* which the editors could not resist printing without again portraying her as an eccentric. Next to Ida's editorial, occupying nearly twice as much space as the text itself, is a photograph in which she appears enraptured in a wide-eyed trance.

Emblazoned over the photo was the headline: "Letter from Strange House. Story of Woman Occupant." Since the column is one of the few surviving documents in—or close to, depending how heavily it was edited—Ida's own words, it is worthwhile to present at length.

HOUSE IS OPEN,
MRS. RUSSELL DECLARES

Writes "Examiner" Denying There Is Mystery
About Her Home by the Ocean.

LIKES LIFE BY THE SEA

Paintings She Has Have No Tinge of Oriental Mysticism; Her Version.

By Mrs. Alexander Russell

When I bought my home at the ocean side it never occurred to me that I was doing anything that was conspicuous, anything that would cause unending comment. One day while I was thinking of moving from my home in town I rode by this property and noted that it was for sale. Seeing its possibilities and loving the ocean I entered into negotiations, which resulted in its purchase. Since then I have improved the place as anyone does a home of which they are fond.

And now I feel a hesitancy in making a personal statement, but as my home and the life in it have been made the subject of public concern I affirm that there is no mystery about either. Our lives are lived as normally and as peacefully as we can make them. The gates are never locked, the house is never closed except when the family has been absent from the city.

It is true that we have an indication on the gate that the grounds are private, but that is simply such a sign as is used at the entrance of any large private residence. The tall fence which has been the subject of criticism was built to keep out but one intruder, and that was the west wind, which seemed bent and determined that we should have no garden. We not only have the high fence outlining the place, but we have fences as ornamental as we can make them throughout the garden, acting as windbreaks.

With all this care we now have an interesting garden, but as soon as a tree dares to grow above the fence the salt-laden west wind burns off the young shoots. The gates are closed, but not locked, because the wind sweeps through them when they are open with such force that the gardener objects. It injures the trees as well as the flowers.

It is curious to me that the impression should have gone forth that there is difficulty in gaining access to my home. My neighbours on the beach know that this is not true. Even strangers often come here to see the Hoffman [*sic*] paintings. In this way I have had the pleasure of meeting several San Francisco and visiting clergymen.

As one of the Hoffman [*sic*] pictures, a head of Christ, which Hoffman [*sic*] called "The Resurrected Christ," is in our little chapel, these visitors have been taken there to see it. In the chapel there is also a reproduction of Guido Reni's painting of the crucifix. I mention these facts to show there is absolutely nothing in the chapel that pertains either to Hindu or Buddhist rites or ceremonies. The room is simply a Christian sanctuary and is no different from those in many other Christian homes.

"The Light of Asia," the painting by Theodore Wores, which was referred to in the article as hanging in the chapel, is in a room adjoining the drawing-room, and was placed there because it could be given a harmonious setting, the room containing only Oriental art. The room is not in any sense used as a shrine.

In an article in "The Examiner" I was constantly referred to as "Mother." No one has ever called me that except my children. I am not known as "Mother Russell," either in my home or by my friends. I have no "disciples," as the writer of the article indicated. I am and have been a student of philosophy and am an ardent seeker of truth and am striving to conform to its demands as far as they are made known to my consciousness.

As I understand the purpose of life, it is not to leave the world, and I am at a loss to know why that impression has gone forth. I believe in self-mastery and self-control, living true to the dictates of an illuminated conscience. This illumination is gained by prayer, which may be termed meditation or communication between the soul and its source—God.

These convictions do not take me or my household out of the world, as my interviewer understood. On the contrary, we are actively interested in the world, in its joys and sorrows. Living by the ocean is not living in isolation. While having the privilege of its beauty, we have the proximity of the city, independent of train and boat. [431]

Though the *Examiner* exposé was certainly exaggerated and in at least some parts fictional, it was not as "scurrilous and untrue in every respect" as Ida's friends and neighbours complained [432]. The reporter's designation of the Russell estate as a religious "colony," for example, was met with opposition. "There is no colony here," said one of the mansion's residents. "We are only a family and not a very large one at that—only nine of us in all." In fact, eighteen people lived at the mansion at this time: Alexander, Ida, and three Russell children; Mary Russell and Mary Crittenden, who identified themselves as governesses when the census enumerator visited earlier in the year; Mary Keeler, listed as the Russells' private secretary; Elise Drexler and her niece, identified as "roomers;" Bertha Christofferson, the housekeeper; and seven servants, four of whom were Japanese. It is unclear which nine of the eleven residents, once the servants are discounted, constituted Ida's self-proclaimed family. What is clearer is that no formal familial relationship bound all of them together. Ida and Alexander were, of course, related by marriage. Their wards, though related to the Russells by neither blood nor law and brought to the mansion "somewhat in the nature of an experiment," were raised as nothing other than the cherished offspring of their foster parents. Elise and her niece Jean were also tied by blood [433]. None of the others, however, was related to the Russells or to each other, and it would be difficult to construe them as a family in any legal or social sense.

All this is to say that if by his use of the word "colony" the *Examiner* reporter meant that a group of unrelated people were residing in a single place and living by a set of commonly-held principles, his description was more accurate than Ida's identification of the mansion denizens as a family. The depiction of the Russell mansion as a colony was in fact not unprecedented. Years earlier, the *San Francisco Chronicle* described it as "a center of devotees of the mystic and where there is a sympathetic understanding of the doctrines of the gentle Buddha." At the same time, the *Examiner*, in characteristically more sensational language, referred to the home of "the Russell cult" as a temple of "sanctified ascetics ... in whom virtue and vice have been annihilated." The *Los Angeles Graphic* chose to portray them as refined patricians rather than occultists, calling the household a "peaceful little colony" of people who "strive to lead a simple and artistic life" [434].

Ida's apology also contained a creative presentation of daily life at the mansion. In it, she crafted a public image very different from the one she fostered privately. Four years earlier she had described her home to the artist Theodore Wores as a place where "an honest effort is being made to heed the admonition of all Buddhas, of all Christs" [435]. But in her 1910 editorial, she presents herself as simple "student of philosophy," a "seeker of truth," a devoted Christian with a proper Christian chapel, the gracious hostess of visiting clergy. While there is no doubt that Ida always held Christ as "the greatest teacher of all" [436], her apology leaves one with the impression that her religious convictions are nothing other than Christian. In some sense this may have been true. As previously noted, though she was a student of Hinduism, Theosophy, and, most ardently, Buddhism, Ida never actually converted to any Eastern creed. She considered religious ideas miscible components of an overriding Truth that, once combined, could better define humanity's relationship with the divine than any single sect or doctrine. It is interesting that in the face of public criticism she should now choose to conceal an enthusiasm for Eastern religion that tended to be fashionable among the smart set of the day. Yet, in her *Examiner* editorial, Ida is careful not to let a single ray of her years-long interest in Buddhism shine through. The only place where she directly mentions the religion is in a denial of its influence on her. The "Light of Asia," which Ida once described as Wores' "divine offspring," was profoundly significant to Ida. In her letter to the *Examiner* it is now described as no more than a wall hanging that conveniently complements other Oriental furnishings in some out-of-the-way annex. Ida, it seems, is intent on portraying her household as conforming to accepted social norms. In presenting a public image of herself as nothing other than a devoted Christian, she was effectively making herself more presentable, more respectable to society at large.

Ida's defense did little to quell the scandal. A few weeks after the exposé's publication, one of the Russells' chauffeurs was tuning up one of their cars when a spark ignited some nearby gasoline and set the entire garage ablaze. Though the structure was detached from the mansion itself, it seemed that the flames would leap to the Oceanside House at any moment. A considerable crowd gathered to witness the imminent destruction of the "House of Mystery" they had read so much about. Five "chemicals" responded to the alarm, though only four actually made it to the mansion. Pulling the heavy engines through the sand was too much for one horse, which dropped dead half a mile from the residence. Despite the fire department's help, the Russells' garage was reduced to ashes, as were all the worldly possessions of the two chauffeurs who lived in apartments above the garage. All that was left of Alexander's limousine, roadster, and touring car were heaps of molten metal. The mansion itself was spared when the high wind changed direction, ceasing to fan the flames and blow sparks toward it. Though deprived of the main event, the spectators who gathered at the mansion's gate were treated to a sideshow: Alexander invited a group of them into the house for a tour. Of course, the exotic shrine was the first thing that people wanted to see, but they went away disappointed—or perhaps relieved that "Hindoo rites" were apparently not being performed in their midst. "The supposed temple for the worship of Buddha was found to be one of the ordinary living-rooms filled with a fine assortment of Indian carvings and statues collected by Mr. and Mrs. Russell in their travels through the Orient" [437].

PART 3

In the years immediately following the *Examiner's* damaging exposé, the community at the Russell mansion changed in a number of ways. Most notably, daily life began to resemble that of a normal family rather than that of a religious community. The Crossleys, who had moved out a few years earlier, were followed by Elise Drexler. Precisely what prompted this end to her fourteen-year association with the Russells is uncertain. Perhaps pressure exerted by her family finally succeeded in estranging her from Ida. Though Elise maintained contact with San Francisco Theosophists for years to come and occasionally looked after the well-being of the Russell wards, she appeared to have completely severed her connection with Ida and those in her community.

It was at this time that Ida also took unambiguous steps to alter her public image. She joined the Women's Athletic Club, the first social club to which she seems to have applied for membership [438]. In another first, she arranged to have her name included in *The Blue Book*, the register of San Francisco society that listed all the prominent families, their addresses, and the hours on which they accepted callers. This public relations effort culminated with the 1915 Panama-Pacific International Exposition. Alexander, as a member of the Ways and Means Committee, had for the previous few years helped organize the event, which would draw international attention to his beloved metropolis. Ida, for her part, was associate director of the Exploitation Department of the Women's Board. It was an organization that identified restaurants and hotels that promised not to take advantage of visitors by raising their rates for the event [439].

While taking a more public role in San Francisco society, Ida did not seem overly eager to have herself associated with Asian religion throughout this period. When Exposition organizers announced the addition of an international gathering of Buddhists at the event, she seems to have taken no part in it. Meant to be reminiscent of the World's Parliament of Religions, which nearly twenty years earlier had played a seminal role in Americans' interest in Asian religions, thirty delegates accepted invitations to speak. Among them were priests from Japan, Ceylon, and elsewhere. Paul Carus, whose interest in the religion had remained constant, took time away from *Open Court* magazine to address the gathering [440]. Unfortunately for those in attendance Swami Mazzinian-anda was present as well. His career in Southern

California had come to an abrupt end just a few years after he shared the podium with Shaku Sōen at Turner Hall. Following a series of *Los Angeles Herald* exposés on local spiritualists swindling their clients, the bogus Buddhist was arrested and imprisoned. Upon release he resurfaced in San Francisco where he confusedly advertised himself as a "yogi adept of the Buddhist Jaina sect" and became a favorite eccentric of journalists seeking a colourful topic on slow news days [441]. At the World's Congress of Buddhism, rather than write up the congress itself, reporters concentrated on a power play in which Mazziniananda wrested control of the event from a better qualified chairman [442]. It is little wonder that Ida Russell wanted little to do with the event, which has been generally forgotten by historians.

During the Panama-Pacific International Exposition, Alexander and Ida hosted several soirées. Their children—they now had seven wards under their protection—were relocated into other rooms of the mansion and their nursery converted into an English-style ballroom. Silk lanterns were strung along the garden paths. The *Examiner's* society page editor gushed over the fête. For the first time, the Russells were presented to the public as one of society's own. No longer followers of a heathen creed, they were "people with a cosmopolitan outlook on life" with an enviable collection of fashionable oriental art.

Names on the guest list tallied in the hundreds. Mayor "Sunny Jim" Rolph, one of Alexander's latest political allies, attended at least one of the dinner parties, as did Hiram Johnson, California's recently reelected governor who three years earlier had run as vice president in Theodore Roosevelt's failed bid for a third term in the White House. Phoebe Hearst attended with her son William Randolph, who had an opportunity to meet the people his paper, the *Examiner*, had demonized only five years earlier. There were also a number of Japanese and Middle Eastern guests, who were requested to attend "in the costume of their country" [443]. Among these exotic guests may have been Nomura Yōzō, who had introduced Ida to Shaku Sōen so many years earlier. He represented Kanagawa Prefecture at the Exposition, displaying sets of forged copper ornaments in the Palace of Manufactures. Since touring the temples of Kyoto and Nara with Ida, Yōzō had built Samurai Shōkai into a thriving, highly respected trading company. Now a very wealthy man, his clientele included Charles Freer of the Smithsonian Institution [444].

During these years Ida would take the children on picnics, driving out to scenic locations along the San Francisco peninsula. Alexander tended not to attend these excursions, preferring to stay home and read the newspaper at one of the large tables in the great hall. Late in the summer of 1917, Ida and the children returned from a picnic lunch among the grassy hills and oak trees of Palo Alto. Alexander asked if their day was enjoyable, to which Ida responded that everyone had a good time and suggested that he join them next time. Then, suddenly changing the subject, she said, "You know, I'm not going to live very long. I'll be dead in two or three weeks." It was a startling thing to say, particularly following such a pleasant outing. Her words, it turned out, were delphic [445].

12

COFFEE & CARBOLIC ACID

1917

PART 1

SŌEN'S plans to return to America for a third missionary tour were regularly delayed by a busy schedule that alternated with bouts of illness. Hale or ailing, he regularly embarked on extended lecture tours throughout Japan and its imperial holdings on the Asian mainland. At one point Sōen was appointed dean, and later president, of Rinzai College, a Zen university in Kyoto. Throughout this period Sōen remained in high demand as a public lecturer. Besides traveling throughout Japan, he journeyed to Taiwan, Korea, and Manchuria—all territories of Japan's growing empire—lecturing at the request of Japanese communities and businesses there. Though much of his work involved encouraging religious sentiment among his fellow Japanese, Sōen also remained keenly interested in propagating Zen among Westerners. He did not need to venture far to do so.

Thomas M. Kirby, a British national raised in Canada, was something of an adventurer. He traveled from community to community working as farmer, lumberjack, cow puncher. Anglican by birth, he at some point converted to Roman Catholicism and entered a monastery. Promptly leaving holy orders he immersed himself in Theosophy which fired an interest in Buddhism. He arrived in Japan sometime around 1913, at which point he added grammar school teacher and magazine editor to his growing list of occupations. He studied with the Pure Land Buddhists but before long became enamoured with Zen. Sōen was away on a lecture tour when Kirby arrived at Engakuji, but on his return heartily welcomed the new student. Sōen ordained him as a Zen monk, making him the first Westerner to formally join the Japanese Zen establishment. The plan was for Kirby to remain in Kamakura for at least two or three years before returning to North America to spread Mahayana Buddhism [446].

Another Westerner who studied under Sōen at this time was Beatrice, the New Yorker whose Buddhist education Sōen had entrusted to Daisetz Suzuki. Shortly after the Zen master's departure from New York, Beatrice Lane embarked on graduate studies at Columbia University that brought her a Master's degree in Political Science. William James, his student George Santayana, Josiah Royce, and George Herbert Palmer numbered among her professors, while Gertrude Stein was a classmate. She continued studying Theosophy and Vedanta, but, with Daisetz Suzuki's ministrations, became increasingly enamoured with Buddhism … as well as with its most immediate expounder. Within the first year of having met each other, Daisetz and Beatrice's relationship had begun to transmute from one of tutelage to romance [447].

Beatrice not only received Daisetz's instruction on Zen, she took an active role in his work. She already exhibited literary flair, having penned an unpublished novel about her college chums [448]. That she now directed her muse's attention to Daisetz's missionary activities is clear from the fact that her handwriting is seen on the proof sheets of *Sermons of a Buddhist Abbot* [449].

When Suzuki returned to Japan in the spring of 1909, his fiancée was not with him. Having completed her studies at Columbia, she received a professorship at Brenau College in Eufaula, Alabama. Across the Pacific, Daisetz was making similar headway. After staying several months at Tōkeiji, the monastery where Sōen lived in semi-retirement, Daisetz was offered a position at Peers' College, a residential school for children of upper class and noble background. He also lectured at the Imperial University for a number of years. Daisetz was not entirely happy with the appointment, in part because he taught English rather than philosophy, but also because it did not pay well. "I should have stayed with you longer, or returned to you when you wrote to me last," he lamented to Paul Carus. "My memory of Lasalle [*sic*] is still green, and I feel frequently like coming back and working in your office" [450].

Though perhaps unsatisfactory from a pecuniary standpoint, Daisetz's teaching provided enough financial stability to invite Beatrice to Japan. Shortly after her arrival in 1911 they were married at the American consulate in Yokohama. Many states at the time enforced laws against Caucasian Americans marrying anyone of Chinese or Japanese descent or citizenry. They did not apply overseas, though this did not prevent the American ambassador from voicing his disapproval of the interracial union [451]. The reception was held at Nomura Yōzō's mansion [452]. The newlyweds lived in Tokyo, regularly visiting Sōen in Kamakura for prolonged visits. On these occasions they lived at Shōden-an, the same hermitage that Ida and Elise, Jean MacCallum, and Louis Howe had inhabited in 1902. Beatrice approached Sōen, asking if he might accept her as his student. The busy bonze, about to depart for one of his lecture tours, suggested that she instead ask the acting abbot of Engakuji. Beatrice soon found herself sitting in meditation alongside the monks of the monastery, wearing a loose-fitting black robe and trying to look as inconspicuous as possible [453].

Inconspicuous, however, was not a word that could easily be applied to Beatrice Suzuki. The Buddhist ideal of compassion is what most attracted her to the religion. This was demonstrated by her graduate research at Columbia on the state care of the elderly poor, as well as her postgraduate certificate in social work. Beatrice's expression of compassion extended beyond her fellow man and reached out to all living organisms. This resulted in an overgrown garden, since she did not want to harm the plants by pruning them. Scolded whenever he tried to take matters into his own hands, Daisetz waited until his wife was out of the house before setting the shears into motion [454]. The expression of Beatrice's compassion also extended to stray animals. She is credited with founding the first animal shelter in Kamakura, which was in fact her own home [455]. Though keeping a strict vegetarian diet much of her life, she fed meat to the many dogs at her house. When she once complained she did not have enough money to purchase food for the animals, Daisetz quietly walked to his bookshelf, removed a rare volume of Buddhist literature, instructed the maid to sell it and use the proceeds to feed the animals [456].

Beatrice was at her least conspicuous when the monks of Engakuji decided to wire the monastery with electricity. Aghast at such a concession to modern technology and worried it would take away from the picturesque beauty of the place, Beatrice would walk from temple to temple shouting that monasteries should not have electric lights. The monks would laugh among themselves at her awkward Japanese, asking each other why she could not see the obvious benefits of an Engakuji with electric power. If Daisetz was embarrassed by his voluble bride, he never showed it. He let her fight the battles she deemed important and never made excuses for her [457].

The pair remained in Tokyo until they were both offered positions at Ōtani University in Kyoto. Beatrice taught English, while Daisetz accepted a professorship in the Buddhist philosophy department. After years of frustration seeking the academic post he so desired, Daisetz had finally achieved his goal. He just needed to wait until he reached his fifties. In addition to their teaching responsibilities, Daisetz and Beatrice embarked on an aggressive pattern of study, writing, and publication that before too long would attract international attention.

In 1916, Sōen was asked to resume his duties as abbot of Engakuji. The monastery was again in a state of decline, populated by few monks, none of whom were qualified to assume the mantle of leadership. Sōen, though living only a short walk away at Tōkeiji, recommended a younger monk be found for the job. Sōen was only 58 at this time, but years of illness left him feeling, and looking, older than his age. However, as the monastery was nearly deserted, no one else could be found. Again abbot of Engakuji, Sōen quickly entrusted the training of monks to an associate. Sōen administered Engakuji from his retirement hermitage at nearby Tōkeiji [458].

It was at this time that Sōen started to make preliminary plans for his third visit to America. Sōkatsu, his missionary to America, had long since abandoned Tomato Ranch and San Francisco. He was now again in Tokyo, mentor of his devoted band of lay followers. Daisetz, of course, was no longer overseas either. Sōen appealed to an associate in New York to help him pen a letter in English which he had never completely mastered [459]. The missive arrived at the Russell mansion, explaining the Zen master's intent to again teach in America and asking whether Ida would once again host his stay in California. Sōen had no way of knowing it, but months before his letter arrived the tranquil life of the Russells had come to a tumultuous halt—literally, overnight.

PART 2

Late one night in the fall of 1917, a bleary-eyed Baldwin Russell was making his way from his bedroom to the mansion's great hall. Mary Keeler, in a terrible state of agitation, had rushed to his room, rousing him with the sobering command: "Get up! Your mother is dying."

Still in his pajamas, the teenager walked to the balcony overlooking the hall. A scene of complete chaos greeted him. Servants ran up and down the stairs on urgent but ultimately futile errands. A desperate voice came from the telephone room where someone was placing a frantic call to Dr. Florence Nightingale Ward. Mary Keeler, already back downstairs, rushed into the room with a pot of hot coffee. In the midst of it all, Ida lay prostrate, motionless, her face swathed in bandages. Keeler tried desperately to induce her to drink, but received no response. By the time Dr. Ward arrived life had already slipped away from Ida Russell. Baldwin may still have been at the balcony as the county coroner jotted down notes for what would be a particularly unusual report [460].

Earlier that same day Ida was the picture of health. She had been busy planning a trip to visit relatives back East, but needed to complete one last task before departing. Rita Krause arrived as scheduled in the early afternoon. She was to apply a "skin peeling" treatment that promised to cast years off Ida's appearance. The therapy was by no means new, being popular among society women around the world for the past several years. It involved completely removing the epidermis. The active agent: a diluted solution of carbolic acid. Once it was applied directly to the skin, the subject's face would be wrapped in plaster. As the acid penetrated, deeply residing blemishes rose to the surface in the form of a scum that would be removed with the wrap after 24 to 36 hours. Pockmarks and wrinkles would also fade away.

It was by no means painless. "The torture I endured while I was encased in this wrapping of paper and plaster is not tellable," testified one horrified subject. "There was no relief until the new skin formed, at the end of several days" [461]. But if successful, the skin peeling treatment could work wonders. Freckles lifted away. Crow's feet and bags completely disappeared from around the eyes. However, vanity could exact a harsh penalty. At the very least, the subject of an improperly executed peeling could wind up with skin so sensitive that it would redden if the slightest breeze blew upon it. Treated skin might also be more prone to wrinkling after the procedure, requiring the subject to re-treat the skin with chemicals every six months. Worse yet, too strong an acid mixture could easily result in permanent disfigurement. It was not unheard of for the subject to be mistaken for the victim of a vitriol throwing. Blood poisoning was also possible, the results of which could be serious illness—or worse.

Given the delicate nature of the procedure, it was highly recommended that specialists apply the skin peeling treatment. Rita Krause was considered just such an expert, having performed the procedure on numerous occasions. Variously described as a dermatologist or a "beauty doctor," Krause managed a parlor on Post Street, not far from the Claxton Gallery where Ida and Sōen first viewed Theodore Wores' "Light of Asia" [462]. In addition to her reputed expertise in skin peeling, Ida had another reason to trust Krause: she had once been in the employ of the Russells, though in what capacity is unclear. Krause, whose husband was an herbalist and dealer in "proprietary medicines," was a professional midwife during the years that most of the Russell wards were born, so perhaps she had a role in delivering or caring for them.

There are mixed accounts of why Ida was willing to subject herself to what would certainly be an unpleasant operation regardless of its outcome. Some reports indicate that Ida, just weeks away from her sixty-first birthday, wanted to remove wrinkles beginning to appear on her throat. Other accounts refer to unsightly blemishes, perhaps age spots. Relatives recall that she had a "disfiguring birthmark" on her face [463]. Such a mark fails to appear on the several photos of Ida that have survived, though she may have learned how to position herself in front of the camera in such a way as to hide the offending mark.

Krause trekked out to the Russell mansion on Thursday, September 20, to apply the burning agent to her client's face. Ida may have mentioned her discomfort for it was common to experience a certain degree of irritation for the first day or two. Krause left the Russell residence, taking the precaution of leaving the phone number of Dr. B. B. Masten, a noted plastic surgeon who often attended to Krause's clients. By mid-afternoon, Ida's state of pain elevated, prompting someone in the mansion to call for his assistance. His examination found a strong heart, normal breathing, and regular pulse. At 5:30 Masten administered an eighth of a grain of morphine to deaden the pain and help Ida rest. The medicine seemed to stabilize her condition, at least enough for Masten to feel comfortable leaving the house at 8 o'clock that evening. Before departing he left strict instructions to give her a cup of black coffee when she awoke.

Ida never regained consciousness. In the hours that followed, her condition steadily worsened, prompting frantic calls, this time to Dr. Ward. She arrived with three of her colleagues. For three hours they tried to revive Ida, using a pulmotor in an attempt to induce breathing. It was all to no avail.

Ida Russell was the third victim of carbolic acid treatment in San Francisco within a two-year period. One of Ward's colleagues accused Masten of injecting his patient with an overdose of morphine, an allegation he denied. Masten insisted that life and death balanced on the lip of the cup of coffee he had prescribed. It would have prevented the carbolic acid from being thoroughly absorbed into the kidneys, he said [464]. A coroner's inquest did not call the nostrum into question. It attributed Ida's death to atheroma and myocarditis, the clogging and inflammation of the heart's arteries. However, the coroner was unable to conclude whether this was the result of carbolic acid entering Ida's bloodstream, an overdose of morphine, or a combination of the two. The coroner's jury investigating the unusual death recommended that the practice of skin peeling be abolished [465]. The jury also recommended that the San Francisco police department investigate the strange death. But Alexander, telephoning the captain of detectives, either requested that the investigation be halted or at least conducted quietly [466]. His wish seems to have been honored for no records of an investigation exist.

Ida's body was cremated, a practice common in the Theosophical circles in which she may have still traveled in her last years. The funeral ceremony was private, probably attended only by residents of the mansion and close friends. Rather than being delivered to the Conner family niche at the Odd Fellows Columbarium, her remains were kept in an urn in the mansion chapel.

PART 3

That winter, Nomura Yōzō was again in San Francisco at the tail end of a business trip. Still among Sōen's most devoted of lay disciples, he may have promised to look in on the Russells before leaving the city. Fifteen years had passed since Yokohama's Kurio King led two unusual women to Kamakura and introduced them to the famous abbot of Engakuji. Like Sōen, Yōzō evidently did not keep in close touch with the Russells for he had no idea that Ida had passed away several weeks earlier. Calling at the mansion, he was led to the upstairs chapel where Ida's ashes were enshrined.

The remains of the adventurous woman Yōzō once led on a cross-country tour of Japan's temples to him seemed lonely in the empty room. He was also under the impression that local churches had refused Ida a Christian burial because she had abandoned Christianity for Buddhism. Approaching Alexander, he requested permission to bring half of Ida's remains back to Japan. Alexander consented. In fact, he may have allowed Yōzō to take all her ashes, for Ida does not seem to have a burial site in the United States [467].

Yōzō was back in Japan in the spring of 1918. With a small bundle tucked under one arm, he climbed the well-worn stone steps that led to the entrance of Tōkeiji where Shaku Sōen now lived a comparatively quiet life. The Zen master was now sixty years old, once again retired, and more than a little frail from the minor but persistent illnesses that pursued him through the latter part of his life. Not long before, he had embarked on a lecturing tour of China. He was gravely ill when he returned and doctors were not certain if he would survive. The Zen master's health rallied, but he was no longer the globe-trotting monk of the Meiji era. Sōen now spent much of his time tending his garden, drinking tea, and honing his considerable skills in the arts of calligraphy and poetry composition. The tranquil life was reflected in poetry Beatrice Suzuki later rendered into English:

> My bamboo hut is low and tiny:
> I sit alone; it is in spring;
> My flowers bloom in rare profusion;
> The breeze is soft the south winds bring.
> But yester eve my friend had promised
> To see my garden blooming fair:
> I sit alone today, but listen
> To gentle rain, and free from care.

[468]

On April 7, 1918, his garden just beginning to bloom, Sōen performed formal Buddhist funeral rites for his American friend. Ida's remains were laid to rest in a bronze coffer and enshrined in a stone lantern, about six feet tall and crowned with three pagodas. It still stands in the garden that was once Sōen's retreat. She is not entirely alone there. A few yards away stands a somewhat more elaborate pagoda containing a handful of earth from a Manchurian battlefield—the memorial of her friend, Uemura Sōkō.

PART 4

Ida's sudden and unexpected death was followed by a period of pandemonium in the Russell mansion. Mary Russell, Sōen's English tutor and Ida's close friend who had been living at the mansion for more than a decade, suffered a nervous breakdown. In October, she was committed to Agnews State Hospital, a psychiatric facility in San Jose [469].

Alexander was grief stricken. Ida once described their marriage as "a relation of love and a union of sympathy and kindness" [470]. His sorrow, combined with a high degree of stress in the vexing months to follow, may have been the root cause of a series of strokes, the worst of which completely paralyzed one side of his body [471].

Ida's estate was valued at roughly $100,000. Subtracting specific bequests in Ida's will, Alexander was left with $65,000 to maintain the mansion and care for his seven wards. This might have been an adequate sum, considering that Ida had owned the title on the mansion, as well as a few other properties. Then claims against the estate began to arrive. There were only a few at first—outstanding accounts from the Central Coal Company, a hardware store, an interior decorator, a dealer in "Oriental goods," and a millinery where Ida purchased hats. Each required relatively small sums to settle. Such demands continued to trickle in until the middle of March 1918, when a very different class of claim began to arrive. Bank of Palo Alto, $4,000. Pacific States Savings and Loan Company, $6,000. Crown City Trust & Savings, $1,000. Banks in Azusa and Vallejo claimed similar amounts. Clara West Jones, $10,150. The loans, the most recent of which had been taken out only a week before Ida's sudden death, were made using the Russell mansion, surrounding land, and other real estate as collateral. Lenders now demanded repayment in full. Alexander's investment brokers were also interested in reimbursement, evidenced in two claims for $7,500 and $15,000 filed by William R. Staats Company, a trader in municipal, corporate, and railway bonds. There was also a claim for $3,000 plus interest from the Pasadena Children's Training Society, as well as those from numerous individuals, some of whom evidently loaned thousands of dollars at a time to Ida [472]. It soon became clear that the estate was in considerable debt. In the year following her death, a total of 113 claims amounted to more than $217,000.

Given Alexander's condition, Mary Crittenden filed papers to be appointed administratrix of the troubled estate and guardian of the children [473]. A judge oversaw the dissolution of the estate to reimburse creditors as much as possible, as well as provide for Alexander and the children who were now dependent on Ida's estate for maintenance.

He ordered the sale of a number of properties: a downtown residence, a mountain retreat on the shore of Lake Alta. The interior furnishings were sold off at auction. Mrs. R. J. Hanna, wife of a Standard Oil Company vice president, bought a painting of Mount Fuji and some of Ida's jewelry, including a $700 diamond ring. William Sesnon, a local oil magnate, purchased a variety of Japanese curios, including a small red shrine, a set of priest's robes, four stone lanterns, and the temple bell that once called the Russell community to prayer. All chapel furnishings went to Edward Hanna, archbishop of San Francisco's Roman Catholic archdiocese. Rita Krause, who must have felt awkward at the auction given her role in Ida's demise, arrived to bid on a chest of drawers Ida had imported from Japan. The irony was complete with the arrival of Mrs. C. S. Stanton, whose husband was publisher of the *San Francisco Examiner*, the paper that had demonized the Russells only eight years earlier. She paid $50 for one of the innumerable Buddha statues on the block and also went home with Ida's Sanskrit dictionary [474].

The House of Silent Light, the embodiment of Ida Russell's philosophy of tranquility and Zen's starting point in America, was the last to go. Mary Crittenden leased the mansion and its surrounding gardens to restaurateur John Tait. When the lease expired a year later, Mary was required to finally sell the real estate along with much of the remaining Oriental furnishings.

PART 5

Tait's-at-the-Beach roared through the 1920s as one of San Francisco's favorite restaurants. The parlor of Alexander and Ida Russell's erstwhile residence, which once rang with conversations on Asian mysticism, was now a busy reception room. The great hall, where silent prayers had been recited before simple vegetarian meals, was transformed into a bustling dining area where elaborate dishes were served. Where a gong once beckoned votaries to prayer, champagne corks burst exuberantly from bottlenecks. The nursery, the center of Ida and Elise's philanthropic experiment, became a dance hall where lively orchestras played jazz.

War-Time Prohibition temporarily prevented John Tait from selling alcoholic beverages at the onetime house of moral and spiritual enlightenment. The enterprising restaurateur, however, was quick to exploit a loophole in the law. He notified his customers that if they brought their own liquor his bartenders would be sure to have ginger ale, tonic water, and soda waiting for them, charging them a modest setup, corkage, and storage fee [475]. Waiters carried hot dishes up the great staircase and along the balcony surrounding the hall, delivering them to intimate little dining rooms that were once bedrooms. Even the chapel, where Ida and her community spent long hours in meditation, now seated Tait's dinner guests, who gazed out large windows at the coastal panorama.

The tavern ranked high among the city's most fashionable restaurants, competing with the Palais Royal, Coppa's, the Cliff House, and Marquard's. In the evenings, Rolls-Royces and expensive Ford saloons lined up at its entry. Theodore Roosevelt, California Governor James Rolph, and a long list of Hollywood actors, sports icons, and foreign nobility numbered among the bistro's well-known and well-publicized patrons. Tea time at Tait's was a very popular event, guests arriving by both automobile and on horseback to sip their brews in the Japanese garden still protected by a towering, fourteen-foot fence.

Remaining unchanged was the atmosphere of art and exoticism that once characterized the House of Silent Light. Tait was careful to maintain much of the mansion's unique appearance. Carved dragons crouched above doorways. Silk screens partitioned the floor space. Teak chairs from China gave guests a place to relax while their tables were prepared. Hundreds of Ida's small Buddha statues peered out from niches around the house. The oriental appearance of the garden was also carefully preserved and visitors—wearing tuxedos and evening gowns—strolled beneath paper lanterns and past dwarf conifers on their way to the tea pagoda. Many of Tait's patrons half-remembered stories of the restaurant's previous incarnation as a mystical temple. Some said that every now and then ghosts emerged from the fog, wandered serenely about the Japanese garden, before they disappeared back into the mist [476].

Tait's-at-the-Beach remained popular for a dozen years. During Prohibition it was a notorious speakeasy where whiskey was served in tea cups [477]. Nonetheless, with less liquor flowing, its main source of revenue dried up. As the 1930s dawned John Tait padlocked the doors and for a time silence again reigned at the House of Silent Light. As the years passed, the abandoned mansion on the ocean beach remained the House of Mystery, once home of some half-remembered cult of a bygone era. Those curious about its history had only to ask "Shorty" Roberts, owner of a nearby tavern. He had lived his entire life in the area and happily regaled patrons with tales of "old Mother Rafael," probably a composite of Gertrude Rayfield, who had sold the property to Ida, and the *Examiner's* "Mother Russell." The mansion, explained the error-prone Shorty [478], then became a private orphanage before it was sold to the wealthy Alexander Russell. Roberts was not alone in his confusion about the history of the place. Herb Caen, an up-and-coming *San Francisco Chronicle* columnist, received a particularly distorted report from John Tait. "Seems that John leased the place from a Mrs. Drexler, a wealthy Philadelphian interested in Buddhism, bud," reported Caen in his folksy style. "Smatterofack (and this hasn't been told) she brought a boy and girl from Chicago, ditto from New Orleans and ditto from N.Y. and raised them out there. Private tutors, piano lessons, the works. These six kids all live in Bay Area [*sic*] now, married and working. The historic place became known as a 'House of Mystery,' says John, because Mrs. Drexler was a strange old lady who wouldn't allow any men on the property; shooed 'em all away personally, in fact" [479].

It seemed no one remembered the old estate as the first place Zen Buddhism was introduced to America. But that was not quite the case. There were still a few.

13

IF IN THE FUTURE NO ONE APPEARS

1936

PART 1

A T an age when most men count the days to their retirement, at sixty-six Dr. D. T. Suzuki seemed to be just reaching the peak of his career. Slender, active, and animated, possessing an inquiring face and a quirky sense of humour, he showed few signs of slowing down. Daisetz was in London in July 1936 to participate in the World Congress of Faiths, an interreligious gathering where he was remembered, by some at least, as the most popular speaker [480]. The Japanese Foreign Ministry then sponsored a lecture tour on which he spoke on Zen Buddhism and Japanese culture at Oxford, Cambridge, Durham, Edinburgh, and London universities [481]. When Daisetz had last been in London, nearly thirty years before, he was on his way home to Japan, completing twelve years as a frustrated editorial assistant for Open Court Publishing. Now D. T. Suzuki was an internationally recognized philosopher, translator, and interpreter of Japanese Buddhism. His *Essays in Zen Buddhism*, published in 1927, established him as the authority on the subject. Following it were translations of and commentaries on the *Lankâvatâra* and *Gandavyūha* Sūtras, presenting some of the fundamental tenets of Mahayana Buddhism and particularly appreciated by Zen Buddhists. A second, then a third set of *Essays* were released. At that point, his scholarly output and international recognition earned him a doctorate of literature from Ōtani University. Most recently, in 1935, he released a complementary pair of books that presented an overview of Zen philosophy (*Introduction to Zen Buddhism*) and Zen ritualism as practiced in Engakuji and other temples (*Training of the Zen Buddhist Monk*). Zen Buddhism, said one Western professor, was finally on the map [482]. D. T. Suzuki was first to put it there.

Yet Daisetz was not simply interested in scholarship, nor was he alone in his efforts. The essay collections that found such an appreciative audience among Western scholars were often first published in *The Eastern Buddhist*. He had founded the magazine upon arriving at Kyoto in 1921. His dozen years of writing, editing, and publishing *The Open Court* magazine made him something of an expert in turning out just such a journal. This was complemented by the understanding of Western religion and psychology he acquired from Paul Carus, as well as the ability to present complex philosophical thought in a generally approachable manner, a hallmark of *The Open Court* [483]. *The Eastern Buddhist* would be published on a regular basis for nearly two decades. Its purpose, however, was not just the presentation of highbrow philosophy. It was also missionary in aspiration. The "bimonthly unsectarian magazine devoted to the study of Mahayana Buddhism" was "aiming at the propagation of Buddhism." Among Daisetz's first backers of this missionary endeavor was Nomura Yōzō, who took out ads for Samurai Shōkai in early runs of the magazine when other advertisers were hard to come by and resources for its publication strained [484].

More practical assistance was nearer at hand. Daisetz and Beatrice considered the propagation of Buddhism to be among the objectives of their marriage. They spent long hours discussing their thoughts on religion, then committing them to writing [485]. She was a prolific author in her own right. Her interests in Asian religion were longstanding. The *Bhagavad Gita* had interested her prior to meeting Daisetz. She read what was available on Theravada Buddhism, but while at Columbia was frustrated with Professors Santayana and Palmer's inability to effectively lecture on Mahayana traditions [486]. At the same time her husband was building an international reputation for his scholarship, Beatrice published two volumes of Buddhist readings, a book on Noh plays and a description of Kōyasan, a Shingon temple that was dear to her.

From its inception, Beatrice co-edited *The Eastern Buddhist*. The magazine was a collaboration between husband and wife, who were equally committed to producing its numbers on a regular basis. "We promised each other that whatever we wrote together would be our child," Daisetz later recalled. "*The Eastern Buddhist* was one such child ..." [487]. Beatrice would frequently contribute articles that, because they were less erudite and more descriptive than those of her husband, complemented Daisetz's more scholarly writing style and appealed to a different audience. Daisetz valued the fact that Beatrice had not been reared in a Buddhist family and inculcated from birth with an Asian way of thinking. "It is for this reason that what she wrote is, from the Japanese Buddhist perspective, fresh and even inspiring," he would later write [488].

Despite years of hard work at the side of her husband, Beatrice's role in the introduction of Zen to the West tends to be either downplayed or ignored. This is unfortunate because she clearly had considerable impact on Daisetz's ability to be as prolific as he was. As far back as 1907 she proofread Daisetz's manuscripts, as well as prepared them for publication. This continued throughout the 1920s and 1930s as the highly educated, highly intelligent (and sometimes highly quirky) Beatrice edited, modified, and corrected the English writings of her increasingly famous husband. This is not to say that Daisetz would have been incapable of preparing English-language manuscripts for publication without Beatrice's assistance. His twelve years in America had bestowed on him a proficient command of the language. However, when it came to writing on Buddhism the two worked together as a team, and as a team they produced more and higher quality writing than either could have accomplished alone. Daisetz's dependence on his wife was underscored when, after her death in 1939, the Eastern Buddhist Society closed and the publication of *The Eastern Buddhist* all but ceased [489]. Without his wife's assistance, Daisetz would produce virtually nothing in the English language for a full ten years. It can safely be said that without the support and assistance of Beatrice, D. T. Suzuki might not have established a reputation for himself in Western academia [490].

Beatrice and Daisetz's work propagating Buddhism in the West was not limited to the publication of an English-language journal. At Ōtani University Beatrice was an enthusiastic teacher who believed most of her students were destined to propagate Buddhism. Perhaps noting the effect that inadequate English skills had on Sōen's missionary endeavors, she believed language training to be absolutely vital to the cause. Her classes were, as a result, rigorous. Instruction was conducted solely in English, much to the dismay of the less linguistically inclined students. She required that students read at least one book in English during their summer break and readily lent them volumes from her library. While at Kyoto she founded the Ānanda Society, a club dedicated to the study of Buddhism in English [491].

It was perhaps inevitable that before long Westerners would begin knocking at the door of the Suzuki household. The first of these seems to have been Ruth Fuller Everett, a Chicago socialite who made a point of obtaining an introduction to Daisetz while on the Asian leg of a round-the world cruise in 1930 [492].

> I sat waiting in the small reception room of the foreign-style house in the northwest section of Kyoto where my taxi-driver had deposited me. The maid who had shown me in and brought me tea had carefully closed the double doors and left me alone in this rather chilly and severe room with its center table and four or five upholstered chairs. Only the several rare and beautiful *kakemonos* hanging on the walls

gave indication that this might be the home of a Japanese scholar. … The door opened quietly and Doctor Suzuki, then Professor Suzuki, came in. Those of you who have met him know well the simple, charming manner of this learned man, his whimsical smile, and his entertaining long eyebrows darting out at astonishing right angles from his high ascending forehead. We had many mutual friends and so, since his excellent command of English permitted of no language problems, fell quickly into easy conversation. Soon Mrs. Suzuki joined us and gradually the talk turned to the subjects that most engrossed us all—Buddhism in general, and then Zen. It was much later in the afternoon, for our talk continued on and on, that Dr. Suzuki said to me in the words so important to my life in the days to come: "If you really want to study Zen, come to Japan. You will learn more in a few months than in America in as many years."
[493]

Were Ida Russell and her nine-month stay at Engakuji at the back of his mind when Daisetz said this? He provided Ruth Everett with some basic instruction in seated meditation and sent her on her way with a copy of *Essays in Zen Buddhism* in her hand. She would return within two years, prepared to follow his advice. Daisetz secured permission for her to live at a nearby monastery, Nanzenji, where she followed Ida Russell's lead by practicing Zen among the monks for three and a half months [494]. Ruth Everett was not alone. Before her second visit to Kyoto, Francis Ormsby and George Colburn, from far-away Idaho, arrived in Kyoto. Ormsby studied at a Baptist college, but turned to Buddhism after hearing a navy doctor speak on the topic. Both Ormsby and Colburn had been ordained as Zen monks in America, given the religious names of Kōun and Mokusai, and came to Japan's ancient capital to complete their training. They proceeded to Daitokuji. Gotō Zuigan, Shaku Sōkatsu's attendant and translator who once shared in his master's San Francisco mission, was now abbot of this head temple and perhaps agreed to teach them. They remained for four months before they were asked to leave. The mendicants proceeded to China, perhaps to Karl Ludvig Reichelt's Christian-Buddhist monastery in Nanking [495].

It is not known if language or cultural differences contributed to the abbreviated stay of the Chicago socialite and Idaho Buddhists. However, proper Zen training takes years, not months. It was with the view of minimizing culture shock, but at the same time providing Westerners a place for extended training in a Zen monastery, that the Zen Hospice was opened in November 1932. It was situated on the grounds of Enpukuji, a monastery near Kyoto. The head abbot promised to train up to five Westerners living there. Applicants for residence should apply to: Mr. Daisetz Teitarō Suzuki.

"The time has now come in Japan to propagate Mahayana Buddhism abroad, especially its form Zen, since Zen is the essence of Oriental culture and preserves most perfectly the original spirit of Buddhism," the Suzukis wrote in a commentary that seriously undermined the "nonsectarian" nature of their publication. To Daisetz and Beatrice, the Zen Hospice was a work of reverse missionary activity. Rather than train and fund missionaries to go to America—and have them arrive handicapped with an insufficient understanding of Western language, culture, and psychology—why not have interested Westerners come to them? "Our purpose is thus to do away with unessentials as far as possible and to concentrate our efforts on what is most vital in the understanding of Zen. As we know, some things in the Zen monastery life can well be dispensed with for foreign students whose habits and ways of living deviate so much from ours. For this reason, it is most desirable to provide them with a simple and quiet place where they can practice meditation, receive instruction in Zen, and gain something of the Zen spirit without contradicting too much of their own way of living" [496].

The Zen Hospice does not seem to have been a long-term success, despite the mayor of Kyoto, president of the Kyoto Imperial University, and a representative of the Ministry of Education all turning out for its opening ceremony. But it marked a fundamental shift in Daisetz's approach to the propagation of Buddhism. Witnessing the limited impact of Sōen and Sōkatsu's efforts to land Zen Buddhism on American soil, he thought it better to take Ida Russell's 1902 stay at Engakuji as a model and make a way for enthusiastic Westerners to receive formal Zen instruction in Japan. After all, Sōen and Sōkatsu's missions to America had been fruitless. Or had they? Daisetz would have an opportunity to see for himself.

PART 2

In London at the World Congress of Faiths, each of the delegates was asked to speak on the subject, "The Supreme Spiritual Ideal." The Canon of Westminster Abbey, chaplain to His Majesty the King, Frank Russell Barrry, declared there to be no greater ideal than the God Who became Man for the deliverance of humanity. The Muslim representative said it was "to believe in one God, who the God of everyone else; that [each individual] is not privileged in any way, that all nations are equal." The rabbi, somewhat redundantly, identified the Supreme Spiritual Ideal as "the supremacy of the spiritual in human life." Sir Sarvepalli Radhakrishnan, future president of India, said "the real spiritual ideal is to develop the divine in us, to perfect ourselves" [497]. Taking the podium, Daisetz admitted he did not know exactly how to approach the topic. "Really I do not know what Spiritual is, what Ideal is, and what Supreme Spiritual Ideal is." He instead talked about his small house and garden in Japan.

That, at least, is how a young editor and Buddhist enthusiast named Alan Watts remembered it [498]. In fact, Daisetz clearly identified non-duality as the Supreme Spiritual Ideal of Zen

Buddhists. He just never said so in as many words. The address marked the turning point Zen Buddhists had passed in presenting religious ideas to unprepared Westerners. Rather than foisting on his audience a lot of technical religious terms and tedious definitions, Daisetz presented his auditors with an analogy. In England and other Western nations, he said, windows are little more than holes in walls that separate inside from out. "The house stands by itself, and so does its occupant. Its occupant is separated from his or her surroundings altogether. There is nature, here am I; you are you, I am I; so there does not seem to be any connection between those two—nature, natural surroundings, and occupants of the house." In traditional Japanese houses, the situation is altogether different. Walls slide away, completely removing one side of the house and opening it right into the garden. In this scenario

> There is no division between house and garden. The garden is a house, a house is a garden. ... And when I look at those trees growing from the ground, I seem to feel something mysterious which comes from the trees and mother earth herself. And I seem to be living in them, and they in me and with me. I do not know whether this communion could be called spiritual or not. I have no time to call it anything, I am just satisfied. [499]

The subtle address earned him a standing ovation.

Crossing the Atlantic in the fall, Daisetz addressed the Japan-American Society of Boston, as well as Harvard University. A girl's high school in Rhode Island invited him to speak, and when he arrived in New York at the onset of winter, he was a guest lecturer at Columbia University. On December 2, 1936, just before departing the city, Daisetz spent a day in Manhattan with the only Zen master teaching in the United States, head priest of the Buddhist Society of America, vice-abbot of Jōfukuin, Sōkatsu's and Shaku's spiritual heir (though temporarily disinherited at the moment)—Sasaki Yeita [500].

When Shaku Sōen, more than thirty-five years earlier, told this sculptor to carve a statue of the Buddha, he had no way of knowing that Yeita would use the American psyche as his medium. Sōkatsu, when he abandoned his California missionary endeavors, did not take quite all his Forgetting Both Society members back with him. "North America is the place where Buddhism will spread in the future," he said to Yeita, known also by his religious name Shigetsu (Pointing at the Moon). "You should stay here and familiarize yourself with the attitudes and culture of this land. ... Be diligent! If in the future no one else appears, the responsibility for bringing Buddhism to America will be yours" [501].

For more than a decade the layman led a wandering existence. At first he had a family to look after. Yeita had married another member of the Forgetting Both Society at Sōkatsu's command. The priest thought it improper to have an unmarried woman traveling abroad with his male-dominated troupe. They moved from San Francisco to an island off the coast of Seattle. It was populated by Native Americans, who must have been more welcoming than the Sasaki family's experience of San Franciscans steeped in a rising anti-Asian sentiment. When not engaged in whatever menial labor he could find, Yeita would explore the Pacific Northwest by foot. "Every evening I used to walk along the riverbed to a rock, chiseled by the current during thousands of years. Upon its flat surface I would practice meditation through the night, my dog at my side protecting me from the snakes" [502].

When his wife returned to Japan, Yeita was again on the road. It eventually landed him in a Manhattan neighbourhood of daytime janitors, dancing girls, and pimps [503]. Rubbing elbows with the Greenwich Village Bohemians and moving in with a petite, attractive actress, he supported himself through art and journalism. Through the 1920s he made a number of trips back to Japan, where he found regular buyers for his literary output, had tense encounters with his now estranged wife, continued his studies under his old master, and always went back to America before his two-year return visa expired. On the last of these visits in 1928 Sōkatsu confirmed him as an officially qualified Zen master and one of his few spiritual successors. He then sent him back across the Pacific with the words: "Your message is for America. Return there!" [504].

Back in New York, Sasaki Yeita now went by Sōkei-an. Sōkatsu gave him the name, a reference to a place where the sixth Zen patriarch lived in China [505], in part because of the fundamental role the sixth patriarch played in bringing Buddhism from India to China. Sasaki Yeita was tasked with doing his part in the eastward spread of Buddhism. Rather than try to build a temple or speak in halls, Sōkei-an, in a practice traditional to Zen masters, waited for students to discover him. It is perhaps not surprising that after three years, few people joined him in his flat for meditation. "Today I see six people. At that time six people were a crowd," he later recalled. "I would say, 'Today was successful.' I was hanging on by a hair. 'One month more! Then I go somewhere else' " [506].

Instead he remained in New York. Perhaps to give his work a sense of organizational validity, he filed papers incorporating the Buddhist Society of America, later renamed the First Zen Institute of America. He took the further step of bestowing on himself additional religious credentials. He asked a friend, another of Sōkatsu's former student now at Daitokuji, to propose his name as a temple priest for the subsect. Sōkei-an, though a qualified Zen master, was technically still a member of the laity. He was appointed vice-abbot of Jōfukuin, a temple he never actually visited. His priestly robes, apparently like the ordination itself, were conveyed by post. When informed of the ordination, Sōkatsu was incensed. Because the mission to America was directed at lay people, Sōkatsu apparently felt Zen ought to be transmitted to them by a layman. He said he had given Sōkei-an his *inka*, the seal confirming his experience of enlightenment, under false pretenses.

Sōkei-an was to return to Japan to be stripped of his status, an order he apparently ignored [507].

The tactics—incorporating the mission and presenting himself as the only Zen master in America—proved effective. Attendance at Sōkei-an's "temple," as he called his apartment *zendō*, slowly increased. By 1935 fifteen people trained under his guidance. The number would double before the end of the decade [508]. The New York students tended to be a verbose, argumentative, and restless bunch. Sōkei-an would introduce them to meditation, sitting in silence for thirty minutes. "And in three days no one came to my place. So five minutes! But that was very long, and I reduced it to one minute, and one young lady fainted!" [509]. Despite such an inauspicious beginning, a core of students soon emerged. One was Edna Kenton, a feminist who wrote books on Jesuit missions, Broadway theater, Native American culture, and family history. Another, Dr. Henry Plakov, was a physician and practicing psychoanalyst with interests in Raja Yoga, Daoism, parapsychology, and Christianity of the Greek Orthodox variety [510]. Word of the Zen master's presence in New York began to spread. Alan Watts, who had authored a book on Zen when he was only nineteen years old, began corresponding with Sōkei-an. Ruth Fuller Everett was also writing him [511]. Both would become his students a few years later.

PART 3

Daisetz spent his final day in New York in the company of Sōkei-an, causing the Manhattan Zen master to arrive at his evening lecture unprepared. Daisetz made his way to Chicago, arriving early in December 1936. Paul Carus had passed away near the end of the Great War, his Victorian-age optimism rattled by the global military action and his German birth grounds for rumors that he concealed a radio that fed intelligence to the Kaiser [512]. In town for nearly two weeks Daisetz spoke at a number of venues, including the Art Institute, housed in the same building where the World's Parliament of Religions had convened at the Columbian Exposition in 1893. Whereas Shaku Sōen's address in the building never directly referenced the Zen sect of Buddhism that he held so dear, Suzuki's lecture—"Zen Buddhism and Far Eastern Culture"—was in no way circumspect [513].

Following lectures at Chicago and Northwestern universities, Daisetz made his way west to California. Before returning to Japan, he stopped by Los Angeles where—in an evening of archery, swordsmanship, and music—he was fêted by members of a local Buddhist organization called the Mentorgarten.

Senzaki Nyogen, perhaps intuiting that he would never again resume work at his Aomori kindergartens, decided to make a fresh start at his Mentorgarten project in 1915. Instead of looking after toddlers at a temple school, he would provide language instruction to adults in San Francisco, much as he had been doing on and off for the past decade [514]. Japanese classes alone could not pay the bills, so he began writing freelance for Japanese newspapers and added one or two other jobs to the mix. Despite this, his pockets always seemed empty. "Ever since I came to America, I have worked like a machine," he complained to a friend in Japan. "Nevertheless, I am still having financial problems." From seven to eleven in the morning he worked as a housekeeper. He went to bed at two o'clock in the afternoon, rising at six to look after a hotel's front desk, books, and switchboard through the night. When the phone ceased ringing regularly—typically between two and five in the morning—he studied. The life of a hotel worker was quite different from that once lived by the simple monk, the rural kindergarten teacher: "Sometimes couples fight, and I have to talk to them. Sometimes I assist the house detective in catching a thief. ... Last night someone came in drunk, so I hit him and took him to bed" [515]. He could never understand why some couples checked in late at night, but only remained in their room for an hour or so before leaving. "Never stay to sleep!" exclaimed the exasperated and innocent monk. Things went from bad to worse when he was talked into investing in a hotel ... and was promptly imprisoned when his American partner accused him of embezzling the profits [516]. His letter to Japan—with the pathetic request, "Perhaps you can ask Chū-san to take this letter to Rōshi and tell him that Senzaki is still alive."—may have been a plea for the Zen master who left him in America to find a means for his return [517]. If so, the letter must not have been delivered, for Sōen never came to the rescue of his careworn student.

In 1922, Nyogen launched into the next phase of his American Mentorgarten project: religious instruction. Having saved $20 from his various jobs, he rented a hall and advertised that he would deliver an address entitled "First Steps in Meditation." People filled the building, but the speaker's accent was so pronounced that his audience could not understand his words. Fortunately he had written out the address beforehand and gave the script to someone else to read. As far as public addresses went, it must have been less than impressive. But as the audience filed out of the hall some left their names and addresses on a sheet he had placed by the exit [518]. Nyogen had his first Zen students.

Over the next five years, teacher and students would meet once a month: January 1st for a New Year party, February 15th for "Nirvana Day," March 3rd to celebrate the Japanese Girls' Festival, April 8th to honor the birth of the historical Buddha. Gatherings were in whatever apartment or residential hotel room he happened to call home. He prepared a simple vegetarian meal for those who came [519].

Throughout this time Nyogen remained in contact with Japan. He submitted a series of articles under the title "News from San Francisco" to be published in a Kyoto newspaper. This caught the attention of a local Zen master, Mamiya Eisō. Visiting San Francisco for three days, he may not have been impressed enough to join Nyogen in his labors but, upon telling others in Japan of his work, managed to raise $300 for his cause [520]. Nyogen burned through the money in a month, moving into a larger apartment and outfitting it as a *zendō*. At the inaugural meeting of the San Francisco Mentorgarten, Nyogen described the place as neither a temple nor school. It was simply a place where studious people could gather for discussions of philosophy, psychology, literature, and Buddhism, "a sort of club for studious people" [521]. Neither was it associated with a particular sect of Buddhism. "Generally speaking, I am a Buddhist, but I do not belong to any sect of the churches. I call myself Zen-Buddhist because Zen is the essence of Buddhism, and I am satisfied with the teaching as far as I have studied it in the past years. I do not belong to any Zen church, and it is not my wish to work as a Minister from certain Zen churches in Japan or of any other country" [522]. Perhaps still conscious of his lack of official permission to teach from the Zen hierarchy in Japan, Nyogen presented himself as a fellow student, adding that he intended to coax a Zen master in Japan to visit and to instruct them all together.

The Mentorgarten would never make Nyogen rich, but donations were apparently sufficient for him to quit his day jobs. He remained in San Francisco for another couple of years, leaving suddenly for Los Angeles sometime between late 1930 and early 1931. The change of venue was apparently due to Nyogen's feelings toward an elementary school teacher attending his classes at the time. She not only sat in classes, but also helped her unmarried teacher with household chores. It is said that Nyogen, now in his mid-fifties, was much taken by this Japanese woman, who was very much his junior. From his collection of Japanese literature, he copied for her a traditional poem that was used in classical times to initiate courtship. Taken aback, the young lady retreated to her home. Friends counseled that she need only provide her admirer with a reply in the negative and the matter would be properly settled. The object of the priest's affections, however, refused to provide a reply of any kind or attend Mentorgarten meetings. Depressed and embarrassed over the state of affairs, Nyogen felt his position in San Francisco was no longer tenable [523].

Nyogen was wholeheartedly welcomed by the Japanese community in Southern California and quickly began attracting the attention of Caucasians as well. At the same time, he maintained contact with his San Francisco sangha, writing and visiting them on a regular basis. He requested that they keep his Northern California *zendō* open, offering a fresh rosebud to his statue of Mañjuśrī each Sunday and Thursday, as well as gather once a month to read and discuss one of his lectures [524]. Between twenty and fifty people attended the Los Angeles Mentorgarten gatherings [525]. Rather than the monthly meetings up north, Senzaki's Southern California students meditated with him daily, from seven until eight in the evening. A dozen or more gathered in San Francisco. Students in both locations included Anton Dahl, a well-known pianist, Mrs. C. I. Chester, an aging chorus girl with the Ziegfeld Follies, Samuel Lewis, whose religious interests included Sufism, and Theosophists Caroline and Agnes Kast, whose "cozy library ... welcomes all truth seekers" [526]. A number of these students were extremely enthusiastic about their new religion. One by the name of either Pearce or Van Steum, later calling herself Sister Dhammadinna, would be among Australia's first exponents of Buddhism [527]. Two men from Nyogen's San Francisco sangha set sail for Ceylon and were ordained as monks in the Theravada tradition. Miriam Salanave of Oakland lived at Daitokuji in Kyoto for several months. Upon her return in 1935 she founded the short-lived Western Women's Buddhist Bureau, which she hoped to turn into a convent [528]. The spiritual wanderings of Paul Fernandez, a former Marxist agitator, had spanned atheism, occultism, Rosicrucianism, and Vedanta:

> But still I could not realize an answer to questions that were obsessing me. About that time a friend of mine took me to

the Mentorgarten to hear a lecture delivered by our Beloved Teacher and Brother, Senzaki-san, but I was not very much impressed. Several days later I was introduced to Senzaki-san by my friend, and right then I made up my mind to try to understand the teachings that this great teacher was giving out to anyone who had eyes to see and ears to hear. So I secretly took him for my teacher. I kept coming here daily, paid particular attention to every word of instruction that he gave and after several months under his able guidance one evening after meditation I suddenly attained a glimpse of Divine Self Consciousness. [529]

Throughout his years in San Francisco and Los Angeles, Nyogen was fond of addressing members of his Mentorgartens as "fellow students." He preferred to present himself as host, rather than as instructor. Nonetheless, it is clear from members like Paul Fernandez that Nyogen was an instructor, and a rather effective one at that. As the years progressed, he would not only lead them in meditation, he would assign them *kōans* and give practical advice on how to respond to them [530]. That Nyogen excited his students' interest in Zen Buddhism is further evidenced by a number who wanted to emulate him by dedicating themselves to the religion as ordained monks. The first of these were Francis Ormsby and George Colburn, the Idaho renunciates who took vows of celibacy, shaved their heads, and sojourned to Kyoto as described above. Following them were at least two women whom Nyogen ordained as nuns [531].

In May 1931 Nyogen had exciting news for his students. For the past ten years, since he had begun the religious work of his American Mentorgartens, he dreamed of having a qualified Zen master join in his work. The dream was about to be fulfilled. Furukawa Gyōdō, who had recently stepped down as abbot of Engakuji, agreed to guide Senzaki and his students. In their younger days he and Nyogen had practiced together at Engakuji, during which time they had become good friends. "He is my senior Brother and a successor to my beloved teacher, Soyen Shaku," Nyogen elatedly wrote his students in San Francisco, adding an implicit criticism of his old master's brief sojourn in America: "He [Furukawa] is coming to settle in his American home for the rest of his life, not to travel for sight-seeing, or so-called 'studying conditions' " [532].

The master arrived in November, but the situation did not seem to be to his liking. It may have been that the makeshift *zendō* in Nyogen's downtown apartment did not impress him. Or perhaps he was shocked by the American students, who meditated in chairs, had never before practiced the *dokusan* interviews that Senzaki so dreaded at Engakuji, and had little to no Japanese language skills. More importantly, perhaps, the former abbot seems to have been upset by Nyogen's formal ordination of his disciples. He believed that such a ceremony ought not to be performed without a special license from the Japanese government, just as priests in Japan were required to receive. Nyogen railed against such officiousness: "The Ordination of a Buddhist is not under the control of any sect. Anyone who has been ordained a Buddhist for ten years, no matter by what sect, has authority to ordain others also. This is one of the precepts of the Buddha himself" [533]. Furukawa Gyōdō resigned as the Mentorgarten's Zen master after only a month and a half. Ogata Sōhaku, who had visited Nyogen before and was impressed by his work in America, was identified as a possible replacement, though he never actually took the post [534]. As the 1930s progressed it became apparent that the white-haired monk of the Mentorgarten would work alone in furthering Shaku Sōen's vision of Zen in America.

14

AT FIRST A WOMAN OPENED
HER INNER EYE

PART 1

I T is no small irony that of all Sōen's disciples, D. T. Suzuki, Senzaki Nyogen, and Sasaki Yeita were the ones most successful in establishing Zen in America. Through the late 1890s and the early part of the new century, Daisetz had been Sōen's eyes and ears in America, not to mention his hands and mouthpiece. The dedicated layman spent years observing and absorbing American life from his small-town setting in the Illinois heartland. He was able to draft articles on Mahayana Buddhism and prepare translations of classic Buddhist texts. Through these he introduced Japanese Buddhism to a Western audience that might otherwise have taken no notice of it. He gained public speaking experience and left LaSalle with printing and publishing expertise that would prove invaluable for much of his long professional life. Yet, when Sōen needed to call on someone to replace Uemura Sōko as the centerpiece of his Zen mission in America he turned to Sōkatsu rather than to Daisetz. It was a decision of questionable wisdom. Daisetz possessed the English language skills that Sōkatsu lacked and were vital to the success of the missionary work. He better understood American culture, psychology, and religion. He had direct experience popularizing Buddhism—both by assisting the Buddhist Mission in San Francisco in 1903, traveling alongside his master two years later, and addressing Green Acre gatherings in 1907 [535]. Perhaps Sōen, like Sasaki Yeita thirty years later, felt Americans would respond better to an ordained priest, someone fully credentialed in the Japanese Zen establishment, as opposed to a humble layman like Daisetz. Or it may have been Sōkatsu's years of experience popularizing Zen among the urban laity of Tokyo that prompted the decision. Whatever the reason and whether or not it was intentional, after 1906 Daisetz was effectively marginalized from Sōen's American missionary endeavors for the remainder of the Zen master's lifetime.

Senzaki Nyogen, for his part, would sometimes claim that Shaku Sōen intentionally left him in America "to do something for Buddhism" [536]. As noted, however, when Nyogen arrived in America Sōen afforded him no role in his missionary emprise. When Sōkō died Nyogen was in no way flagged to take his place. And when Sōkatsu arrived Nyogen took lessons from him rather than struggle at his side to establish an American chapter of the Forgetting Both Society. As the years passed, it seems Sōen completely lost track of the student he left in San Francisco with no clear means of supporting himself or returning to Japan. Nyogen, however, never forgot his master or ceased to revere him. Each year, Nyogen composed a new poem to Sōen's memory and held a commemoration ceremony introducing the old master to his students. "It was like a dream, but I can see him vividly even now," he would say nearly fifty years after he bid Sōen farewell from the Russell mansion. "Zen monks should think the beginning is the ending, so every morning I think I am still a novice monk in 1896 waiting to enter his *sanzen* room, apprehensive of his severity as he guides me over the rough path" [537].

Nyogen sent to Japan for copies of Sōen's writings. Patiently translating the old script, he produced a small corpus of Sōen's sermons, mottos, poetry, and autobiographical notes. Some of his Mentorgarten sermons were based on these. In this way Shaku Sōen became known to new generations of Zen practitioners.

Sasaki Yeita was virtually unknown to Sōen, little more than a face in Sōkatsu's crowded *zendō*. When Sōkatsu returned to Japan he had no particular objective to further Sōen's aim of building up a presence for Zen in America. Yet, members of Yeita's First Zen Institute would become an incubator for some of the most active and charismatic Zen teachers in America.

Strangely these three unexpected successors of Shaku Sōen never seriously attempted to combine their energies, activities, and resources. Instead, they operated independently. When encountering one another, as during Daisetz's 1936 sweep across the United States, they remained affable and voiced appreciation of the other's work. But one never seemed to trust the others enough to join forces.

At the time Nyogen was hunting for a Zen master to teach at his Mentorgarten, he need not have looked any further than New York. Unlike the masters he scouted in Japan, Sōkei-an could communicate in English and ardently desired to teach Zen to Americans. The two knew each other well enough for Nyogen to periodically look after Sōkei-an's children [538]. Perhaps Nyogen's desire to have a fulltime master for his Southern California Mentorgarten conflicted with Sōkei-an's desire to remain in his adopted Manhattan home. Perhaps Nyogen was concerned about Sōkei-an's lack of priestly qualifications before his ordination and his nebulous status as a Zen master after Sōkatsu disinherited him. The problem, in truth, was probably more of a personal nature. Nyogen could be something of a prude when it came to the lifestyle of Buddhist priests, maintaining that they should not drink, smoke, or marry. Sōkei-an was guilty of at least the latter two faults, as Nyogen would have seen them. Sōkei-an, for his part, considered Nyogen an "egotistical ass" and was not afraid to say as much to his face [539]. Daisetz was more specific. He recalled Nyogen as commanding a poor understanding of Zen, saying that is why Shaku Sōen forbade him from teaching [540]. Both Nyogen and Sōkei-an, while appreciative of Daisetz's seminal work in bringing Zen to the attention of the American reading public, considered his writing too highbrow for many of those attending their meetings [541]. Sōkei-an was also critical of Daisetz's ability to effectively communicate Zen in his whirlwind lecture tours: "The tea ceremony is what Americans think Japan is, and when Dr. Suzuki takes seventy-five dollars for a lecture, he must give them that and not Zen" [542].

Each acted like a man underconfident about his own qualifications, bent on undermining the authority of the others to strengthen his own position. They seemed loath to recognize that they all shared a common lineage, each tracing his missionary activities back to a master they equally venerated. Daisetz, Nyogen, and Sōkei-an shared something else in common as well— something they did not seem prepared to acknowledge. Each would not have been able to play his role in Buddhism's eastward migration were it not for Ida Evelyn Russell.

PART 2

Ida Russell's 1902 visit to Japan had revitalized Sōen's interest in overseeing Zen's spread to the West. After the Parliament of Religions, Sōen had only one American sympathizer with whom he was in regular contact. His friendship with Paul Carus had resulted in a number of articles and, thanks to Daisetz, a book or two that presented his views on Buddhism to America. But Open Court Publishing was a family business, a small company with limited distribution. Its publications may have been able to raise an eyebrow or two among a well-educated minority, but they would not be able to create a groundswell for Buddhism in America. Ida's arrival at Engakuji and subsequent friendship with Sōen introduced him to a very different type of sympathizer. Here was a woman who was not only prepared to write or expound on Buddhism but to fold it into her everyday life. And the Buddhist practice that appealed to her most was meditation—the very hallmark of the Zen sect. As Sōen got to know her and learn that there were other Americans interested in meditation, he immediately began planning his second American mission. Had Ida not arrived at Engakuji it is unlikely Sōen would have seriously entertained the possibility of bringing Zen to America. Ida's interest in Zen inspired Sōen to again take part in Buddhism's spread east and, more importantly to him perhaps, Zen's introduction to America.

Ida Russell's suggestion that Sōen teach at her little commune did not immediately result in a group of Zen practitioners, nor did her enthusiasm for undertaking the study of *kōans* and *zazen* produce a vocal American advocate for the sect in America. However, Sōen's nine-month sojourn at her mansion had a considerable amount of indirect impact on the future of his American missionary endeavors. Her invitation for Sōen to visit her in 1905 resulted in Senzaki Nyogen's departure for America—a trip he would not have made were he not given the opportunity to follow his master there. Sōen's excursion to the East coast resulted in Daisetz meeting, and subsequently falling in love with, Beatrice Lane. Without her writer's muse, academic background, passion for Buddhism and Theosophy, and years of hard work at his side, Daisetz would have been unable to produce the many English writings that would eventually make him an international cause célèbre. It was the work produced by this collaboration with Beatrice—not his earlier writings through Open Court Publishing—that became widely known to the general public [543]. Finally, without Sōen in San Francisco preparing the way for Sōkatsu to follow, Sasaki Yeita would certainly have remained in Japan and never have played his role in the establishment of Zen in America.

Daisetz Suzuki, who possessed a subtle mind when he applied it to interpreting Buddhist teachings, did not seem to appreciate Ida Russell's importance in the establishment of Zen in America. "Japanese consider this a big deal because it was the first time a *hakujin* (Caucasian) participated in *sanzen*," he commented late in his life. "But it was not very significant. She had a lot of money, a little intelligence, and so-called religious faith" [544]. To Daisetz, Ida was enamoured by the Orient, but her grasp of Asian spirituality was superficial in the extreme. This was evident in Ida's view of *dokusan* as an esoteric practice for the initiated elite, rather than as a discipline that could lead any individual to spiritual enlightenment. She did not allow others in her community to practice *dokusan*. In the nine months that Sōen lived in San Francisco, it seems that she practiced *dokusan* nine times, most of the sessions occurring within a brief three-week period. When Ida fell ill in mid-September of 1905 her personal interviews with Sōen ceased, and she never seems to have resumed them in the remaining six months of the Zen master's stay. Daisetz took a dim view not only of the chatelaine of the House of Silent Light but also of the general importance of Sōen's second visit to America. "*Rōshi's* propagation of Zen in America was not fruitful," he said. "People give *Rōshi* credit for propagating Zen across America for the first time, but in fact his impact was not so great. It did not bring forth a fruitful result" [545].

Senzaki Nyogen was more generous when it came to acknowledging Ida Russell's contribution to the establishment of Zen in America. Perhaps it was because his San Francisco and Los Angeles Mentorgartens tended to attract numerous women who, like Ida, had interests in Buddhism and meditation fired by previous experiences with alternative religions. Or he may have been seeking a way to put his students' spiritual pursuits in a historical context, providing them with a set of religious predecessors to whom they could relate. Nyogen remembered Ida to his students as "our sister in the Dhamma" and "gate-opener of Zen here in America" [546]. In describing Zen's spread east from India, he noted that a woman—a nun named Zongchí (Soji)—was among the first group of Chinese to take up the practice of meditation. Likewise, when the teaching reached Japan it was a woman—the Empress Danrin—who became the first Zen student. Ida was the latest in an ancient line of women whose religious interests facilitated the spread of Buddhism: "Here in America, at first, a woman opened her inner eye in studying Zen" [547].

Nyogen not only likened Ida Russell to Zongchí and Empress Danrin, but to Huineng, a central figure in Zen history. Because he was from a southern region of China, whose peasant population was considered uncouth and foreign to the cultured north, Huineng was believed incapable of achieving enlightenment. Not only was he enlightened, but he became the sixth patriarch of the Zen sect which he and his followers propagated in China. Sōen penned a poem on Huineng, which he dedicated to Ida. Nyogen rendered it in this way:

> The Fifth Patriarch told a new monk,
> "Southern monkeys have no Buddha-nature."
> That monk proved that he had Buddha-nature
> By becoming the Sixth Patriarch.
> In any part of the globe
> Where there is air, a fire can burn.
> Someday my teaching will surely go to the West,
> Led by you.
>
> [548]

The last line, "Led by you," was apparently an invention, since the verse does not exist in the Japanese version [549]. Regardless of whether Sōen, Nyogen, or a latter-day Mentorgartener was the source of the line, the audience of the poem—Senzaki's students and others practicing Zen in America—would interpret it the same way. Just as Huineng, a foreigner unfamiliar with Buddhism, was able to achieve enlightenment, Sōen was convinced that Americans could also appreciate the religion. And just as

Huineng's disciples propagated Buddhism on one continent, Sōen anticipated Ida Russell and those coming after her would play a similar role in America, helping Buddhism spread to the Western world.

At the same time, Nyogen was realistic about Ida's actual direct impact on the establishment of Zen in America. If he knew this was because she had been frustrated with Daisetz's translations or viewed Buddhism as but one part of her synthetic religion he did not let on. Instead he explained that Shaku Sōen was such a great man, such a profound teacher that even his direct successors in Japan were but flickering candles to his raging flame. How then, was the implication, could someone who had received his guidance for only a few months hope to carry on his work? "Besides, Mrs. Russell died a few years after the teacher left, therefore her fruit of meditation was not ripened enough to give to others" [550].

Nyogen probably had no clear idea of when Ida actually died, that she had practiced meditation long before meeting Sōen, or that she never had any intention of passing on her "fruit of meditation" to anyone beyond her little circle of friends. Even if he did know these details, they probably would not have mattered much to him. It was more important to him that his American students had a religious history, a lineage of sorts to call their own. Mrs. Alexander Russell should be to them "the pioneer Zen-student in America," someone they could admire and honor for what she attempted to accomplish [551].

PART 3

It was perhaps with this sentiment in mind that on a crisp spring day in San Francisco Nyogen dropped a handful of cards in a mail box [552]. He was in the city for an extended visit at the request of his original Northern California Mentorgarten students. The home of one-time communist Paul Fernandez became his temporary *zendō* as he led his students in an intensive seven-day meditation retreat (*sesshin*). Speaking engagements at the Theosophical Society in San Francisco, Memorial Library of Philosophy in Berkeley, Buddhist temple in Mountain View, and a Japanese school in Redwood City kept him on the move. He conducted a commemoration for Robert Smith, one of his first Mentorgarten students who died suddenly and unexpectedly in Japan, and ordained two more lay disciples. One of them, Nellie Holbrook, now owned the "Silent Light" calligraphy that Sōen wrote for Ida and once hung at the entrance to her property. While visiting Agnes Kast he may have heard about her friend Katherine Ball, who was in Japan and would soon be making a pilgrimage to Ida's memorial in Kamakura. The humble stone lantern that housed Ida's remains was apparently known as the Russell Shrine Temple at this time [553].

Luncheons in Palo Alto, Los Altos, and elsewhere made for a busy schedule. Busy, but not out of the ordinary. Sermons, ordinations, funeral services and memorials had been part of his priestly duties in California for more than a decade. It was perhaps to offer his students something a little different that he drafted the invitations written on the cards:

> A Buddhist Pilgrimage led by Senzaki Nyogen, in memory of Soyen Shaku, the pioneer Zen-master in America, will start at 12 o'clock, March 29, 1936, at the end of the Number 12 car line, Ocean Beach. Take your lunch along.

Senzaki was fond of conducting such "pilgrimages." In Los Angeles he led students from one Buddhist temple to another— there were about a half dozen of them at this point—paying homage to the statues and relics housed in each [554]. He equated it to the pilgrimage routes trafficked by Buddhists in Japan.

Ten people disembarked from the Number 12 streetcar and made their way south along the beach to the old Russell estate. A couple of years after prohibition had forced John Tait to close his restaurant, ownership of the property changed and it reopened as the Edgewater Beach Club. A notorious gambling establishment, police raids soon drove it out of business too. The mansion was not quite abandoned when Nyogen brought his fellow pilgrims to the site. The stables, which once housed the Russells' cart horses, were now leased to a local equestrian club. Besides the riders picking up their horses for a gallop along the coast, picnickers arrived on weekends. Protected by the winds, they munched their lunches behind the fourteen-foot fence that still encircled the property. An elderly recluse, acting as caretaker, sometimes could be seen peering from the broken windows and into the garden, once meticulously maintained but now running wild [555].

Entering the neglected estate, Nyogen led his followers through the parlor where Ida was once questioned on astral travel by *Examiner* reporters, past the hall where she expounded her thoughts on quietude, up the grand staircase, and into the room that had served as Shaku Sōen's private chamber. There Nyogen conducted a brief memorial service for his old master, following it up with a prepared speech in his easy-going, rambling style. Shaku Sōen, he said, was a man of "strong vibration" who possessed "the will of a hero, and the heart of a child." He recounted how he had studied under the old master for five years in the late nineteenth century, sharing with them a few memories of Engakuji, its abbot, and his personality. He recounted how one of his old Aomori Mentorgarten pupils who became a monk at Engakuji had comforted Sōen during his last illness and looked after his grave. "This monk also died last winter, and I am now left alone in this strange land."

Nyogen concluded the pilgrimage, admonishing his students to keep the four vows of Buddhism and composing a poem for the occasion:

> I was the most stupid and stubborn fellow among the
> disciples of Soyen Shaku.
> His kind heart, however, always kept me somewhere in
> the corner, and never gave me up.
> I am still a stupid and stubborn monk, showing no
> change but my white hair.
> Seventeen years after his death, I came to this memorial
> place where there he stayed ...
> The American Sangha followed me, together with
> Japanese students and friends, to pay homage to
> Soyen Shaku, the pioneer Zen-teacher in the
> Occidental countries ...
> The spring breeze also joined us along the road of the
> ocean side, and it is now lingering in the garden of
> this memorial place, blowing gently like the
> compassion of the great teacher himself.

Reciting a few prayers in Pāli, he concluded the pilgrimage. The eleven American Buddhists made their way out, returning to the daylight and leaving the empty house to its silence. "How we enjoyed our lunch in the garden," he later said to the students who did not join the outing, "I will leave to your imagination."

AFTERWARDS

PART 1

IDA Russell's remains are still interred in the stone lantern outside the little house that was once Shaku Sōen's retirement hermitage. While Uemura Sōkō's memorial, also still standing, is prominent and well-marked, Ida's burial site is unidentified. Few people at Tōkeiji remember it as the resting place of the student Sōen once named Keikaku, the first Westerner to formally practice Zen.

*

Alexander Russell—to whom Sōen gave the Buddhist name Sōkan—did not long survive his wife. When required to lease out his mansion, he, Mary Crittenden, and his seven wards removed themselves to a smaller house downtown. A nurse was hired to care for Alexander, who by this time was bedridden. A final stroke brought his life to a close in 1919.

*

Sōen was able to enjoy his flowering garden for only one more season after conducting Ida Russell's funeral. Weakened by piercing facial pains triggered by neuralgia and the throat infection that had long afflicted him, he was diagnosed with acute heart disease in 1918. For a few months he relaxed his ever-hectic lecture schedule, but he was unable to entirely abandon his work. In February 1919 he toyed with the idea of attending the World's Peace Conference to be held in Paris later that year. Following the event he planned to return to America on a westward, round-the-world journey. However, Sōen's health steadily deteriorated in the following months, making international travel impossible. He instead embarked on a series of lecture trips within Japan, ignoring doctor's orders not to exert himself. "For the sake of the Dharma this has to be done at any cost," he wrote [556]. The cost was high. Upon his return home, fever and chills alternately coursed through his body. The monk no longer needed a doctor to tell him to avoid the podium. Coughing fits left him so exhausted that he no longer had the strength to lecture. Sōen continued to entertain visitors, both Japanese and those from abroad. Daisetz, faithful to the end, regularly arrived to translate. In early August, Sōen briefly slipped into a coma, then rallied and continued to make diary entries through the middle of the month. He died at midday on November 1, 1919. He was 60 years old.

Sōen's funeral a month later was an unusually grand affair, attended by many of the prominent citizens and dignitaries who had attended his lectures over the years. Members of Engakuji bestowed on him the posthumous title "Restoring Founder of the Temple" (Chūkō Kaizan) for making the place internationally famous. His tomb is in the wooded cemetery behind Tōkeiji, at the top of a steep stone stairway bounded by bush clover of which Sōen was particularly fond. A serene statue of Amitâbha Buddha, shaded by a maple tree, guards the ashes [557]. To one side is engraved a verse by Sasaki Nobutsuna, Sōen's celebrated poetry instructor:

> When I ask the clouds, the clouds drift away.
> When I ask the wind, the wind flies away.
> So what should I do?

*

On a cold December day in 1940, a fire started somewhere inside the abandoned Russell mansion. Exactly how no one was ever able to explain. The caretaker and his family safely escaped as the flames spread from room to room. Black smoke, billowing from the collapsing roof, attracted thousands of spectators and 140 firemen to the three-alarm blaze. Despite their efforts, the entire structure, along with much of the huge encircling fence, was completely consumed [558]. Long after the embers cooled, city workers leveled the low tor on which the mansion once stood. Lines of row houses were then built, obliterating all trace of the place where Zen Buddhism was introduced to America.

PART 2

After moving out of the Russell residence in 1914, Elise Drexler—whom Sōen named Keimyō—erected a new manor house in Woodside. In this bucolic setting of rolling hills and pasture lands on the San Francisco Peninsula, she established not only her residence but also a home for crippled and sickly children. Incorporated as the Hospital and School for Convalescent Children, it was popularly known as Drexler Hall. Situated on forty acres of land, the institution provided medical attention to the ill, as well as a rudimentary education and vocational training for the permanently handicapped. Unlike the taking in of children at the Russell mansion, Drexler Hall made no pretext of providing a home-like milieu for disadvantaged children. The juveniles were inmates of a benevolent—but institutional—organization. Despite this significant difference, Drexler Hall carried forward the torch of Ida and Elise's experiment in practical philanthropy. It took in children whose heredity had left them lame or infirm, placing them in an environment where medical care, primary school education, and vocational training would hopefully make them self-sufficient. Drexler Hall operated for fifteen years, caring for nearly six hundred children, often at no cost to their families. Many left the institution with practical training in tailoring, stenography, or woodworking [559]. The Great Depression brought an end to the institution, but Elise remained active in children's charities for years to come. She lived on Russian Hill until her death in 1951, aged 85.

*

Dr. Louis Howe—Sōgen—had not been available to assist Ida Russell in her dying hours. At the outbreak of World War I, he joined the Army medical service. Stationed on the front lines in France, grisly amputations occupied too much of his 20-hour shifts. Upon his discharge he served on Drexler Hall's board of directors and remained closely associated with his aunt's other philanthropic pursuits. But like many war veterans, Major Howe was much changed when he returned from the battlefields. The vegetarianism and teetotaling purity from his days at the Russell manor was replaced by addictions to morphine and alcohol. With a considerable struggle he eventually gave up the former, though it proved more difficult to set aside the whiskey that helped dim memories of wartime horror. He died in 1933 at the age of 52 [560].

*

Jean MacCallum—Keichō—remained at her aunt's side for the rest of her life. Upon Elise's death, much of the $950,000 remaining from the Drexler fortune passed on to this lifelong companion. When she passed away in 1970 at 85, she, like her aunt before her, provided modest bequests to each of the Russell wards [561].

PART 3

When Daisetz Suzuki returned to Japan in the first days of 1937 he also returned to his pattern of aggressive publishing. Over the next two years four more books would issue forth from his pen. Among them was *Zen Buddhism and Its Influence on Japanese Culture*, which under a later abbreviated title remains one of the many D. T. Suzuki books still widely available. Another is *Sermons of a Buddhist Abbot* (renamed *Zen for Americans* after it entered the public domain), the records of Shaku Sōen's lectures during his second and final visit to America.

In early 1939, Beatrice Lane Suzuki was diagnosed with cancer, to which she fell victim later the same year. Over the ensuing years,

Daisetz continued his prolific writing career. But without his wife's assistance for the first decade after her death he published mainly in Japanese. His contribution to Japanese scholarship was officially recognized by his election to the Japan Academy, reception of the Cultural Medal, an opportunity to deliver a lecture before the Emperor, and posthumously received rank in the imperial court.

In 1949, at the age of 79, Daisetz Suzuki showed few signs of slowing down. He lectured at the University of Hawai'i for a quarter. The next year saw him teaching at Claremont College, then moving to New York to teach at Columbia University. He would remain there for six years. During this period, the octogenarian traveled extensively, presenting papers at conferences and workshops throughout Europe and America. He exchanged thoughts with Carl Jung, Martin Heidegger, Karl Jaspers, Erich Fromm, Arnold Toynbee, and other intellectual luminaries of the twentieth century. This, combined with his mild manner, quizzical smile, and playful sense of humour, made him something of a media celebrity. The *New Yorker* printed an extensive profile of this ancient sage in bow tie and bifocals. *Vogue* magazine interviewed him, as did numerous radio and television reporters. Beatnik intellectuals read voraciously from his books, adopting the elderly, bemused scholar as part spiritual stepfather, part mascot.

Daisetz's analytical approach to Zen, his interpretation of it as something beyond religion, and his position that it is almost impossible to separate Zen from Japanese culture earned him harsh criticism at times. But his works remained popular until—and beyond—the end of his days. D. T. Suzuki ended his long, productive life in 1966 at the age of 96.

*

Except for the war years, when he was interred in Heart Mountain, Wyoming, Senzaki Nyogen led his Mentorgarten students until his death. This came in 1958 when he was 82 years old. Nakagawa Sōen, abbot of Ryūtakuji and executor of Nyogen's estate, furthered his friend's work in America. He reorganized the Mentorgarten into the Los Angeles Bosatsukai (later California Bosatsukai), trained American students visiting his monastery in Japan, and, through his successor Eidō Tai Shimano, founded a Zen monastery that is still nestled in the Catskill Mountains [562].

*

Sōkei-an once said, "When Dr. Suzuki dies, I will celebrate [his] funeral service in my temple. Suzuki has done a service for Zen" [563]. He was never able to fulfill this vow. His health deteriorated when he was ordered to an internment camp in 1942. His distressed students eventually gained his release, but he passed away in their presence in 1945 shortly after his return to New York.

Ruth Fuller Sasaki (four years after the death of her first husband she married Sōkei-an, in part to secure his release from the camp) was a leading light at the First Zen Institute, which to this day continues to teach Zen to New Yorkers. She later moved to Japan to study under Shaku Sōkatsu's disciple Gotō Zuigan, who eventually ordained her as a priest. Probably taking Daisetz's Zen Hospice as a model, she founded a *zendō* for Westerners interested in practicing Zen in Japan.

*

Sōkatsu, on his return from America, was briefly appointed abbot of Engakuji. He continued to train hundreds of lay people through various incarnations of the Forgetting Both Society, which flourished until he abruptly ordered its closure shortly after World War II. He retained his health into his eighties, teaching advanced students who came to him for instruction. He passed away in 1954, aged 85 [564].

Years earlier, in 1928, when he sent Sōkei-an back to America to cultivate the interest in Zen, he warned his student to be diligent. He planned to one day personally appraise how well Sōkei-an had accomplished his mission of spreading Zen to America: "Shigetsu-san, five hundred years from now I shall be born again to see the condition of this country" [565]. Sōkatsu was not the only one to anticipate checking back on his comrades.

*

Mary Crittenden devoted the remainder of her life to raising Ida Russell's sons and daughters. Despite the assistance of others, she found it impossible to support all of them on the limited income that came from Ida's estate. Two of the children, twelve-year-old Margaret and five-year-old Stuart, were placed with other families who are said to have adopted them. Katherine was lodged in a convent for nearly two years before rejoining Mary and the others. Baldwin, nearly an adult when his mother died, fell in love, moved to Southern California, and followed his father's footsteps as a salesman.

With little money at her disposal, Mary moved the children to Oakland where the cost of living was more reasonable. Having seen them all reach adulthood, she prepared a handwritten will and testament [566]. The household furniture and other effects left over from the Russell estate were to be divided among the children. She advised them to keep track of a few shares of stock in a music company, now worthless but perhaps eventually regaining their value. The "priestess Teaset"—the antique once owned by the Mikado's sister and that Sōen had given to Ida—should be sold as it might fetch them $200.

But pecuniary matters were of little importance to her. "Never mind these material things," she wrote in her last words to the children of Ida Russell. Instead, she looked forward to the day when she would be once again reunited with them and the other residents of the House of Silent Light. "Be your best and look high. I'll meet you all in another life."

APPENDIX

Annotations

1 The autobiography of Huineng is contained in the first section of the *Platform Sūtra*, also known as the *Sūtra of the Sixth Patriarch*. See Thomas Cleary, trans., *Sūtra of Hui Neng: Grand Master of Zen*, Boston: Shambhala, 1998.

2 Shaku Sōen, *Bankoku shūkyō taikai ichiran*, in *Seironto shi sonohoka: Sōen Zenji jiden*, volume 10, Tokyo: Heibonsha, 1930, p. 122.

3 Barrows 1893, p. 68.

4 Druyvesteyn 1976, p. 31.

5 Druyvesteyn 1976, p. 33.

6 Jin Zen Hokutsu, March 17, 1893, in *Journal of the Maha-Bodhi Society*, Calcutta: Maha-Bodhi Society, May 1893, p. 7.

7 Ketelaar 1991, p. 44.

8 Barrows 1892, p. 568.

9 Ketelaar 1991, p. 46.

10 Ketelaar 1990, p. 159.

11 Furuta Shōkin 1967, pp. 74-75. Ketelaar describes Shaku Sōen and his fellow Japanese delegates as generally unpublished prior to representing Buddhism at this World's Parliament of Religions. See Ketelaar 1991, p. 49. This, however, was not the case. Upon his return from Ceylon in the late 1880s, Sōen published *The Buddhism of the Southwest* (Seinan no bukkyō). See Jaffe 2004, p. 83. Sōen also published a series of lectures (Bukkyō kōenshū) in 1889 and *Travels in Ceylon* (Seirontō shi) in 1890.

12 Jin Zen Hokutsu, March 17, 1893, in *Journal of the Maha-Bodhi Society*, Calcutta: Maha-Bodhi Society, May 1893, p. 7.

13 *Gokoku* quoted in *Japan Weekly Mail*, Yokohama: Jappan Mēru Shinbunsha, December 31, 1892, as quoted in *Journal of the Maha-Bodhi Society*, Calcutta: Maha-Bodhi Society, March 1893 p. 5.

14 *Journal of the Maha-Bodhi Society*, Calcutta: Maha-Bodhi Society, May 1893 p. 7.

15 *Wind Bell*, San Francisco: Zen Center, Fall 1969 volume 8, p. 7; Tsunemitsu 1994, p. 222.

16 Senzaki and McCandless 1961, p. 96.

17 Akizuki 1992, p. 103.

18 Akizuki 1992, p. 103.

19 Shaku Sōen to Kōsen, January 25, 1888, Senzaki Papers, University of California, Berkeley.

20 *Journal of the Maha-Bodhi Society*, Calcutta: Maha-Bodhi Society, October 1893, pp. 5-6.

21 Snodgrass 2003, p. 78; Nagao 1931, p. 94.

22 *Japan Weekly Mail*, Yokohama: Jappan Mēru Shinbunsha, November 4, 1893, p. 539.

23 Inoue 2000, p. 75.

24 Barrows 1893, p. 61.

25 For a detailed analysis of the efforts listed here see Snodgrass 2003.

26 Verhoeven 1997, p. 369.

27 John Henry Barrows to Dharmapala in *Journal of the Maha-Bodhi Society*, Calcutta: Maha-Bodhi Society, May 1893 p. 4.

28 Shirato 1963, pp. 97ff.

29 Shirato 1963, pp. 99-100.

30 Barrows 1893, pp. 829-831. Portions amended against Neely 1893.

31 Shaku Sōen 1930, p. 138; Shaku Sōen, "Reflections on an American Journey," *The Eastern Buddhist*, Kyoto: The Eastern Buddhist Society, Autumn 1993, p. 132; Ketelaar 1991, p. 49.

32 Ketelaar 1990, p. 151.

33 Barrows 1893, pp. 115-116.

34 Barrows 1893, p. 95.

33 *Journal of the Maha-Bodhi Society*, Calcutta: Maha-Bodhi Society, November 1893, p. 6.

36 *Journal of the Maha-Bodhi Society*, Calcutta: Maha-Bodhi Society, October 1982 p. 8; November 1893, pp. 3-7.

37 More than thirty years later Charles Strauss was corresponding with editors of Buddhist periodicals in Britain, criticizing them for unduly favoring Mahayana over Theravada traditions. See *The Eastern Buddhist*, April 1930, p. 281. Strauss also maintained an active dialog on Buddhism with Paul

Carus, some of which is preserved in the letter boxes of the Open Court Archives at Southern Illinois University, Carbondale.

38 Snodgrass 2003, p. 221.

39 Ketelaar 1991, p. 49.

40 Unless otherwise noted, the description of Belmont Hall presented in this chapters is derived from articles in the following newspaper issues: *Los Angeles Times*, February 17, 1895, p. 10; February 19, 1895, p. 10; April 5, 1895, p. 8; April 6, 1895, pp. 6, 8; April 11, p. 8; April 14, p. 10; April 22, 1895, p. 6; April 23, 1895, p. 6; April 24, 1895, p. 3; April 24, 1895, p. 6; April 25, 1895, p. 8; April 27, 1895, p. 10; July 6, 1895, p. 8; January 9, 1896, p. 8; June 30, 186, p. 10; October 7, 1896, p. 10; February 15, 1897, p. 8; March 26, 1897, p. 8; March 27, 1897, p. 9; March 28, 1897, p. 23; March 30, 1897, p. 9; March 31, 1897, p. 5; April 1, 1897, p. 5; April 2, 1897, p. 8; April 3, 1897, p. 9; April 4, 1897, p. 11; April 6, 1897, pp. 6, 8-9; April 7, 1897, p. 9; April 8, 1897, p. 5; April 8, 1897, p. 6; *Los Angeles Herald*, April 24, 1895, p. 7; March 27, 1897, p. 10; March 28, 1897, p. 12; March 30, 1897, p. 8; March 31, 1897, p. 10; April 1, 1897, p. 10; April 2, 1897, p. 10; April 3, 1897, p. 10; April 4, 1897, p. 24; April 5, 1897, p. 10; April 7, 1897, p. 10; *Los Angeles Express*, April 23, 1895, p. 1; April 26, 1895, p. 5; March 31, 1897, p. 1; April 1, 1897, p. 1; April 2, 1897, p. 1; April 3, 1897, p. 1.

41 *Los Angeles Herald*, April 1, 1897, p. 10.

42 *Los Angeles Herald*, April 2, 1897, p. 10.

43 *Los Angeles Herald*, April 2, 1897, p. 10.

44 Personal Property Tax Role, *San Francisco Municipal Reports*, 1876-1877. San Francisco Public Library, San Francisco History Room, 218.

45 *Los Angeles Times*, April 24, 1895, p. 3.

46 Baptismal book, Parish of St. John, Bangor, Maine. Pacific Preparatory School enrollment list, University of the Pacific archives, Stockton, California. *San Francisco Chronicle*, September 22, 1917, p. 10.

47 *Los Angeles Times*, February 17, 1895, p. 10.

48 *Los Angeles Times*, February 17, 1895, p. 10. See also *Los Angeles Times*, April 6, 1897, p. 9: "'Her main teachings were exhortation upon rendering one's self at ease, to have as little to do with the outside world as possible;' that is, to throw yourself into an entirely passive state…. 'And not exert your mind except when absolutely necessary; not to reason.'"

49 *Los Angeles Herald*, March 28, 1897, p. 12.

50 *Los Angeles Herald*, April 2, 1897, p. 10.

51 *Los Angeles Times*, April 6, 1897, p. 8.

52 *Los Angeles Times* April 2, 1897, p. 8.

53 *Los Angeles Times*, October 10, 1890, p. 7; May 27, 1893, p. 4; June 23, 1894, p. 4; July 5, 1895, p. 1l.

54 *Los Angeles Herald*, April 2, 1897, p. 10; *Los Angeles Times*, April 2, 1897, p. 8.

55 *Los Angeles Times*, October 7, 1896, p. 10.

56 *Los Angeles Times*, March 27, 1897, p. 23.

57 *Los Angeles Times*, April 3, 1897, p. 9.

58 *Los Angeles Herald*, April 2, 1897, p. 10.

59 *Los Angeles Times*, April 2, 1897, p. 8.

60 *Los Angeles Times,* February 17, 1895, p. 10.

61 *Los Angeles Herald*, March 26, 1897, p. 12.

62 *Los Angeles Herald*, March 26, 1895, p. 12.

63 *Los Angeles Times*, March 31, 1897, p. 5.

64 Los *Angeles Times*, March 30, 1897, p. 9.

65 Ketelaar 1990, p. 159.

66 *Dentō*, August 1893, as quoted in Ketelaar 1991, p. 47.

67 *New York Times*, August 19, 1894, p. 4.

68 *Japan Weekly Mail*, Yokohama: Jappan Mēru Shinbunsha, December 2, 1893, p. 658.

69 Tsunemitsu 1994, p. 223.

70 Furuta 1967, p. 77.

71 Senzaki Nyogen, "Kyogaku," August 4, 1934, p. 10, Senzaki Papers, University of California, Berkeley.

72 Sawada 1998, pp. 130, 142.

73 Holz 2002, p. 56.

74 Sasaki Shigetsu, Sōkei-an, *Cat's Yawn*, New York: First Zen Institute of America, July 1940, p. 3; See also Holz 2002, pp. 72-73.

75 Holz 2002, pp. 56, 59.

76 Akizuki 1992, p. 97. There is no indication Sōen made a regular habit of visiting brothels and even Akizuki has doubts about this anecdote.

77 *Sō* is the Buddhist reading of Chinese character "*shū*," the first part of which appears in the word *shūkyō*, "religion." The second syllable of the name comes from the compound *enzetsu*, "to preach or to give a stirring lecture." Historically the name has been rendered Soyen, the 'y' being inserted to offset the syllables after the long vowel. In modern time the accepted Romanization is Sōen. In 1870s the Meiji government required

that Buddhist clerics take surnames. Sōen took Shaku, the Japanese transliteration of Śākya, the historical Buddha's clan name. Jaffe 2004, p. 80.

78 Senzaki Nyogen, "Speech on Buddhism," November 11, 1935, p. 2, Senzaki Papers, University of California, Berkeley.

79 Henderson 1993, p. 90.

80 Tsunemitsu 1994, p. 223; Snell to Carus, September 1, 1893 in Verhoeven 1997, p. 307.

81 Carus 1897, p. 83. Henderson 1993, p. 92.

82 *Chicago Daily Tribune*, Chicago: Tribune Company, November 15, 1897, p. 8.

83 Henderson 1993, p. 89ff.

84 Tsunemitsu 1994, p. 222.

85 Shaku Sōen to Paul Carus, December 17, 1895, The Open Court Archives, Southern Illinois University, Carbondale; D. T. Suzuki to Paul Carus, May 14, 1896, The Open Court Archives, Southern Illinois University, Carbondale.

86 Henderson 1993, p. 100; Shaku Sōen to Paul Carus January 15, 1896, The Open Court Archives, Southern Illinois University, Carbondale.

87 Furuta 1967, p. 79.

88 Shimano 1978, p. 101.

89 Shirato 1963, pp. 104-107.

90 Shimano 1978, p. 10.

91 Tanahashi and Chayat 1996, p. 5.

92 Fields 1992, p. 170

93 Shimano 1978, p. 119.

94 Shimano 1978, p. 119.

95 "Early Memories," *The Middle Way* 39, November 1964, p. 106.

96 Nishimura 1973, p. 58.

97 Akizuki 1992, p. 176.

98 Akizuki 1992, p. 174.

99 Inoue 1989, volume 1, p. 466.

100 Akizuki 1992, p. 174.

101 Inoue 2000, pp. 110ff.

102 Uemura Sōkō to Suzuki July 18, 1903, in Inoue 1989, p. 467,

103 Militz 1904, pp. 77-78.

104 *San Francisco Chronicle*, November 15, 1968, p. 23.

105 The only document that identifies Clarence Crossley as Ida Russell's secretary is a slip of paper entitled "Aunt Ida's 'menage,'" written by Alexander Russell's niece, Janet Russell Phillips, and kept in the private collection of Susan Stetson Clarke. The document contains a number of errors, misidentifying the Norwegian housekeeper as Swedish and the Japanese cook as Chinese, so perhaps Clarence Crossley's role as secretary is also inaccurate. In any event, the 1910 census identifies Mary C. Russell as a secretary, a role she could have taken over from Clarence Crossley who left the Russell mansion in the summer of 1906.

106 *San Francisco Call*, March 28, 1901, p. 12.

107 "Studying Universal Art," unidentified newspaper clipping in Daisy MacCallum Scrapbook, Mendocino Historical Society, Mendocino, California.

108 Simmons 1987, p. 130, referencing *Christian Science Journal* article of November 1887.

109 *San Francisco Examiner*, September 15, 1910, p. 1.

110 *Los Angeles Express*, April 1, 1897, p. 1.

111 Angels crop up consistently in articles about Ida Russell. In the Belmont Hall documents, Josephine Holmes is variously described as claiming she is the reincarnation of an angel or periodically possessed by one. Much later, Elise Drexler would be referred to as the "financial angel" in such a way that implies that is the way the Russell community referred to her. (*San Francisco Examiner*, September 15, 1910, p. 2.) Then there is the aforementioned note about guardian angels that Ida wrote to her niece. Despite all these references, it is not possible to describe exactly what Ida believed concerning the angelic host.

112 Ida Russell to Theodore Wores, May 10, 1906, in private collection of A. Jess Shenson.

113 Jaffe 2004, p. 81.

114 The author is indebted to conversations with archivists at the Henry S. Olcott Memorial Library and Archives for information pertaining to the Russells' membership records.

115 Fryer 1901, p. 251.

116 *Light of Dharma* subscription book, Buddhist Churches of America archives, Japanese-American National Museum, Los Angeles.

117 Tada 1990, p. 31.

118 "Buddha Shrine Worshipped in House of Mystery," *San Francisco Examiner*, September 15, 1910, p. 1

119 Marie Louise Burke, *Swami Vivekananda: His Second Visit to the West*, Calcutta: Advaita Ashrama, 1973, p. 279.

120 Vivekananda, *The Complete Works of Swami Vivekananda*, Calcutta: Advaita Ashrama, 1989, volume 6, pp. 37-40; volume 4, pp. 227-237.

121 *San Francisco Chronicle*, November 15, 1968, p. 23.

122 *San Francisco Examiner*, September 15, 1910, p. 2.

123 Shaku Sōen 1993, p. 140.

124 "Alexander Russells Buy Great Painting," *San Francisco Examiner*, March 2, 1906, p. 7. Late in his life Baldwin Russell made direct reference to these morning baths in the ocean, which in his case was prescribed to rid him of a fever. Tape-recorded recollections of Baldwin Russell, in private collection of Paul and Jan Russell.

125 Autograph book of Janet Russell, in private collection of Ann-Marie Cunniff; also quoted in Mary Russell Stetson Clarke, *Russells in America*, Melrose, MA: Hilltop Press, 1988, pp. 135-136.

126 *Los Angeles Herald*, April 2, 1897, p. 10.

127 Autograph book of Janet Russell, in private collection of Ann-Marie Cunniff.

128 Shaku Sōen 1993, p. 140.

129 Shaku Sōen 1993, p. 140.

130 *San Francisco Examiner*, September 18, 1910, p. 20.

131 Julian St. John, "Voice of Silence," *Pacific Theosophist*, volume 6, no. 10, January 1897 (misprinted as volume 11, no. 1), p. 12.

132 "Golden Gate Lodge, American Section, T. S.," *Light of Dharma*, volume 1, no. 5, December 1905, p. 32.

133 Militz 1904, p. 28.

134 Militz 1904, pp. 77-78.

135 *San Francisco Examiner*, September 15, 1910, p. 1.

136 Clarke 1988, p. 133; Shaku Sōen 1993, p. 140.

137 "Kelley Family Album," *Mendocino Historical Review*, volume 6, no. 3, December 1981, Mendocino Historical Research Inc., Mendocino, Calif., pp. 4-5; Bailey Millard, *History of the San Francisco Bay Region*, American Historical Society Inc., Chicago, Illinois, 1924, volume 2, pp. 121-123.

138 "Wanda McFarland," Biographical Index Card File, Mendocino Historical Society, Mendocino, California.

139 Bruce Levine, *Mendocino County Remembered: An Oral History*, volume 2, Mendocino: Mendocino County Historical Society, 1973, p. 18. Also "Wanda McFarland," Biographical Index Card File.

140 *San Francisco Chronicle*, November 15, 1968, p. 23.

141 *San Francisco Chronicle*, May 19, 1901, p. 24.

142 *San Francisco Chronicle*, November 15, 1968, p. 23. Theodore Besterman, *The Mind of Annie Besant*, London: Theosophical Publishing House, pp. 215-221.

143 Shirato 1963, pp. 241-242

144 Personal conversation with Dr. Howe's nephew and namesake, Louis Philippe Howe of San Jose, California.

145 See Bickford Brooks, "Biography of Benjamin Brooks," March 22, 1936, California Historical Society archives. Also see *San Francisco News*, December 2, 1940, p. 3; "Benjamin Sherman Brooks" in Bailey Millard, *History of the San Francisco Bay Region*, volume 2, Chicago: American Historical Society Inc., 1924, pp. 56-57; F. R. Adams, "House of Mystery," *The San Franciscan*, April 1928, pp. 22, 27.

146 Colville's San Francisco Directory and Gazetteer of 1856-1857, quoted in *Oakland Tribune*, September 4, 1960, p. C-l. See also Muscatine, 1975, p. 232. Note: The *Tribune* article refers to the Oceanside House as Ocean House. The two roadhouses were often confused with one another, the latter being situated next to a racetrack a few miles inland.

147 Bickford Brooks, "Biography of Benjamin Brooks," March 22, 1936, California Historical Society archives; *San Francisco Examiner*, September 15, 1910; *San Francisco Chronicle*, May 19, 1901, p. 24.

148 Shirato 1963, pp. 241-242.

149 Shaku Sōen 1993, p. 141. In this account Sōen does not mention Nomura Yōzō by name, only noting that Ida Russell's Japanese guide introduced the two to each other. See also Inoue 2000, p. 115.

150 "Gaijin no sanzen zanmai" ("Foreigners Absorbed in Sanzen"), *Zenshū*, Kyoto: Baiyōshōin, volume 94, January 1903, p. 46.

151 Shirato 1963, p. 242.

152 Sasaki, Cat's Yawn, July 1940, p. 7.

153 Hearn, 1894, pp. 62-70. See also Hartshorne, 1902, pp. 21-29, 64-79.

154 Sasaki, *Cat's Yawn*, July 1940, p. 3.

155 Hermann Keyserling, *Travel Diary of a Philosopher*, New York: Harcourt, Brace & Co., 1925, p. 228.

156 Shaku Sōen 1993, p. 140.

157 Shaku Sōen 1993, p. 140.

158 Shaku Sōen 1993, p. 141; also Inoue 1989, p. 336.

159 Inoue 2000, p. 128.

160 Inoue 2000, p. 115.

161 Shaku Sōen 1993, pp. 141-142.

162 Among the most popular modern books to provide details of Ida Russell's stay at Engakuji is Fields 1992, pp. 168-169. Unfortunately, Fields presents a particularly confused account of Sōen's early experience teaching Zen to Westerners, saying that prior to the Russells' arrival he had already allowed a group of three Americans to live at his monastery. "From these Americans, who ate barley gruel with the monks and sat a full *sesshin* [monastic retreat], Sōen had learned something about how to guide foreigners in Zen." Fields is paraphrasing Furuta 1967. Furuta, in turn, drew from a personal letter in which Sōen describes his three American visitors (See Shaku Sōen to Kitamura Eki, August 3, 1902, Nagao 1931, p. 155). What Fields failed to realize and Furuta failed to note was that the three Americans Sōen described in his letter are in fact Ida Russell, Elise Drexler, and Louis Howe. There is no evidence that Sōen allowed any other group of Westerners to live at Engakuji before Ida's arrival.

163 Daisetz Teitarō Suzuki, *Training of the Zen Buddhist Monk*, New York: University Books, 1965, pp. 91ff.

164 Akizuki 1992, p. 173. Note: Ida and Elise are sometimes remembered as staying in the *Koji-rin*, the dormitory for lay practitioners. This is highly unlikely. Sōen's determination not to spare Ida from the harsh realities of monastic life would not have included requiring her to live in the communal dormitory inhabited solely by male monks.

165 Shaku Sōen 1993, p. 142.

166 Keyserling 1925, p. 228.

167 Shaku Sōen 1993, p. 142.

168 Furuta 1967, p. 79.

169 Uemura Sōkō, *Zen Ken ikō* (Posthumous Writings of Zen Ken), Tōkeiji: Kamakura, 1908, pp. 106-107.

170 Shaku Sōen, "First step in meditation," Senzaki Papers, University of California, Berkeley.

171 Shaku Keishun, ed., *Ryōgakutsu nenji den* (Chronological life of Ryōgakutsu), Daichūji, 1952, p. 204. See also Tōkeiji, p. 22.

172 Shaku Sōen 1993, p. 143. See also Furuta, p. 79, where Alexander Russell is mistakenly identified as studying at Engakuji.

173 Inoue Zenjō, *Tōkeiji*, Kamakura: Tōkeiji, 1997, p. 466. See also Akizuki 1992, p. 173.

174 "Gaijin no sanzen zanmai" ("Foreigners Absorbed in Sanzen"), *Zenshū*, Kyoto: Baiyōshōin, volume 94, January 1903, p. 64.

175 *San Francisco Examiner*, September 15, 1910, p. 2.

176 *Los Angeles Times*, February 17, 1895, p. 10.

177 *Los Angeles Express*, April 1, 1897, p. 1.

178 Shaku Sōen introduction to Senzaki's "Grass in the Field" in Fields 1992, p. 171. For a different translation see Senzaki Nyogen, et al., *Namu Dai Bosa*, New York: Zen Studies Society, 1976, p. 8.

179 Senzaki 1976, p. 9.

180 Fujimoto Kōjō, "Tōzen Zenkutsu no hito" (The Zen Man of the Eastward-facing Hall: The life of Senzaki Nyogen), *Zen Bunka*, 1986, volume 120, pp 133-137; volume 121, pp. 124-134; volume 122, pp. 121-132. Senzaki Nyogen may have latched onto his grandmother's taunts as a means of psychologically disassociating himself from a Japan he later left behind and which was increasingly unfamiliar to him. References to a Russian or Chinese father were presented in collections of his writings, such as *Namu Dai Bosa* (1976) and *Like a Dream, Like a Fantasy* (1978). However, *Endless Vow* (1996), compiled by the same editor as *Like a Dream* and perhaps following the lead of *Bukkyō tōzen: Taiheiyo o wattata Bukkyō* (1990), notes that the Fukaura city records show Aizo born to a clearly Japanese family.

181 Tanahashi and Chayat 1996, p. 3.

182 Fujimoto 1986, volume 121, p. 131.

183 Tanahashi and Chayat 1996, p. 5.

184 Fujimoto 1986, volume 121, p. 134.

185 Shirato 1963, p. 243.

186 Uemura 1908, p. 87.

187 Shirato 1963, p. 243.

188 Shaku Keishun 1952, p. 60.

189 Shaku Sōen 1993, p. 142.

190 Uemura 1908, p. 102.

191 For much of her adult life Ida Russell adjusted her year of birth back by five years. The date of birth that often appears on official documents, March 10, 1862, conflicts with her enumeration, at three years old, in the 1860 census. Though a birth certificate no longer exists, Ida's baptismal record, kept in the archives of St. John's Catholic Church in Bangor, Maine, lists her date of birth as March 10, 1857.

192 "Autobiography of Soyen Shaku," Senzaki Papers, UC Berkeley.

193 Uemura 1908, 100.

194 Uemura 1908, 92.

195 Uemura 1908, 114.

196 Shirato 1963, p. 241ff.

197 "Gaijin no sanzen zanmai" ("Foreigners Absorbed in Sanzen"), *Zenshū*, Kyoto: Baiyōshōin, volume 94, January 1903, p. 64.

198 Inoue 2000, p. 116.

199 *Japan Weekly Mail*, Yokohama: Jappan Mēru Shinbunsha, December 20, 1902, p. 694.

200 Inoue 1989, volume 1, p. 336.

201 Shaku Sōen 1993, p. 143; Shirato 1963, p. 242.

202 Inoue Zenjō, "Sōen Zenji no shōgai" (Life of Sōen Zenji"), *Zen Bunka*, Kyoto: Institute for Zen Studies, volume 50, October 1968, p. 26.

203 Shaku Sōen, "Breadth of Buddhism," *The Open Court*, January 1900.

204 D. T. Suzuki to Shaku Sōen, June 11, 1898, in Inoue Zenjō, *Suzuki Daisetsu no hito to gakumon* (The Personality and Scholarship of Daisetz Suzuki), Tokyo: Shunjūsha, 1992, p. 141.

205 Uemura 1908, pp. 84, 103. Uemura Sōkō visited Ida at both the Imperial Hotel in Tokyo and Grand Hotel in Yokohama at the time she was also said to be living at Engakuji.

206 D. T. Suzuki to Shaku Sōen, November 21, 1899, in Inoue 1992, p. 147.

207 D. T. Suzuki to Paul Carus, September 17, 1903, The Open Court Archives, Southern Illinois University.

208 D. T. Suzuki to Paul Carus, August 4, 1903, The Open Court Archives, Southern Illinois University.

209 D. T. Suzuki to Paul Carus, August 30, 1903 and September 17, 1903, The Open Court Archives, Southern Illinois University.

210 Thomas Tweed, *American Encounter with Buddhism*, Bloomington: University of Indiana Press, 1992, pp. 51, 67-68.

211 *San Francisco Chronicle*, August 30, 1903, p. 36.

212 *San Francisco Call*, October 10, 1910, p. 7. It is possible that a number of these destinations were reached prior to Ida, Elise, and Louis Howe's arrival in Yokohama in July 1902. A number of sources indicate that Japan was Ida's last port of call on her 1902 voyage. See Inoue 1989, p. 336; Akizuki, p. 173. See also Clarke 1988, pp. 133-135.

213 *San Francisco Chronicle*, May 24, 1963, p. 20 quoting unnamed article.

214 Inoue 1968, p. 17.

215 Uemura Sōkō to D. T. Suzuki, July 18, 1903, in Inoue 1989, p. 466-467.

216 Ueumura 1908, p. 273.

217 Inoue 1989, p. 467.

218 Inoue 1997, p. 467.

219 Shaku Sōen, "Inauguration of So-yen Shaku," Senzaki Papers, University of California, Berkeley.

220 Shaku Sōen, "Arbitration Instead of War," *Neely's History of the Parliament of Religions and Religious Congresses at the World's Columbian Exposition*, Walter Houghton, ed., Chicago: F. T. Neely, 1893, pp. 797-798.

221 Snodgrass 2003, p. 78-79.

222 See the account of Uchiyama Gudō, in Brian Victoria, *Zen at War*, New York: Weatherhill, 1997, pp. 38-54.

223 Respect for the imperial government was a trait that Sōen shared with his former teacher. Kōsen Imakita maintained "an attitude of modest deference" to the Japanese government and "routinely expressed reverence for the *kami* and their imperial 'descendents.'" See Sawada 1998, p. 120. Sawada observes that Kōsen rarely criticized government policy in public, making rare and delicately worded exceptions when legislation directly impacted monastic life and practices.

224 Shaku Sōen to Kōsen, April 14, 1887, Senzaki Papers, University of California, Berkeley.

225 Shaku Sōen to Kitamura Zen'eki, February 6, 1904, in Furuta 1967, pp. 79-80.

226 Shaku Sōen, "At the Battle of Nan-Shan Hill," in Soyen Shaku, *Sermons of a Buddhist Abbot*, New York: Samuel Weiser, 1971, pp. 196-203.

227 Victoria 1997, p. 29. Reference is to *Heimin Shinbun*, No. 34, August 7, 1904.

228 Shaku Sōen, "Address Delivered at a Service Held in Memory of Those Who Died in the Russo-Japanese War," in Soyen Shaku 1971, p. 206. See also Furuta 1967, p. 80ff.

229 Soyen Shaku 1971, pp. 198-199.

230 See *Cassell's History of the Russo-Japanese War,* London: Cassell, 1904 or 1905, volume 2, pp. 335ff.

231 Letter to Amakuki Sessan, in Nagao Sōshi, ed., *Sōen Zenji to sono shūi* (Sōen Zenji and his Surroundings), Tokyo: Ōzora-sha, 1993, p. 246.

232 Furuta 1967, p. 81.

233 Akizuki 1992, p. 175.

234 Yamamoto Ryōkichi to D. T. Suzuki, August 27, 1905, in Inoue 1989, volume 1, p. 34.

235 Shaku Sōen to Amakuki Sessan, in Nagao 1931, p. 247.

236 *Japan Weekly Mail*, Yokohama: Jappan Mēru Shinbunsha, March 3, 1894, p. 276.

237 Shaku Sōen, *Ōbei unsui ki* (A Monk's Diary of Travels in the West), Tokyo: Kinkōdō Shoseki, 1907, June 12, 1905, pp. 3-4.

238 "En route to America," Shaku Sōen, June 1905, Senzaki Papers, University of California, Berkeley; Fields 1992, p. 168

239 Shaku Keishun 1952, p. 208.

240 Shaku Sōen's introduction to "Grass in the Field," in *Namu Dai Bosa*, New York: Zen Studies Society, 1976, p. 8.

241 Inoue 1997, p. 380.

242 Inoue 1997, p. 382.

243 *San Francisco Examiner*, March 2, 1906, p. 7.

244 *San Francisco Call*, April 15, 1911, p. 25. Also *San Francisco Chronicle*, July 6, 1913, p. 38.

245 Uemura 1908, p. 111.

246 "Indenture," December 12, 1923, Private collection of Janice and Paul Russell.

247 "Russell Home is Scene of Garden Fête," *San Francisco Examiner*, August 15, 1915, p. 24. Additional details of the mansion's furnishings can be gleaned from the extensive probate records in the archives of the San Francisco Superior Court.

248 Clarke 1988, p. 135.

249 Shaku Sōen to Ōta Jōshō, June 28, 1905, Nagao 1931, p. 184.

250 Shaku Sōen 1907, July 27, p. 15.

251 Shaku Sōen to Ōta Jōshō, June 28, 1905, in Nagao 1931, p. 185.

252 Will of Ida Russell, October 17, 1917, San Francisco Superior Court Archives. Also, tape-recorded recollections of Baldwin Russell, c. 1990, in private collection of Paul and Janice Russell.

253 Shaku Sōen 1907, June 27, 1905, p. 14.

254 Unless otherwise noted, details of Sōen's life at the Russell house are from Shaku Sōen 1907, June 27, 1905.

255 *San Francisco Chronicle*, September 22, 1917, p. 10.

256 *San Francisco Examiner*, September 15, 1910, p. 2.

257 Ida Russell to Theodore Wores, in private collection of A. Jess Shenson, San Francisco.

258 The author is indebted to Inoue Zenjō, the current *jūshoku* of Tōkeiji, who in August 2002 shared his insights into the organizational structure of Zen monasteries and the history of Engakuji and Kenchōji.

259 Ida was not alone in misidentifying Sōen. Numerous erroneous, and often amusing, titles were heaped onto him during his stay in America. To the *Los Angeles Herald* he was "head of the Buddhist religion," ("Buddhist Temple for Los Angeles," *Los Angeles Herald*, September 18, 1905, p. 2), while to the *Los Angeles Examiner* he was "Lord Abbot of Engakyni and Kene Hoji of the Shyana sect." ("Japanese Exponent of Buddhism Here," *Los Angeles Examiner*, September 18, 1905, p. 5) "Shyana" is probably the reporter's attempt at dhyana, the Sanskrit word for meditation and cognate of the Japanese word "Zen." Following his first visit to the United States, Sōen was mistakenly identified as the "archbishop of the Zen Buddhist sect" (*Neely's History of the World's Parliament of Religion*, p. 36).

260 Shaku Sōen to Kōsen, April 14, 1887, Senzaki Papers, University of California, Berkeley.

261 Shaku Sōen 1907, June 11, 1905, p. 2.

262 Shaku Sōen 1907, June 15, 1905, p. 8.

263 Tada 1990, pp. 21, 31.

264 Shaku Sōen to Ōta Jōshō, June 28, 1905, in Furuta 1967, p. 81, also in Nagao Daigaku, Sōen 1931, p. 185.

265 Shaku Sōen to Ōta Jōshō, June 28, 1905, in Furuta 1967, p. 81.

266 Questions and Answers, 1936, Senzaki Papers, University of California, Berkeley.

267 Fields 1992, p. 169.

268 Return of sale of personal property, April 2, 1919, Probate Documents for the Estate of Ida E. Russell, San Francisco Superior Court Archives.

269 *Los Angeles Graphic*, March 10, 1906, p. 9, in private collection of A. Jess Shenson.

270 J. M. Heinrich Hofmann to Elise Drexler, June 8, 1904, and January 9, 1905, Box 438, File "Hofmann Paintings," Shelf BB-8, Cage 2, The Riverside Church Archives, New York.

271 Clarke 1988, p. 135.

272 Autograph book of Janet Russell, in private collection of Ann-Marie Cunniff.

273 D. T. Suzuki to Carus, undated, 1905, The Open Court Archives; D. T. Suzuki to Yamamoto Ryōkichi, in Inoue 1989, volume 1, p. 334.

274 *San Francisco Call*, January 6, 1913, p. 12.

275 *San Francisco Examiner*, May 18, 1919, p. 50.

276 Tada 1990, p. 31

277 Tape-recorded recollections of Baldwin Russell, in private collection of Paul and Janice Russell.

278 Shaku Sōen 1907, November 21, 1905, p. 64.

279 See Clarke 1988, pp. 71, 82.

280 Alexander's nieces, who would visit the mansion later that year, also came to know Elise Drexler as "Aunt Lee," even though there was no blood relationship between the Russells and the Drexler or Kelley families. See Clarke 1988, p. 134.

281 "Kelley Family Album," Mendocino Historical Review, volume 6, no. 3, December 1981, Mendocino Historical Research Inc., Mendocino, Calif., p. 6.

282 *San Francisco City Directory*, San Francisco: Langley Publishing, 1892, p. 83.

283 "Drexler Left Estate Worth Many Millions," *San Francisco Call*, August 25, 1899, p. 14.

284 Tada 1990, p. 31, quoting from *Shin sekai nikkan*, a Japanese-language newspaper in San Francisco.

285 F. R. Adams, "House of Mystery," *The San Franciscan*, April 1928, pp. 22, 27.

286 *San Francisco Chronicle*, May 18, 1919, p. 50.

287 Mary Stetson Clarke, Notes from conversation with Mildred Burnham Russell, in private collection of Susan Stetson Clarke; also Clarke 1988, p. 135.

288 Shaku Sōen 1993, p. 140.

289 Pryse 1896, pp. 267-268.

290 Greenwalt 1955, p. 54.

291 Waterstone 1995, pp. 292, 318.

292 Shaku Sōen 1907, July 11, p. 20.

293 Shaku Sōen to Carus, July 18, 1905, The Open Court Archives.

294 Soyen Shaku 1971, p. 67

295 Soyen Shaku 1971, p. 68.

296 Soyen Shaku 1971, pp. 69-78.

297 Akizuki 1992, p. 176.

298 Clarke 1988, p. 135.

299 Jaffe 2004, p. 83.

300 Shaku Sōen 1896. See also Dornish, 1969, pp. 30-33.

301 Shaku Sōen 1907, August 14, p. 34.

302 Shaku Sōen 1907, September 18, p. 45.

303 Classified advertisement, *Los Angeles Herald*, September 17, 1905, p. 3.

304 *Los Angeles Times*, January 18, 1907, p. 112.

305 *Los Angeles Herald*, September 18, 1905, p. 2.

306 "Buddhist Temple for Los Angeles," *Los Angeles Herald*, September 18, 1905, p. 2.

307 Shaku Sōen 1907, September 19, p. 46.

308 Shaku Keishun 1952, p. 78.

309 D. T. Suzuki to Carus, November 7, 1905, The Open Court Archives.

310 D. T. Suzuki to Carus, November 23, 1905, The Open Court Archives.

311 Okamura and Ueda 1999, p. 66. See also D. T. Suzuki to Shaku Sōen, October 27, 1906, in Inoue 1992, p. 164.

312 Uemura 1908, pp. 86, 91.

313 Akizuki 1992, p. 176.

314 Furuta 1967, p. 85.

315 Shaku Sōen to Amakuki Sessan, in Nagao 1993, p. 248.

316 D. T. Suzuki to Carus, July 15, 1905, The Open Court Archives.

317 D. T. Suzuki to Yamamoto Ryōkichi, in Inoue 1989, p. 334. Elsewhere Daisetz described Ida Russell as "the main character of a certain religious group who had several followers." Akizuki 1992, p. 173.

318 Akizuki 1992, p. 176.

319 Daisetz Suzuki to Shaku Sōen, June 11, 1898, in "Daisetz sensei letters written while staying in America," in Inoue 1992, p. 141. See also Bandō Shōjun, "D. T. Suzuki's Life in LaSalle," in *The Eastern Buddhist*, volume 2, no. 1, August 1967, p. 143.

320 Daisetz Suzuki to Shaku Sōen, June 11, 1898, in "Daisetz sensei letters written while staying in America," Inoue 1992, p. 141.

321 Furuta 1967, p. 83

322 D. T. Suzuki to Carus, September 26, 1905, The Open Court Archives.

323 Shaku Sōen to Nakahara Shūgaku, October 20, 1905, in Nagao 1931, p. 186.

324 Inoue 2000, p. 131.

325 Shaku Sōen 1907, January 14, 1906, p. 83.

326 Inoue 2000, pp. 131-134. Reference is to *Asahi Shinbun* article, June 16, 1937.

327 Uemura 1908, p. 273, quoting the *Tokyo Asahi Shinbun*, October 5, 1906.

328 *Iyō Maru* Passenger Manifest, Seattle, Washington, July 21, 1905, Japanese American National Museum, Los Angeles.

329 Sasaki 1969, volume 8, p. 8. See also Fields 1992, p. 172.

330 Commemoration of So-yen Shaku, 1954, Senzaki Papers, University of California, Berkeley.

331 See Shaku Sōen 1907, November 9, p. 62; November 21, p. 64; January 16, p. 84; February 4, p. 88; March 11, p. 98.

332 "Senzaki Nyogen in America," Senzaki Papers, University of California, Berkeley.

333 Shaku Sōen to Shaku Taibi, December 28, 1905, in Nagao 1931, p. 130.

334 Shaku Sōen to Shaku Taibi, December 28, 1905, in Nagao 1931, p. 188.

335 Clarke 1988, p. 125.

336 Janet Russell Phillips, "Aunt Ida's 'menage,'" in private collection of Susan Stetson Clarke.

337 Clarke 1988, p. 153.

338 Clarke 1988, p. 136.

339 Sōen to Shaku Taibi, December 28, 1905, in Nagao 1931, p. 188.

340 D. T. Suzuki to Yamamoto Ryōkichi, September 26, 1905, in Inoue 1989, volume 1, p. 334.

341 D. T. Suzuki to Carus, November 7 and November 23, 1905, The Open Court Archives. See also Henderson 1993, p. 106.

342 Shaku Sōen to Shaku Taibi, December 28, 1905, in Nagao 1931, p. 190.

343 Accounts about Sōen's visit to the Claxton Gallery conflict. It is Ida Russell who, in a letter to Theodore Wores, recounts the event as is generally presented in this book. However, Sōen recorded in his diary that "Mr. Russell" accompanied him to see "Light of Asia." This seems strange considering Alexander's apathetic interest in Asian spirituality. Perhaps the discrepancy can best be explained as a typographical error on the part Sōen or the company that would later publish his diary.

344 Ferbraché 1968, pp. 44-46.

345 Ida Russell to Theodore Wores, February 19, 1906, in private collection of A. Jess Shenson, San Francisco.

346 Ida Russell to Theodore Wores, February 19, 1906, in private collection of A. Jess Shenson, San Francisco; *Shaku Sōen Ōbei unsui ki* (A Monk's Diary of Travels in the West), Tokyo: Kinkōdō Shoseki, 1907, p. 9l.

347 Shaku Sōen 1907, March 10, 1906.

348 Fujimoto 1986, p. 127.

349 Inoue 2000, p. 128.

350 Inoue 2000, p. 126.

351 Shaku Sōen to Amakuki Sessan, in Nagao 1931, p. 247.

352 *San Francisco Call*, March 29, 1897, p. 3.

353 Clarke 1988, p. 145.

354 Passenger manifest, *SS Manchuria*, June 27, 1905, Los Angeles Public Library.

355 Shaku Sōen to Carus, July 18, 1905, The Open Court Archives, Special Collections, Morris Library, Southern Illinois University Carbondale.

356 *Los Angeles Examiner*, September 18, 1905, p. 5; Shaku Sōen 1907, September 18, p. 45.

357 Hori Kentoku 1908.

358 Shaku Sōen to Tanase Zenji, January 1, 1906, in Nagao 1931, p. 119.

359 D. T. Suzuki to Yamamoto Ryōkichi, in Inoue 1989, p. 331.

360 Shaku Sōen 1907, December 5, 1905, p. 69; See also Kadota 1990.

361 Soyen Shaku 1971, p. 9.

362 D. T. Suzuki to Carus, March 31, 1906, The Open Court Archives.

363 Shaku Sōen, "Niagara Falls I," Senzaki Papers, University of California, Berkeley.

364 D. T. Suzuki to Carus, April 3, 1906, The Open Court Archives.

365 D. T. Suzuki to Carus, April 3, 1906, The Open Court Archives.

366 Program of Meetings of the National Geographic Society, Season of 1905-1906, National Geographic Society archives, Washington D.C.

367 *San Francisco Chronicle*, June 5, 1904, Sunday Supplement, p. 5.

368 Shaku Keishun 1942, p. 83.

369 Murakata 1975, pp. 90ff. Also see Murakata 1971, pp. 7-8.

370 Shaku Sōen 1907, April 5, 1906, pp. 128-133. See also Inoue 2000, p. 137; Desk Diary of Theodore Roosevelt, Theodore Roosevelt Collection, Houghton Library, Harvard University.

371 Akizuki 1992, p. 180; Nagao 1931, p. 480, indicates that she died in San Francisco en route to Japan.

372 Beatrice Lane's mother, Emma Erskine Hahn, reputedly of an aristocratic Scottish family, shared her daughter's interests in Asian religions. Both women were vegetarians and walked freely in Theosophical and Vedanta circles. Emma was particularly active in the Bahá'í faith, at one time helping guide a small gatherings of Connecticut farmers that "met often to read the Tablets and Prayers." See Emma Hahn to Alfred Lernt, March 3, 1915, Bahá'í Archives. See also Beatrice Lane Suzuki 1929.

373 Between 400 and 1,000 people attended this meeting. Some sources claim that Vivekananda, the Vedanta Society's charismatic founder, introduced Sōen and lectured on the life of the Buddha at this event. See Inoue 2000, p. 137. It would have been a nostalgic event for Sōen, who had met the Indian swami at the Parliament of Religions thirteen years earlier. However, Vivekananda died in 1902, so this meeting could not have occurred.

374 "At the Seashore," Senzaki Papers, University of California, Berkeley.

375 D. T. Suzuki to Yamamoto Ryōkichi, September 26, 1905, in Inoue 1989, p. 332.

376 Amakuki 1990, p. 122.

377 D. T. Suzuki to Shaku Sōen, November 21, 1899, in Inoue 1992, p. 148.

378 Suzuki to Sōen, November 21, 1899, in Inoue 1992, p. 148.

379 D. T. Suzuki to Carus, March 9 and March 21, 1901, The Open Court Archives. See also Henderson 1993, pp. 105, 181; and Verhoeven 1997, pp. 373-374.

380 Amakuki 1990, p. 121.

381 Suzuki to Yamamoto Ryōkichi, Inoue 1989, p. 344.

382 Suzuki to Yamamoto Ryōkichi, Inoue 1989, p. 332.

383 D. T. Suzuki to Yamamoto Ryōkichi, in Inoue 1989, p. 347.

384 A photograph of Daisetz's room in the Ramsey house shows "Light of Asia" centered above his desk. *The Eastern Buddhist*, volume 15, no. 1, Spring 1982, p. 137.

385 Ida Russell to Theodore Wores, May 10, 1906, in private collection of A. Jess Shenson, San Francisco.

386 Ferbraché 1968, p. 45.

387 Tape-recorded recollections of Baldwin Russell, in private collection of Paul and Janice Russell.

388 *San Francisco Examiner*, May 27, 1906, as referenced in Tweed 1992, p. 206.

389 Furuta 1967, p. 82.

390 Tsunemitsu 1976, volume 2, p. 110.

391 Passenger Manifest of *Tango Maru*, Port of Seattle, August 22, 1906, Japanese American National Museum, Los Angeles.

392 Sasaki 1993, p. xv.

393 Tsunemitsu 1976, p. 111, Tada 1990, p. 61.

394 Holz 2002, p. 88.

395 Tada 1990, p. 61.

396 Nagao 1931, p. 251.

397 Shaku Sōen to Amakuki Sessan, January 5, 1907, in Nagao 1931, p. 203.

398 Shaku Sōen to Tatsumi Eijirō Sept 9, 1908 in Nagao 1931, p. 243.

399 Tsunemitsu 1994, p. 224.

400 Furuta 1967, p. 84.

401 Inoue 2000, pp. 158-160.

402 Tsunemitsu 1994, p. 226.

403 Holz 2002, p. 88.

404 *Wind Bell*, San Francisco: Zen Center, Fall 1969 volume 8, p. 12.

405 Tsunemitsu 1976, pp. 107ff.; Miura and Sasaki 1967, p. 225.

406 Tada 1990, p. 21, 61; Ikeda, p. 107ff; Sasaki 1940, p. 19; Tsunemitsu, pp. 225-226; Fields, pp. 174-179; Miura and Sasaki 1967, p. 225; "Sōkei-an," *Zen Notes*, First Zen Institute of America, volume 5, May 1958, p. 2; Sasaki 1969, p. 12.

407 Senzaki Nyogen in America, Senzaki Papers, University of California, Berkeley.

408 Tada 1990, p. 61.

409 Senzaki Nyogen in America, Senzaki Papers, University of California, Berkeley.

410 D. T. Suzuki to Shaku Sōen, October 27, 1906, in Inoue 1989, p. 163.

411 The authors had promised "will locate source."

412 Nomura 1908, pp. 35-40. Also see *San Francisco Examiner*, April 4, 1908, p. 4; *San Francisco Call*, April 5, p. 40.

413 Tsunemitsu, p. 226, notes "Though he (Sōkatsu) had, through his master, Sōen, the support of the Russells in San Francisco, the farm failed because of his own and his followers' inexperience." It is unclear what form of support the Russells may have provided Sōkatsu or for how long. The author, unfortunately, does not cite his sources.

414 "Gives Building for an Island," clipping from unidentified newspaper dated December 1907; "Two Big Ranch Deals Closed," clipping from unidentified newspaper dated May 24, 1919; "L. P. Drexler," *Weekly Commercial Review*, April, 24 1890, in Kelley Family file, Mendocino Historical Society.

415 Tsunemitsu 1976, p. 107ff.

416 *Santa Barbara Morning Press*, February 8, 1907, p. 4; *Santa Barbara Morning Press*, May 27, 1906, Special Edition, p. 3; Myrick 1991, pp. 239-240.

417 *San Francisco Examiner*, September 15, 1910, p. 2.

418 Unless otherwise noted the source of the material relating to the *San Francisco Examiner* reporters' visit to the Russell mansion is taken from *San Francisco Examiner*, September 15, 1910, pp 1-2.

419 *San Francisco Examiner*, December 16, 1919. Also day book of Ida Russell, fragments, in private collection of Paul and Janice Russell.

420 Tape-recorded recollections of Baldwin Russell, in private collection of Paul and Janice Russell.

421 *San Francisco Call*, September 30, 1906, p. 21.

422 Clarke 1988, p. 131.

423 *San Francisco Examiner*, March 2, 1906, p. 7.

424 Brechin 1999, p. 210.

425 *San Francisco Chronicle*, November 15, 1968, p. 23.

426 *San Francisco Chronicle*, November 15, 1968, p. 23.

427 *San Francisco Call*, September 12, 1911, p. 2; also October 4, 1910, p. 7.

428 *San Francisco Call*, September 2, 1911, p. 10.

429 *San Francisco Call*, September 3, 1911, p. 52. See also September 2, 1911, p. 10; *History of The Bay of San Francisco*, volume 1, Chicago: The Lewis Publishing Co., 1892, p. 632.

430 *San Francisco Call*, September 26, 1910, p. 14.

431 *San Francisco Examiner*, September 18, 1910, p. 20.

432 *San Francisco Call*, September 26, 1910, p. 14.

433 Though Bertha Christofferson was unrelated to any of the others in the mansion, she was undoubtedly dear to Elise Drexler. Christofferson passed away sometime after 1910 and her remains are now interred, unmarked save in the record books, in the Drexler mausoleum at Cypress Lawn Cemetery in Colma, California.

434 *San Francisco Chronicle*, March 2, 1906; *San Francisco Examiner*, March 2, 1906, p. 7; *Los Angeles Graphic*, March 10, 1906, p. 9, in private collection of A. Jess Shenson.

435 Ida Russell to Theodore Wores, May 10, 1906, in private collection of A. Jess Shenson.

436 *San Francisco Examiner,* September 15, 1910, p. 2.

437 *San Francisco Chronicle*, November 19, 1910, p. 18.

438 Notes from conversation with Mildred Burnham Russell, by Mary Stetson Clarke, in private collection of Susan Stetson Clarke.

439 Simpson 1915, p. 173.

440 (No author) *Buddhist Churches of America*, Chicago: Nobart Press, 1974, volume 1, p. 50.

441 Interestingly, in 1911 Mazzinianada officiated at the Buddhist ordination ceremony of three Americans. Though there is good cause to question the validity of the ceremony, his followers were apparently the first native Americans ever ordained as Buddhists. Among the swami's last known "spiritual" acts was to attempt contact with the spirit of recently deceased Sir Arthur Conan Doyle. He died penniless in an Oakland apartment, claiming to be more than one hundred years old. *San Francisco Call*, July 25, 1911, p. 9. See also Abbott 1909, pp. 82-84; *San Francisco Chronicle*, November 6, 1920, p. 10; March 28, 1930, p. 13; April 5, 1930, p. 12; July 9, 1930, p. 1; July 10, 1930, p. 2; July 17, 1930, p. 3; December 10, 1931, p. 11.

442 *San Francisco Call*, August 3, 1915, section 2, p. 1; "A Company of High Buddhists Convene," *San Francisco Call*, August 2, 1915, p. 6; *San Francisco Chronicle*, August 3, 1915, p. 8; *San Francisco Bulletin*, August 2, 1915, p. 2; August 3, part 2, p. 1.

443 *San Francisco Examiner*, August 13, 1915, p. 9; August 15, 1915, p. 24.

444 Shirato 1963, p. 244; Hakurankwai Kyōkwai (Société des Expositions) 1915, p. 181.

445 Tape-recorded recollections of Baldwin Russell, in private collection of Paul and Janice Russell. Note: Baldwin Russell recalled this event more than seventy years after his mother's death, when he was in his nineties. In his reminiscences he sometimes confuses how old he was when a particular event took place, stating, for example, that he was about ten when Shaku Sōen visited the mansion. He was, in fact, no older than four. Many other recollections of his early life are perfectly accurate and can be verified by separate sources. The story of Ida Russell prophesying her own death is not among these, however. If part of the family mythology rather than its actual history, Baldwin Russell's anecdote of his mother in the role of Cassandra at the very least shows the profound impression she could make on other people.

446 Jeff Shore, "Japanese Zen and the West: Beginnings," unpublished paper presented to the International Conference on Buddhism in the Modern World at Fo Kuang Buddhist Monastery, Taiwan, December 25-29, 1990, p. 62ff. A Japanese version was published in *Hanadai Kenkyū kiyō*, no. 24, 1992, pp. 43-85. Hunter 1971, pp. 132-152; Rawlinson 1997, p. 613, quoting Samuel Lewis, *Sufi Vision and Initiation*; Furuta 1967, p. 86. Kirby returned to Canada the following year. He claimed to have had a *satori* experience while in Japan and to have been appointed as a qualified

teacher of Zen Buddhism. However, by 1920 he was in San Francisco where he attached himself to the Pure Land's Buddhist Mission. The following year, Kirby accepted an offer to teach English at a Pure Land college in Hawai'i. He regularly preached at the Mission, calling himself Archbishop Kirby, Ph.D., and conducting ceremonies remembered as crass, pompous, and pretentious. In his sermons he railed against Christianity. Leaving Hawai'i in the mid-1920s, he traveled back to Japan, Europe, and eventually Southeast Asia, abandoning Buddhism somewhere along the way. He ended his days penniless, embittered, and alone at a Salvation Army camp in Sri Lanka, describing Buddhism as fit only for the "dirty Niggers of Ceylon."

447 The earliest known evidence of Daisetz's romance with Beatrice is a letter to Yamamoto Ryōkichi from April 1907, exactly a year after the couple first met. See Inoue 1989, volume 1, p. 51.

448 Lane 1940, p. 12.

449 *Sermons of a Buddhist Abbot*, proof sheets, Southern Illinois University, Morris Library, Special Collections, The Open Court Archives.

450 D. T. Suzuki to Carus, February 23, 1911, and December 29, 1912, The Open Court Archives.

451 D. T. Suzuki's friends in Japan also disapproved of the union, arguing that supporting an American wife in Japan would be exorbitantly expensive. See Inoue 1989, pp. 51, 53, 58.

452 Akizuki 1992, p. 184.

453 Beatrice Lane Suzuki 1940a, pp. 168-169.

454 Akizuki 1992, pp. 187-188.

455 Abe 1986, p. 221.

456 Akizuki 1992, p. 189.

457 Okamura and Ueda 1999, p. 224.

458 Furuta 1967, pp. 88-89.

459 The Authors had promised to locate source.

460 Tape-recorded recollections of Baldwin Russell, in private collection of Paul and Janice Russell.

461 *San Francisco Chronicle*, May 3, 1902, p. 9.

462 *San Francisco Chronicle*, September 22, 1917, p. 10.

463 Clarke 1988, p. 135.

464 *San Francisco Chronicle*, September 22, 1917, p. 10.

465 *San Francisco Examiner*, October 2, 1917, p. 1.

467 Shirato 1963, p. 244. Beatrice Lane Suzuki later recalled that only Ida's heart was brought to Tōkeiji, though there is no evidence to support this macabre assertion. Beatrice Lane Suzuki 1930, p. 253. Beatrice Suzuki may have been thinking of writer Thomas Hardy, whose heart was buried separately from the rest of his body just two years before Beatrice's statement. According to the biographical card file in the San Francisco Public Library, half of Ida's remains were placed in a columbarium at the Odd Fellows Cemetery in San Francisco. The remains of Ida's parents, Robert and Elizabeth Conner, were also interred at the Odd Fellows columbarium at the time of her death. But the Conner remains were later removed and their current location is unknown. Perhaps half of Ida's remains rest with those of her parents in some unknown or now-destroyed cemetery in the United States. Of all his immediate family, only Alexander Russell's ashes remain at the Conner/Russell family niche at San Francisco Columbarium. He is not entirely alone, for the remains of Robert Allan Fairchild, the husband of one of his wards, were interred in the niche in 1927.

468 "Poems by the Late Right Reverend Soyen Shaku," *The Eastern Buddhist*, October-December 1924, volume III, no. 3, p. 273.

469 Probate Documents for the Estate of Ida E. Russell, San Francisco Superior Court Archives.

470 *Los Angeles Herald*, April 2, 1897, p. 10.

471 Tape-recorded recollections of Baldwin Russell, in private collection of Paul and Janice Russell.

472 Probate Documents for the Estate of Ida E. Russell, San Francisco Superior Court Archives; see also Book of Mortgages, volume 435, p. 55, and Book of Deeds volume 998, p. 178 and volume 1048, p. 178, Office of the Recorder, San Francisco.

473 *San Francisco Examiner*, July 31, 1918, p. 1.

474 Return of sale of personal property, April 2, 1919, Alexander Russell file, San Francisco Superior Court, Records Office.

475 Walker 1999, p. 28. See also *San Francisco Examiner*, November 12, 1920, p. 1.

476 See *San Francisco Chronicle*, May 18, 1919, p. 50; F. R. Adams, "House of Mystery," *The San Franciscan*, April 1928, pp. 22, 27; *Oakland Tribune*, September 4, 1960, p. C-1; *San Francisco Chronicle*, November 8, 1968, p. 26; August 4, 1931, p. 1.

477 *San Francisco Examiner*, November 12, 1920, p. 1.

478 *San Francisco Chronicle*, December 2, 1940, p. 12.

479 *San Francisco Chronicle*, December 4, 1940, p. 17.

480 Abe 1986, p. 105.

481 Abe 1986, p. 221.

482 Abe 1986, p. 100.

483 Abe 1986, p. 110.

484 Samurai Shōkai advertisement, *The Eastern Buddhist*, January/February 1923, volume 2, no. 5, inside back cover.

485 Akizuki 1992, p. 186.

486 Akizuki 1992, p. 183.

487 Editorial, *The Eastern Buddhist*, volume 4, no. 1, May 1971, p. 6.

488 Lane 1940, viii.

489 Editorial, *The Eastern Buddhist*, volume 4, no. 1, May 1971, p. 6.

490 Okamura and Ueda 1999, p. 230; See also Taylor 1995, page unknown. http:
www. baysidechurch. org/studia/print. cfm? ArticleID =129 & detaiI =l

491 Okamura and Ueda 1999, pp. 223-225.

492 Fields 1992, p. 188.

493 "Ruth Fuller Sasaki," *Zen Notes*, volume 25, no. 10, 1978, pp. 1-2.

494 *Bukkyō nenkan* [Buddhist annual], Tokyo: Bukkyō nenkan-sha, 1932, p. 268.

495 See "Two Take Buddhist Vows," *Los Angeles Times*, June 16, 1930, p. 1; Senzaki Nyogen, "Farewell to the Old Year," December 31, 1931, p. 6, Senzaki Papers, University of California, Berkeley; *Zenshū*, volume 38, pp. 21-23, 28-35. D. T. Suzuki's diary entry for July 24, 1931, indicates that the two monks called on him to say the monks of Daitokuji asked them to leave by the end of the month. The author appreciates the assistance of Wayne Yokoyama, who possesses a copy of Suzuki's 1931 diary, for this information.

496 "The Zen Hospice," *The Eastern Buddhist*, volume 6, no. 2, June 1933.

497 Millard 1936, pp. 429-437.

498 Abe 1986, p. 191.

499 Millard 1936, pp. 432-433.

500 Sasaki 1993, p. 6.

501 Sasaki 1993, p. xv.

502 Sasaki 1993, p. xvi.

503 Holz 2002, pp. 150-151.

504 Holz 2002, p. 129.

505 Holz 2002, p. 141.

506 Sasaki 1993, p. 83.

507 Holz 2002, p. 250.

508 Review of *Zen Eye*, *The Eastern Buddhist*, volume 29, no. 1, Spring 1996, p. 295.

509 Holz 2002, p. 133.

510 "Wer War Dr. Henry Plakov? Zurich: Zentrum fur Zen-Buddhismus," http :

www. zzb Zurich . ch/bib liothek/p lato v_w . pdf

511 Holz 2002, pp. 15, 146.

512 Henderson 1993, p. 164.

513 *Chicago Tribune*, December 8, 1936, p. 21.

514 "What is the Mentorgarten," 1928, Senzaki Papers, University of California, Berkeley.

515 Tanahashi and Chayat 1996, p. 6.

516 Senzaki Nyogen in America, Senzaki Papers, University of California, Berkeley.

517 Tanahashi and Chayat 1996, p. 6.

518 "Senzaki Nyogen in America," Senzaki Papers, University of California, Berkeley.

519 "Senzaki Nyogen in America," Senzaki Papers, University of California, Berkeley.

520 The paper is identified as *Chūgai Nippō* in Fujimoto 1986, volume 122, p. 129.

521 "What is the Mentorgarten," June 3, 1928, Senzaki Papers, University of California, Berkeley.

522 "What is the Mentorgarten," June 3, 1928, Senzaki Papers, University of California, Berkeley.

523 This is the first time this account of Nyogen's rationale for leaving San Francisco has been presented in English. Its source is Fujimoto 1986, volume 122, pp. 131-132. The article was written by a novelist who visited San Francisco and interviewed elderly residents who remembered the series of events. It is an unusual story given that Nyogen was adamant that Buddhist priests should remain celibate and he consistently identified himself as a Buddhist priest. However, there is no other account for Nyogen's change of venues so this story should at least be taken into consideration.

524 Senzaki to Sangha of San Francisco, March 25, 1931, Senzaki Papers, University of California, Berkeley.

525 Los Angeles Times, June 16, 1930, p. 1; Senzaki Nyogen, "Farewell to the Old Year," December 31, 1931, p. 6.

526 "A Thursday evening at Mu-so-an," Senzaki Papers, University of California, Berkeley.

527 *Los Angeles Times*, November 4, 1932, p. A2; *Los Angeles Times*, June 19, 1933, p. A2; "Why I Became a Buddhist," July 29, 1931, Senzaki Papers, University of California, Berkeley; Paul Croucher, *A History of Buddhism in Australia*, Kensington: New South Wales University Press, 1989, p. 38.

528 "Farewell to the New Year," December 31, 1931, p. 6, Senzaki Papers, University of California, Berkeley. See also Rawlinson 1997, p. 500.

529 "Why I Became a Buddhist," July 29, 1931, Senzaki Papers, University of California, Berkeley.

530 "How to Study Ko-an," January 30, 1936, Senzaki Papers, University of California, Berkeley.

531 *Los Angeles Times*, June 16, 1930, p. 1; *Los Angeles Times*, June 19, 1933, p. A2.

532 "Senzaki to San Francisco Sangha," May 14, 1931, Senzaki Papers, University of California, Berkeley.

533 Senzaki Nyogen, "Kyōgaku," August 4, 1934, pp. 7-8, Senzaki Papers, University of California, Berkeley.

534 Senzaki Nyogen, "Farewell to the New Year," December 31, 1931, p. 6, Senzaki Papers, University of California, Berkeley.

535 Suzuki's address at Green Acre was entitled "Zen Method of Spiritual Discipline." Green Acre Conference Programs, 1907, Bahá'í Archives. En route to the conference, he resided for several weeks at the home of what he called "my American Buddhist sympathizers." This was in fact the house that Beatrice shared with her mother in rural Stamford, Connecticut. D. T. Suzuki to Carus, July 17, 1907, The Open Court Archives.

536 "Rōshi Day," November 7, 1943, Senzaki Papers, University of California, Berkeley.

537 "Commemoration of So-yen Shaku," 1954, Senzaki Papers, University of California, Berkeley.

538 Holz 2002, p. 10.

539 Fields 1992, p. 184

540 Akizuki 1992, p. 178.

541 Abe 1986, p. 100.

542 Holz 2002, p. 156.

543 Switzer 1985, p. 31.

544 Akizuki 1992, p. 176.

545 Akizuki 1992, pp. 176-178.

546 "Rōshi Day Commemoration," Nov. 7, 1943, Senzaki Papers, University of California, Berkeley.

547 "Buddhism and Women," 1948, Senzaki Papers, University of California, Berkeley.

548 "To Mrs. Russell," Senzaki Papers, University of California, Berkeley; see also Fields 1992, p. 170.

549 Shaku Keishun 1952, p. 204. See also Tōkeiji, p. 59.

550 "Questions and Answers," April 7, 1936, Senzaki Papers, University of California, Berkeley.

551 "Questions and Answers," April 7, 1936, Senzaki Papers, University of California, Berkeley.

552 Unless noted otherwise, the source of this section is "Home Coming Gift," March 31, 1936, Senzaki Papers, University of California, Berkeley.

553 See Satō Zenchū 1935, in the special collections library at Stanford University. The book is inscribed with a dedication addressed to Katherine Ball, a Theosophist and noted authority on Asian art. (See *San Francisco Chronicle*, October 21, 1936, p. 34; *San Francisco Chronicle*, February 19, 1929, p. 12.) It gives the location of Ida Russell's remains, identifies the stone lantern Sōen erected as the "Russel Shrine Temple" [*sic*], and a contains a piece of poetry that Sōen composed perhaps with Ida in mind:

> "If the Truth be transmitted from heart to heart
> It will become blooming into flowers and singing like birds,
> Pleasant to your eyes and ears."

It is unknown how Katherine Ball knew of Ida, but given their common interests in art, Japan, and Theosophy, as well as their common age, they were very likely friends.

554 Fields 1992, p. 183.

555 *San Francisco Chronicle*, December 2, 1940, p. 1; *San Francisco News*, December 2, 1940, p. 3.

556 Furuta 1967, p. 90.

557 See Kaneko and Morrell 1983, volume 10, no. 2/3, p. 223; see also Inoue Zenjō, *Tōkeiji*, p. 23.

558 *San Francisco Chronicle*, December 2, 1940, p. 1; *San Francisco News*, December 2, 1940, p. 3; *San Francisco Chronicle*, August 4, 1931, p. 1.

559 *San Francisco Examiner*, January 30, 1916, p. 35. See also "Our Private Schools: Drexler Hall," *The Tall Tree*, Palo Alto: Palo Alto Historical Society, volume 1, October 1952, p. 2; *Palo Alto Times*, January 29, 1916. See also Articles of Incorporation of Hospital and School for Convalescent Children at Palo Alto, January 28, 1918, State of California, Office of the Controller, Sacramento, California.

560 *San Francisco Chronicle*, January 22, 1933, p. 9. Also author's personal conversation with Dr. Howe's nephew and namesake, Louis Philippe Howe of San Jose, California.

561 Last Will and Testament of Elise A. Drexler, filed November 16, 1951, San Francisco Superior Court; Last Will and Testament of Jean MacCallum, February 24, 1970, San Francisco Superior Court.

562 Senzaki 1976, pp. 5ff; Fields, p. 217ff.

563 Holz 2002, p. 135.

564 "Shaku Sōkatsu," *Zen Notes*, volume 18, no. 12, December 1971, pp. 1-8.

565 Holz 2002, p. 126.

566 Mary A. Crittenden to Russell children, Oct. 24, 1933, in private collection of Paul and Janice Russell.

References

Abbott, David P.
>   1909——"Fraudulent Spiritualism Unveiled," in Julian Hawthorne, ed., *The Lock and Key Library: Classic Mystery and Detective Stories*. New York: Review of Reviews Co.

Abe Masao 阿部正雄
>   1986——*A Zen Life: D. T. Suzuki Remembered*. New York: Weatherhill

Adams, F. R.
>   1928——"House of Mystery," *The San Franciscan*, April 1928, pp. 22, 27.

Akizuki Ryōmin 秋月龍珉
>   1992——*Sekai no zensha: Suzuki Daisetsu no shōgai* (Zen Philosopher: The Life of Daisetz Suzuki). Tokyo: Iwanami Shoten

Amakuki Sessan 天岫接三, et al.
>   1990——*Zensō ryūgaku kotohajime* (Initiation of a Zen Monk Studying Abroad). Kyoto: Zen Bunka Kenkyūjō

Bandō Shōjun 坂東性純
>   1967——"D. T. Suzuki's Life in LaSalle," *The Eastern Buddhist*, volume 2, no. 1

Barrows, John Henry
>   1892——"The Religious Possibilities of the World's Fair," *Our Day*, volume 9. Boston: Our Day Publishing Company
>   1893——*World's Parliament of Religions*, volume 1, Chicago: Parliament Press,

Besterman, Theodore
>   1927——*The Mind of Annie Besant*. London: Theosophical Publishing House, pp. 215-221.

Brechin, Gary
>   1999——*Imperial San Francisco*. Berkeley: University of California Press

Bukkyō nenkan-sha
>   1932——*Bukkyō nenkan* [Buddhist annual]. Tokyo: Bukkyō nenkan-sha, 1932. Edited by Horiguchi Giichi.

Burke, Marie Louise

1973——*Swami Vivekananda: His Second Visit to the West*. Calcutta: Advaita Ashrama

Carus, Paul
1897——*Buddhism and Its Christian Critics*. Chicago: Open Court Publishing Co.

Clarke, Mary Russell Stetson
1988——*Russells in America*. Melrose, MA: Hilltop Press

Croucher, Paul
1989——*A History of Buddhism in Australia*. Kensington: New South Wales University Press

Dornish, Margaret
1969——*Joshu's Bridge: D. T. Suzuki's Message and Mission*. PhD dissertation, Claremont Graduate School.

Druyvesteyn Kenten
1976——*The World's Parliament of Religions*, PhD dissertation. University of Chicago

Ferbraché, Lewis
1968 ——*Theodore Wores: Artist in Search of the Picturesque*. San Francisco, CA: n. p.

Fields, Rick
1992 ——*How the Swans Came to the Lake*. Boston: Shambhala Publications

Fryer, John
1901——"Buddhist Discovery of America," *Harper's Monthly*. New York: Harper & Brothers, July 1901

Fujimoto Kōjō 藤本光城
1986——"Tozen Zenkutsu no hito" ("The Zen Man of the Eastward Hall: The Life of Senzaki Nyogen"), *Zen Bunka*

Furuta Shōkin 古田紹欽
1967——"Shaku Sōen: The Footsteps of a Modern Japanese Zen Master," in *The Modernization of Japan*, volume 8. Tokyo: Japan Society for the Promotion of Science

Greenwalt, Emmett
1955——*California Utopia: Point Loma 1897-1942*. San Diego: Point Loma Publications

Hakurankwai Kyōkwai (Société des Expositions)
1915——ed., *Japan and Her Exhibits at the Panama-Pacific International Exposition*. Tokyo: Hakurankwai Kyōkwai, Japan

Hartshorne, Anna C.
    1902——*Japan and Her People,* volume 1. Philadelphia: John C. Winston
    & Co.
Hearn, Lafcadio
    1894——*Glimpses of Unfamiliar Japan*, volume 1. Boston: Houghton
    Mifflin & Co.
Henderson, Harold
    1993——*Catalyst for Controversy: Paul Carus of Open Court.* Carbondale:
    Southern Illinois University Press
Holz, Michael
    2002 ——ed., *Holding the Lotus to the Rock: The Autobiography of Sōkei-an,
    America's First Zen Master.* New York: Four Walls Eight Windows.
Hori Kentoku 堀謙徳
    1908——"Ryōga rōshi beikoku junkyō shi" ("Journal of Ryoga Rōshi's
    Travels in America"), *Zenshū*, volume 39, September 15, 1908
Hunter, Louise
    1971 ——*Buddhism in Hawaii.* Honolulu: University of Hawai'i
Inoue Zenjō 井上禅定
    1968——"Sōen Zenji no shōgai" (Life of Sōen Zenji"), *Zen Bunka,*
    volume 50, October 1968. Kyoto: Institute for Zen Studies
    1989——ed., *Suzuki Daisetsu mikōkai shokan* (Unpublished Letters of
    Daisetz Suzuki), volume 1. Tokyo: Zen Bunka Kenkyūjō
    1992 ——*Suzuki Daisetsu no hito to gakumon* (The Personality and
    Scholarship of Daisetz Suzuki). Tokyo: Shunjūsha
    1997——*Tōkeiji.* Kamakura: Tōkeiji
    2000——*Shaku Sōen den.* Kyoto: Zen Bunka Kenkyūjō
Isshu Miura and Ruth Fuller Sasaki
    1967——eds., *Zen Dust.* New York: Harcourt, Brace & World
Jaffe, Richard
    2004——"Seeing Śākyamuni: Travel and the Reconstruction of Japanese
    Buddhism," *Journal of Japanese Studies* 30, Winter 2004. Seattle: University
    of Washington Press
Kadota Akira
    1990——*Kanaye Nagasawa: A Biography of a Satsuma Student.* Kagoshima:
    Kagoshima Prefectural Junior College
Kaneko, Sachiko and Robert E. Morrell
    1983——"Sanctuary: Kamakura's Tōkeiji Convent," *Japanese Journal of
    Religious Studies*, June-September 1983, volume 10, no. 2/3

Kashiwahara Yūsen and Sonoda Kōyū 柏原祐泉, 薗田香融
　　1994——eds. *Shapers of Japanese Buddhism*. Tokyo: Kōsei Publishing.
　　Originally published as *Nihon meisō retsuden*, 1968.
Ketelaar, James
　　1990——*Of Heretics and Martyrs in Meiji Japan: Buddhism and its Persecution*.
　　Princeton: Princeton University Press
　　1991——"Strategic Occidentalism," *Journal of Buddhist-Christian Studies*,
　　volume 11. Honolulu
Keyserling, Hermann
　　1925—*Travel Diary of a Philosopher*. New York: Harcourt, Brace & Co.
Lane, Beatrice (B. L. Suzuki)
　　1940a——*Impressions of Mahayana Buddhism*. Kyoto: The Eastern Buddhist
　　Society
　　1940b——*Seiren bukkyō shōkan*. Kyoto: Suzuki Teitarō
Militz, Annie Rix
　　1904——*Primary Lessons in Christian Living and Healing*. New York:
　　Absolute Press
Millard, A. Douglas
　　1936——ed., *Faiths and Fellowship*. London: J. M. Watkins
Millard, Bailey
　　1924——*History of the San Francisco Bay Region*, volume 2, Chicago:
　　American Historical Society Inc.
Murakata Akiko
　　1971——*Selected Letters of Dr. William Sturgis Bigelow*. George Washington
　　University, dissertation
　　1975——"Theodore Roosevelt and William Sturgis Bigelow: The Story
　　of a Friendship," *Harvard Library Bulletin*. Cambridge: Harvard University
　　Library, volume 23, no. 1, pp. 90-108
Muscatine, Doris
　　1975——*Old San Francisco*. G. P. Putnam's Sons, New York
Myrick, David
　　1991 *Montecito and Santa Barbara: The Days of the Great Estates*, volume 2.
　　Glendale: Trans-Anglo Books
Nagao Daigaku 長尾大學
　　1931——ed., *Sōen Zenji shokan shū* (Letters of Zen Master Sōen). Tokyo:
　　Nishōdō
Nagao Sōshi 長尾宗軾

1993——ed., *Sōen Zenji to sono shūi* (Sōen Zenji and his Surroundings). Tokyo: Ōzora-sha. Originally published in 1923.

Nishimura Eshin 西村惠信

1973——*Unsui*. Honolulu: University of Hawai'i Press

Nomura Michi 野村みち

1908——*Sekai isshū nikki* (Diary from My Around the World Trip). Yokohama: Nomura Michi

Okamura, Mihoko and Ueda Shizuteru 上田閑照

1999——comp., *Daisetsu no fūkei: Suzuki Daisetsu to wa dare ka* (Daisetz and His Surroundings: Who was Daisetz Suzuki?). Kyoto: Tōeisha

Pryse, James M.

1896——"The Children of Theosophists," *The Path*, December 1896

Rawlinson, Andrew

1997 ——*Book of Enlightened Masters*, Open Court

Sasaki Shigetsu, Sōkei-an 佐々木指月

1940——*Cat's Yawn*, New York: First Zen Institute of America

1969——"Excerpts from 'Our Lineage,'" *Wind Bell*, volume 8, no. 1-2, Fall 1969. San Francisco: Zen Center of San Francisco

1993——*The Zen Eye: A collection of Zen talks by Sōkei-an*. New York: Weatherhill

Satō Zenchū 佐藤禅忠

1935——*Suiun kō* [The Life of a Zen Novice], [Ōfuna-chō (Kanagawa Prefecture)]: n.p., in the special collections library at Stanford University.

Sawada, Janine Anderson

1998——"Political Waves in the Zen Sea: The Engaku-ji Circle in Early Meiji Japan," *Japanese Journal of Religious Studies*, volume 25, nos. 1-2, Spring 1998

Senzaki Nyogen 千崎如幻

1976—*Namu Dai Bosa*. New York: Zen Studies Society

Senzaki Nyogen and Ruth Strout McCandless

1961—*Iron Flute*. Rutland, VT: Charles E. Tuttle Co.

Senzaki Nyogen, et al.,

1976 ——*Namu Dai Bosa*, New York: Zen Studies Society

Shaku Keishun 釋敬俊

1952 ——ed., *Ryōgakutsu nenji den* (Chronological life of Ryōgakutsu). Daichūji

Shaku Sōen (Soyen Shaku) 釋宗演

1893——"Arbitration Instead of War," *Neely's History of the Parliament of Religions and Religious Congresses at the World's Columbian Exposition*. Walter Houghton, ed. Chicago: F. T. Neely

1896——"Doctrine of Nirvana," *Open Court*, December 24, 1896, volume 10, no. 487, p. 51-68

1907——*Ōbei unsui ki* (A Monk's Diary of Travels in the West). Tokyo: Kinkōdō Shoseki

1924——"Poems by the Late Right Reverend Soyen Shaku," *The Eastern Buddhist*, October-December 1924, volume III, no. 3. Translated by Beatrice Lane.

1930——*Bankoku shūkyō taikai ichiran*, in *Seironto shi sonohoka: Sōen Zenji jiden*, volume 10. Tokyo: Heibonsha

1971——"At the Battle of Nan-Shan Hill," in Soyen Shaku, *Sermons of a Buddhist Abbot*, New York: Samuel Weiser. Originally published in the December 1904 issue of *The Open Court*.

1976—Introduction to "Grass in the Field," in *Namu Dai Bosa*. New York: Zen Studies Society

1993——"Reflections on an American Journey," *The Eastern Buddhist*, volume 26, no. 2: pp. 136-148. Kyoto: The Eastern Buddhist Society

Shimano Eidō 嶋野栄道

1978——ed., *Like a Dream, Like a Fantasy: The Zen Writings and Translations of Nyogen Senzaki*. Tokyo: Japan Publications

Shirato Hideji 白士秀次

1963——*Nomura Yōzō den*. Yokohama: Nomura Mitsumasa

Shore, Jeff

1990——"Japanese Zen and the West: Beginnings," unpublished paper presented to the International Conference on Buddhism in the Modern World at Fo Kuang Buddhist Monastery, Taiwan, December 25-29. A Japanese version was published in *Hanadai Kenkyū kiyō*, no. 24, 1992, pp. 43-85

Simmons, John

1987——*The Ascension of Annie Rix Militz and the Home(s) of Truth*, dissertation, University of California at Santa Barbara

Simpson, Anna Pratt

1915——*Problems Women Solved, Being the Story of the Woman's Board of the Panama-Pacific International Exposition*. San Francisco: The Woman's Board

Snodgrass, Judith

2003——*Presenting Japanese Buddhism to the West: Orientalism, Occidentalism, and the Columbian Exposition*. Chapel Hill: University of North Carolina Press

Soyen Shaku (Shaku Sōen) 釋宗演
1971——*Sermons of a Buddhist Abbot*. New York: Samuel Weiser. Originally published in 1907.

St. John, Julian
1897——"Voice of Silence," *Pacific Theosophist*, volume 6, no. 10, January 1897

Suzuki, Beatrice Lane
1929——In Memoriam: Emma Erskine Lane Hahn [Kyoto:] n. p.
1930——"Temples of Kamakura III," *The Eastern Buddhist*, volume 5, no. 2-3, April 1930

Suzuki, Daisetz Teitarō 鈴木貞太郎, 鈴木大拙
1965——*Training of the Zen Buddhist Monk*. New York: University Books

Switzer, A. Irwin
1985——*D. T. Suzuki: A Biography*. London: The Buddhist Society

Tada Minoru 多田稔
1990——*Bukkyō tōzen: Taiheiyō o wattata Bukkyō* (Buddhism from West to East: Buddhism Crossed the Pacific Ocean). Tokyo: Zen Bunka Kenkyūjō

Tanahashi Kazuaki and Roko Sherry Chayat
1996——eds., *Endless Vow: The Zen Path of Sōen Nakagawa*. Boston: Shambhala

Tsunemitsu Kōnen 常光浩然
1976——*Meiji no Bukkyō* (Meiji Buddhism), volume 2. Tokyo: Hyōronsha
1994——"Shaku Sōen," in *Shapers of Japanese Buddhism*. Tokyo: Kōsei Publishing

Tweed, Thomas
1992——*American Encounter with Buddhism*. Bloomington: University of Indiana Press

Uemura Sōkō 植村宗光
1908——*Zen Ken ikō* (Posthumous Writings of Zen Ken). Tōkeiji: Kamakura

Verhoeven, Martin

1997——*Americanizing the Buddha: The World's Parliament of Religions, Paul Carus, and the Making of Modern Buddhism*. PhD dissertation, Madison: University of Wisconsin

Victoria, Brian

1997——*Zen at War*. New York: Weatherhill

Vivekananda

1989——*The Complete Works of Swami Vivekananda*, 8 volumes. Calcutta: Advaita Ashrama

Walker, Clifford James

1999——*One Eye Closed, the Other Red*. Barstow, CA: Backdoor Publishing

Waterstone, Penny

1995—*Domesticating universal brotherhood: feminine values and the construction of Utopia, Point Loma Homestead*. PhD dissertation, University of California, Los Angeles

EDITORIAL POSTSCRIPT

Reminiscences. We first met Brian and Hidemi Riggs while doing research at the D. T. Suzuki archives at the Matsugaoka Bunko in Kamakura, Japan. The Matsugaoka Bunko was situated on top of a hill called Matsugaoka. The Riggs team was doing research at the bottom of the hill at the Shaku Sōen archives at Tōkeiji. It's often assumed the Matsugaoka Bunko was founded by D. T. Suzuki and indeed it has played an important role in promoting his legacy in Japan after his death. In fact it's part of the legacy of Shaku Sōen who set aside a trust fund to build a Zen library he wished to be called the Matsugaoka Bunko. We believe the original funds were part of a monetary gift of $5,000 he received as a farewell gift from Ida Russell and Elise Drexler upon departure from the House of Silent Light in March 1906. He refers to this exact sum in his travelogue *Ōbei unsui-ki*, 1907, a record of his leisurely round-the-world journey of 1905-1906 through America and Europe. It is likely that this sum was earmarked for establishing a Zen library from the very beginning. When D. T. Suzuki arranged to meet briefly with Elise Drexler in San Francisco just before he boarded a ship back to Japan in December 1936, she must have enquired about it. His recollection of Shaku Sōen's dream to build a Zen library led him to locate the trust fund and use it to establish the Matsugaoka Bunko on the hill above Tōkeiji. The anteroom of the library, where we all had tea, has a row of large photographs on display of people who were important to D. T. Suzuki's career. While Shaku Sōen was one of them, it does not show the two people who shared his dream to establish the Matsugaoka Bunko.

Illustrations. There are only a few photographs used in the book. The oldest is the 1890 newspaper photograph of the Oceanside House. This is the actual House of Silent Light. We were able to locate the photograph with the help of Woody LaBounty, who has famously worked with San Francisco historical photo archives. He directed us to the San Francisco Public Library which helped us to arrange for permissions.

Next is the 1903 group photo of Ida Russell, Shaku Sōen, Elise Drexler, and Louis Howe at Engakuji, Kamakura. Engakuji is the Zen monastery where the San Francisco group spent the entire winter months living the Zen life from October 1902 to April 1903. The photograph first surfaced in a 2018 exhibition by Keiō University, Tokyo, marking the centennial of Shaku Sōen's passing. Oikawa Kenji and Tōkura Takeyuki, who were members on the staff of Keiō's online journal, helped us to obtain permission from Tōkeiji, Kamakura.

The third photo is of D. T. Suzuki's upstairs room at the John Ramsey house on Marquette Street in LaSalle, IL, circa 1907. It was actually taken by Suzuki himself, probably for the purpose of wooing his American fiancée whose college graduation photo is prominently displayed on the desk. What interests us more is the image of Theodore Wores' Kamakura Daibutsu on the wall. "The Light of Asia" painting was purchased by Ida Russell in 1906 and was once on display at the Oceanside House where Suzuki first saw it. The digital photograph of the room was sent to us by Matsuda Shūya on behalf of the Matsugaoka Bunko.

Brian Riggs was the first to identify the Wores' painting on the wall of Suzuki's room when the photograph of the room appeared in an article in *The Eastern Buddhist.* For a better image of the painting, see "Wores's Great Painting," *Los Angeles Graphic,* volume 24, number 10 (March 10, 1906), pp. 8–9, compiled in the archive .org database. We refrain from including it here since it is impossible for us to locate the actual painting. For a long time Theodore Wores had it on display at an art gallery in San Francisco.

If any prospective buyer were to enquire the gallery owner would inform them the price was $5,000, a ridiculous price that Wores thought no one would be able to afford. In February 1906, Mrs. Ida Russell went to see the painting with Shaku Sōen and made up her mind to purchase it.

Acknowledgments. We wish to acknowledge our debt of gratitude to Dr. Desmond Biddulph and Darcy Flynn, editors of *The Middle Way*, who set the wheels in motion for the eventual publication of this book. Our thanks also to Elizabeth Kenney and Jonathan Earl for professionally editing important portions of the main text; Thomas Kirchner for significant corrections to the Zen data; and John C. Maraldo, whose *Saga of Zen History*, 2021, was a real eye-opener when it came to gleaning an insight into the Western mind's historic descent into Zen. Finally, Brian and Hidemi, we hope that you are happy with the way your book has turned out. This volume, symbolising your love, will indeed make a wonderful gift to the world! Lastly, we wish to express our thanks to fellow researchers Reverends Robert T. Oshita and Patricia Oshita, former Buddhist chaplains of the California State Assembly, for contributing a timely review of this book to *The Middle Way*.

Wayne S. Yokoyama, EDITOR
KAKEN researcher, D. T. Suzuki studies

Captions for photographs on the following page. Above: Oceanside House, 1890. Courtesy of San Francisco History Center, San Francisco Public Library. *Below:* Suzuki's room in LaSalle, IL. Courtesy of The Matsugaoka Bunko.